The European Science Foundation (ESF) acts as a catalyst for the development of science by bringing together leading scientists and funding agencies to debate, plan and implement pan-European scientific and science policy initiatives. It is also responsible for the management of COST (European Cooperation in the field of Scientific and Technical Research). ESF is the European association of 76 major national funding agencies devoted to scientific research in 29 countries. It represents all scientific disciplines: physical and engineering sciences, life, earth and environmental sciences, medical sciences, humanities and social sciences. The Foundation assists its Member Organisations in two main ways. It brings scientists together in its Scientific Forward Looks, Exploratory Workshops, Programmes, Networks, EUROCORES (ESF Collaborative Research Programmes), and European Research Conferences, to work on topics of common concern including Research Infrastructures. It also conducts the joint studies of issues of strategic importance in European science policy and manages, on behalf of its Member Organisations, grant schemes, such as EURYI (European Young Investigator Awards).

It maintains close relations with other scientific institutions within and outside Europe. By its activities, the ESF adds value by cooperation and coordination across national frontiers and endeavours, offers expert scientific advice on strategic issues, and provides the European forum for science.

D1153740

# Audiences and Publics:
## When cultural engagement matters for the public sphere

**Changing Media, Changing Europe Volume 2**

Edited by Sonia Livingstone

**intellect**™
Bristol, UK
Portland, OR, USA

 FSC Mixed Sources
SA-COC-001695
© 1996 FSC A.C.

First published in the UK in 2005 by

Intellect Books, PO Box 862, Bristol BS99 1DE, UK

First published in the USA in 2005 by

Intellect Books, ISBS, 920 NE 58th Ave. Suite 300, Portland, Oregon 97213-3786, USA

A catalogue record for this book is available from the British Library

Electronic ISBN 1-84150-923-X / ISBN 1-84150-129-8 ISSN. 1742-9439

Cover Design: Gabriel Solomons

Copy Editor: Heather Owen

*Printed and bound in Great Britain by 4edge Ltd, Hockley. www.4edge.co.uk*

# Foreword

This volume is the product of a major Programme under the title 'Changing Media - Changing Europe' supported by the European Science Foundation (ESF). The ESF is the European association of national organizations responsible for the support of scientific research. Established in 1974, the Foundation currently has 76 Member Organisations (research councils, academies and other national scientific institutions) from 29 countries. This programme is the first to be sponsored by both the Social Sciences and the Humanities Standing Committees of the ESF, and this unique cross-disciplinary organization  reflects the very broad and central concerns which have shaped the Programme's work. As co-chairpersons of the Programme it has been our great delight to bring together many of the very best scholars from across the continent, but also across the disciplinary divides which so often fragment our work, to enable stimulating, innovative, and profoundly important debates addressed to understanding some of the most fundamental and critical aspects of contemporary social and cultural life.

The study of the media in Europe forces us to try to understand the major institutions which foster understanding and participation in modern societies. At the same time we have to recognize that these societies themselves are undergoing vital changes, as political associations and alliances, demographic structures, the worlds of work, leisure, domestic life, mobility, education, politics and communications themselves are all undergoing important transformations. Part of that understanding, of course, requires us not to be too readily seduced by the magnitude and brilliance of technological changes into assuming that social changes must comprehensively follow. A study of the changing media in Europe, therefore, is indeed a study of changing Europe. Research on media is closely linked to questions of economic and technological growth and expansion, but also to questions of public policy and the state, and more broadly to social, economic and cultural issues.

To investigate these very large debates the Programme is organised around four key questions. The first deals with the tension between citizenship and consumerism, that is the relation between media, the public sphere and the market; the challenges facing the media, cultural policy and the public service media in Europe. The second area of work focuses on the dichotomy and relation between culture and commerce, and the conflict in media policy caught between cultural aspirations and commercial imperatives. The third question deals with the problems of convergence and fragmentation in relation to the development of media technology on a global and European level. This leads to questions about the concepts of the information society, the network society etc., and to a focus on new media such as the internet and multimedia, and the impact of these new media on society, culture, and our work, education and everyday life. The fourth field of inquiry is concerned with media and cultural identities and the relationship between processes of homogenisation and diversity. This explores the role of media in everyday life, questions of gender, ethnicity, lifestyle, social differences, and cultural identities in relation to both media audiences and media content.

In each of the books arising from this exciting Programme we expect readers to learn something new, but above all to be provoked into fresh thinking, understanding and inquiry, about how the media and Europe are both changing in novel, profound, and far reaching ways that bring us to the heart of research and discussion about society and culture in the twenty-first century.

Ib Bondebjerg

Peter Golding

# Contents

# Author Biographies

## Máire Messenger Davies

Máire Messenger Davies is Professor of Media Studies and Director of the Centre for Media Research in the School of Media and Performing Arts at the University of Ulster, Coleraine. She has a BA in English from Trinity College Dublin and a PhD in Psychology from the University of East London and taught in universities on both sides of the Atlantic before joining the University of Ulster in 2004. Her most recent book is *'Dear BBC': Children, television-storytelling and the public sphere,* published by Cambridge University Press, 2001; she is currently writing *Small Screen, Big Universe: Star Trek as television*, with Professor Roberta Pearson, for the University of California Press.

## Daniel Dayan

Daniel Dayan is Director of Research at the Centre National de la Recherche Scientifique. He has taught media sociology and film theory at various universities including Stanford, Institute d'Etudes Politques, Paris, USC-Cinema, Annenberg School for Communications, EHESS, University of Oslo, University of Geneva. His books include *Western Graffiti* (Clancier-Guenaud, 1982), *Media Events* (with E. Katz, Harvard University Press, 1992), *En Busca del Publico* (1997), and *Despacio Publico in Imagenes* (with I. Veyrat-Masson, 1998). He is currently working on two projects concerning the rhetoric of terrorism and the role of specular processes in media theory.

## Kirsten Drotner

Kirsten Drotner is Professor of Media Studies at the Centre for Media Studies, University of Southern Denmark, and founding director of the Centre for Child and Youth Media Studies and DREAM (Danish Research Centre on Education and Advanced Media Materials). Among her extensive publications are *English Children and their Magazines, 1751-1945* (Yale, 1988); *Medier for fremtiden: børn, unge og det nye medielandskab* [Media for the future: children, young people and the changing media landscape] (Hoest, 2001); *Disney i Danmark: at vokse op med en global mediegigant* [Disney in Denmark: growing up with a global media giant] (Hoest, 2003); and *Researching Audiences* (London: Arnold, 2003, with K. Schroeder, C. Murray and S. Kline). Her current research interests include mobile media and the development of digital learning resources.

## Sonia Livingstone

Sonia Livingstone is Professor of Social Psychology in the Department of Media and Communications at the London School of Economics and Political Science. She has published widely on the subject of media audiences. Her recent work concerns children, young people and the Internet, as part of a broader interest in the domestic, familial and educational contexts of new media access and use. Books include *Making Sense of Television* (2nd edition, Routledge, 1998), *Mass Consumption and Personal Identity* (with Peter Lunt; Open University Press, 1992), *Talk on Television* (with Peter Lunt; Routledge, 1994), *Children and their Changing Media Environment* (edited with Moira Bovill, Erlbaum, 2001), *The Handbook of New Media* (edited with Leah Lievrouw; Sage, 2002), *Young People and New Media* (Sage, 2002), and, her current project, *Children and the Internet* (Polity, in preparation for 2006).

## Mirca Madianou

Mirca Madianou teaches at the Faculty of Social and Political Sciences and is a Fellow of Lucy Cavendish College, University of Cambridge. She holds a PhD in Media and Communications from the London School of Economics and Political Science on the relationship between the media and national and transnational identities in Greece. This research forms the basis of her book entitled *Mediating the Nation* (UCL Press, 2005). Until September 2004 she was a Mellon Postdoctoral Fellow at the Department of Anthropology, University College London, working on television news consumption, cultural citizenship and everyday life in the UK. Other research interests include new media and migration, the social and intimate uses of mobile phones and the Internet, and the development of the subfield of media anthropology.

## Sabina Mihelj

Sabina Mihelj is Lecturer in Media, Communication and Culture at Loughborough University. She gained her PhD in Anthropology of Everyday Life - Media Studies, from Institutum Studiorum Humanitatis Ljubljana Graduate School of the Humanities in 2004. Her major research interest is the relationship between modern media and collective identities (especially national and religious) in contemporary societies. She has researched the role of mass media in the rise of nationalism in socialist Yugoslavia and the constitution of new nation-states in its territory in the 1990s, with a particular emphasis on the coverage of migration, culture and religion, and is currently developing publications based on this research.

## Ulrike Meinhof

Ulrike Hanna Meinhof, Professor of German and Cultural Studies at the University of Southampton, is a specialist in discourse analysis with a strong interest in cultural identities and cultural mediation. She has (co-)written and edited many books and articles in this area, including *Language Learning in the Age of Satellite Television* (OUP, 1998)*; Worlds in Common?* (with Kay Richardson, Routledge, 1999); *Intertextuality and the Media* (ed. with J. Smith, Manchester University Press, 2000); *Living with Borders* (ed. Ashgate, 2002). She is the co-ordinator of two large interdisciplinary research projects funded by the European Commission's fifth framework: one is a study of people living in (South-) Eastern border communities straddling the old and new EU nation-states (2000-2003, see http://www.borderidentities.com for resulting publications); another investigates cultural policies in seven ethnically diverse capital cities in Europe (2003-2005, see http://www.citynexus.com).

## Dominique Mehl

Dominique Mehl is Research Director at the CNRS and is affiliated to the Centre d'Etude des Mouvements Sociaux (Ecole des Hautes Etudes en Sciences Sociales) in Paris. Her fields of research include urban, medical, political and family sociology. For several years, since her work on social movements and change, she has focused on studies of mass culture. In particular, she analyses the evolving interaction between the public and private spheres of life, including questions of how the media orchestrate discussion about behaviour and how speech and expertise combine to shape public space. Recent publications include: *La télévision de l'intimité* (Seuil, 1996), *Naître? La controverse bioéthique* (Bayard, 1999) and *La bonne parole* (La Martinière, in press).

## Roberta Pearson

Roberta E. Pearson is Professor of Film Studies and Director of the Institute of Film Studies at the University of Nottingham. She is a cultural historian who has authored, co-authored and co-edited numerous books and articles on popular culture forms and figures, such as the early cinema, *Batman*, Shakespeare and *Star Trek*. Most pertinent to this project is her co-authored book *Reframing Culture: The Case of the Vitagraph Quality Films* (Princeton University Press, 1993) which considers the implied audiences of early American cinema.

Sonia Livingstone

# Introduction

*Alice began to get rather sleepy, and went on saying to herself, in a dreamy sort of way, "Do cats eat bats? Do cats eat bats?" And sometimes, "Do bats eat cats?" for, you see, as she couldn't answer either question, it didn't much matter which way she put it.1*

Following Alice, this volume asks, when is an audience a public and when is a public an audience? Or, how does it come about and with what consequences that publics are mediated or that audiences participate as a public? The contributors to this volume have been intrigued to note how difficult it is to think about any dimension of social life - from the grand concerns of democracy and culture to the apparently mundane but equally consequential matters of ordinary beliefs, emotions and identity in everyday life - without reference to the notion of 'public'. Centuries of English-speakers have come to preface numerous concepts with the term 'public' - public participation, public sector, public opinion, public interest, even public convenience. The conceptual vocabulary of other languages is somewhat similar, although certainly not identical. If one reflects on the everyday uses of the term 'public', it is clear that despite the many dimensions of publicness, there are some crucial commonalities. 'Public' refers to a common understanding of the world, a shared identity, a claim to inclusiveness, a consensus regarding the collective interest. It also implies a visible and open forum of some kind in which the population participates in order that such understandings, identities, values and interests are recognised or contested.

Our starting point is the contention that the understandings, values and identities of the public (or publics), together with the fora in which these are expressed, are increasingly mediated - technologically, materially, discursively. Moreover, the forms of mediation are themselves changing, with the public being mediated by ever more diversified, pervasive and subtle forms of mass and, recently, interactive communication. This ushers in not just a technological shift in communicative forms but also a social shift: the media are ever less sequestrated to discrete domains (of leisure, of political news, etc.) but act to blur traditional boundaries between work and leisure, education and entertainment, domestic and civic, local and global.

We ask whether and how this mediation of publics matters by exploring the intersection between hitherto distinct fields - one concerning publics, the other concerning media audiences. These research questions have been stimulated by the empirical observation that publics are increasingly mediated, moving ever closer to audiences, while audiences are increasingly diffused and diverse, no longer contained within the private sphere. As befits a volume in this series, emerging as it has done from the European Science Foundation's *Changing Media, Changing Europe* Programme, these changes are analysed by the contributors to this volume in relation to historically and culturally-specific shifts in turn-of-the-century Europe.

These changes include, first, the transformation of the long-standing alignment between public, audience and nation, disturbed by transnational flows of money, people, technology, information and culture. Within the European context, publics and audiences are conceptualised in relation to the mass-market diffusion of imported - typically American - media contents, these influencing policy initiatives to strengthen the European market. Central in cultural terms is the legacy of public service broadcasting (and its contemporary dilemmas), together with the traditional 'fourth estate' role of the press (and the variety of factors threatening this) - both theorised in relation to the public sphere. Meanwhile these debates occur in a context of technological and market innovation, the development of interactive or narrowcast rather than mass audience media technologies potentially undercutting or reorganising the collectivity inherent in conceptions of both audience and public. One must also note the broader shift from a focus on the individual nation towards an increasingly inclusive conception of a unified Europe, including the notion of the European or transnational public sphere.

Many of these changes are insightfully theorised in the conceptual terms of late modernity - individualisation, privatisation, commercialisation, globalisation. These then represent the themes that variously guide the chapters in this volume. The contributors have met on a series of occasions over the last five years to discuss the relations between audiences and publics.[2] The intention has not been to generate an agreed position so much as to engage in conceptual clarification in order to construct a framework which makes sense of a diversity of empirical phenomena – both those we ourselves are researching and others increasingly to be found in the literature. These empirical phenomena appear to be ambiguous, hybrid, confusing even, and often contested. Rather than treating them as messy objects to be tidied away into distinct categories (public, audience, mass, crowd, consumer, citizen, etc.), we chose to focus our meetings on bringing them to the fore, making them central rather than peripheral to our account of wider trends in the mediation of social relations and cultures.

As we hope is evident in the dialogue threaded through this volume, the contributors have sought to develop these conceptual debates by asking some *Alice in Wonderland* questions that move beyond asking whether public and audience are distinct or identical. These questions concern the boundaries or relations among concepts. They also concern the nature of the social phenomena referred to by these concepts - and their relation to others much debated in media and communications - the public sphere, civil culture, civil society, the personal and the political. Since, unlike Alice, we think it matters which way around the questions are put, we have asked ourselves the following:

*When is an audience acting so as to participate in, or to constitute, a public?* This is to ask about the audience as a collectivity rather than an aggregate of individuals, and about an engagement with media texts that includes but goes beyond the moment of reception. For example, when a public service broadcaster addresses the nation, how does audience membership mediate public opinion and with what consequence? If teens discuss sexuality in chat-rooms, do they thereby create a public forum? If the talk show audience becomes so engaged with the issue that some of them write to their local politician, does this effect a shift from audience to public? Indeed, can the media bring new publics into being?

*When does it matter that a public is also an audience?* Given that the knowledge, interests and activities of publics are increasingly mediated, does their status as an audience alter their activities as a public? When and why do certain publics come to rely on the media to sustain their common understanding, interaction style and purpose? For example, if a pre-existing group moves its face-to-face discussions into an online forum, does this alter the nature of the discussion? At what point in the media coverage of a politician's speech is the occasion reduced to one of publicity? Will forming a minority radio station help a pre-existing immigrant group to mobilise?

We can ask these *Alice in Wonderland* questions also in the negative.

*When is an audience not a public?* An audience may not be a public because the media or the elites deny this possibility via strategies of gate-keeping or exclusion, whether for political or commercial reasons. Or, the media might attempt but fail to transform an audience into a public, as in various e-democracy initiatives. Or, audiences may not wish to become publics, satisfied to engage with the media purely for reasons of identity, pleasure, knowledge, lifestyle.

*When is a public not an audience?* As a complex range of media becomes ever more thoroughly embedded in all aspects of daily life, it is arguable that there are no unmediated moments or spaces or social relations, this forcing us to refer to the media in any discussion of the definition and activities of publics. But one might still wonder why some publics rely less on the media than others. Or, why face-to-face communication plays a greater or lesser role in different publics?

In the first chapter, I explore the relations between audiences and publics, noting that in some intellectual traditions these terms are mutually opposed, that some instead focus on phenomena situated on the borderline between audience and public, while in yet other traditions, audiences are subsumed within a broader conception of 'the public' or 'publics'. Following an analysis of the key words 'audience' and 'public' as these have been used within the field of media and communications, this chapter argues for a recognition of the ways in which the activities of publics rest upon, indeed are sustained and resourced by, the activities of people in private. Hence the activities of publics cannot be divorced, analytically or empirically, from those of private individuals. And since these activities - which include thinking, feeling, talking, interacting, acting - occur in a thoroughly-mediated environment, they also cannot be divorced from the activities of people as audiences. The chapter concludes by reviewing recent research concerned to examine whether and when the media are used by audiences, conceived as 'citizen-viewers', to bridge the increasingly permeable boundary between the private domain and the civic or, arguably, the public sphere.

The semantic space of 'audiences' and 'publics' is widened in Daniel Dayan's chapter to include spectators, crowds, communities, activists, militants and witnesses, all terms which address, as he puts it, 'the focussing of collective attention'. He proposes that some publics are there for anyone to see. Their key features are visibility, dramaturgy and performance for they belong in a theatrical model of the public sphere. These are the 'publics' most often contrasted with audiences, for audiences he argues require professional mediation in order to become visible even to themselves and so to stake a claim to being a public. He further distinguishes 'meaning-making audiences', catalyzed into existence as an imagined community (a kind of public) by and through the process of viewing, from 'consumer audiences', for whom the collective fiction that characterises them has been imagined for them by others and which, therefore, draws no commitment from them though they may take pleasure in it. All, however, are collective formations that rely on processes of imagination for their very existence. Hence in different ways, the media are crucial to today's publics (and audiences) in inviting, shaping and managing the focusing of collective attention and, hence, the construction of the collective fictions through which publics come into being, perform and, eventually, die.

The chapters that follow bring into focus some of the ambiguous empirical phenomena situated variously on the borderline between audiences and publics, thereby opening up the particular and yet everyday ways in which publics are mediated and audiences become - or do not become - engaged in ways that matter in the public sphere. Dominique Mehl takes as her subject the widely discussed and apparently paradoxical situation in which people's most intimate, even taboo thoughts and feelings are publicised to the nation in the talk show studio, creating, as she puts it, a subjectivised, individualised 'public sphere of exhibition'. This new 'public/private space' is populated not by experts but by the figure of the witness; it is no longer centred on the process of deliberation so much as on that of display; the outcome is less the conclusion of an argument than an experiment in lifestyles. And yet, these programmes attract a particularly active audience - or, as she terms it (see the multi-lingual account of these keywords in the appendix to this volume), a particularly active public. The chapter concludes by seeking validation for the activities of this audience-as-public by broadening traditional conceptions of citizenship so as to recognise the ways in which public discussion is routinely but crucially sustained by private experience.

If the talk show is traditionally denigrated as emblematic of the improper publicisation of private life (or, conversely, the privatisation of the public sphere), the news is traditionally valued as a primary, even the only, form through which the media address audiences as citizens rather than as consumers or private individuals. Daniel Dayan argued in his chapter that publics are defined in relation to an identifiable object of collective attention - an issue, a programme of action, a constituency. Mirca Madianou takes as her starting point that normative project which is the ultimate object of television news, namely the nation-state. Through detailed ethnographic work with audiences in Greece, she uncovers diverse ways in which members of both majority and minority groups (Greek, Greek Cypriot, Turkish-speaking) are positioned, and position themselves, in response to the public address of national and international news. She argues that engagement as a citizen includes emotional as well as cognitive participation in the mediation of public affairs and that, for some people, the media's invitation to participate instead results in a 'switching off' - an audience ceasing to be part of a public. This is explicable in part at least by a mismatch between the imagined citizen inscribed in the textual address and the actual, contextualised, ethnically-diverse citizens of the news audience.

Some audiences actively participate from the comfort of their living rooms, others display their domestic conflicts in the glare of the television studio, and yet others express their relation to the public sphere by switching off from its dominant media. However, a much longer tradition links audiences to publics through participation in live events as managed institutionally by theatres, concert halls, political meetings and so forth. The next two chapters draw on the tradition of research developed for mass-mediated audiences to re-examine these live, co-present audiences.

Ulrike Meinhof asks about the social and cultural competences required to perform in public, drawing on ethnographic work to inquire into the process whereby a public is initiated within the particular context of a distinctive yet also ambiguous phenomenon, namely the live performance of 'roots' or 'world' music in a Western cultural setting. Having followed a Malagasy artist and politician - itself a highly meaningful combination given our present project - across a range of European and African performance contexts, she reveals a series of steps by which an audience is reconfigured as a public. This is achieved through 'strategies of involvement', a carefully sequenced set of linguistic, emotional and performative moves by which the artist manages the 'collective attention' of the audience, inviting them not 'just' to participate as an audience but also initiating them in the steps required to transform themselves into a public.

A music festival such as that discussed by Ulrike Meinhof reveals the workings of popular culture and popular audiences, linking these to opportunities for the popular expression and mobilisation of civic concerns. Roberta Pearson and Máire Messenger Davies further unsettle the easy opposition between audiences (or masses) and publics (or citizens) by switching the focus to a high culture setting, that of the theatre. As they observe in their empirical work, the same people at one time participate in the often-denigrated audience for popular television shows such as Star Trek and, at another other time, participate in the often-admired audience for plays by literary figures such as J.B. Priestley. Indeed, both audiences and actors - one such actor providing an empirical focus for their research - routinely cross discursive boundaries of taste and value as they move in and out of different audiences in public and private settings. This has implications for a further arena in which relations between audiences and publics are debated, that of the policy and funding for public events. Roberta Pearson and Máire Messenger Davies draw on the concept of cultural citizenship to theorise cultural participation in relation to questions of access, rights, even heritage.

The last two chapters in this volume move away from the very public spaces of live events and turn to those most private of spaces - the child's bedroom, and the personalised space of mobile media - to examine how these too raise issues of public participation and the public sphere. In Chapter 7, my starting point is the persistent valorisation of the public over the private in many polar opposites. Yet empirical research with children and young people persistently reveals the value they place on the private - as secret, as beyond surveillance, as personalised, even a pleasure in branded and commercialised entertainment. In offering, then, a 'defence of privacy', I distinguish three underlying dimensions along which public/private matters are often discussed and, indeed, confused, in academic and policy circles as well as in ordinary discourse - public sector/commercial, connected/withdrawn, visible/hidden. Empirically, it is evident that these produce tensions in the everyday lives of children and their families as they come to terms with the new media in their homes and bedrooms. I suggest that each represents a Habermasian interpenetration of once-distinct social spheres, each with different pressures and challenges, raising crucial questions of interest or profit, of participation or retreat, and of governance and accountability or of invasions of privacy. It is concluded that the media, especially interactive, personalised media, contribute towards the blurring or renegotiation of several versions of the 'public'/'private' boundary which should be kept distinct if we are to recognise their various implications for agency, sociality and responsibility.

Kirsten Drotner pursues the challenge of understanding new forms of media in her chapter, for these are increasingly mobile media, media that create an individual and private experience within and across public spaces. Unlike the Walkman or Discman, however, the mobile phone not only separates but it also connects people, simultaneously withdrawing them from their immediate physical location in order to draw them into another set of connections, potentially just as 'public' as that from which they have absented themselves. In reviewing the emerging empirical analyses of mobile phone use, she argues that as the spatial and temporal boundaries of sociality become increasingly permeable, communicative connectivity is becoming more important than that previous theme so stressed by ethnographic researchers of static media (television, personal computer) – communicative context. Some have argued that the notion of audience is inappropriate here – after all, there is no broadcaster as yet (though the nature of mobile communication is, of course, set to changes further) – but Kirsten Drotner argues, on the contrary, that mobile communicators are indeed audiences, if more flexible, adaptable, and performative than ever before. Are they, she then asks, also 'portable publics', or are the new opportunities for civic or democratic participation exaggerated? Ending with a challenge to media researchers to get mobile also, following their objects – audiences, publics, communities, activists – wherever they go, she reminds us that while new technologies pose some old and familiar questions for the field, they also prompt a fascinating agenda for further research.

Finally, we end by reflecting on a persistent and fascinating theme that has threaded through our work in preparing this volume, that of language and its relation to concepts. Having begun with the realisation that the relation between audiences and publics as we initially conceived it is in significant ways peculiar to the English language, we then asked ourselves not only about the terms for 'audiences' and 'publics' in other languages, but also about how these terms variously fit within a wider semantic field in each language (encompassing masses, crowds, communities, viewers, etc.). Importantly, this then led us to consider whether and how the English (or American) conceptions of audiences, media and publics have been translated, exported even, thereby influencing the academic discourse through which the mediation of publics is conceptualised in other languages and in intellectual traditions. Since this project threatened to take over our discussions entirely, requiring of us considerable linguistic and historical skills, we have restricted our ambitions here to an accounting for key terms and usages in several languages. Our aim is to alert the reader of media and communications research, especially those who read only in English, to the issue of translation, for this is by no means a mere practicality but rather a matter of some theoretical consequence.

Rather than presuming a consensual framework, the authors in the present volume have found it productive to position their work at the intersection of debates about audiences and debates about publics. Each is deeply concerned with questions of citizenship, power and the public, variously seeking out contemporary ramifications of such questions in the ambiguous and shifting ground of mediated culture, pursuing themes of identity, hybridity, cultural citizenship, borderlands and the everyday. Each develops a complementary dimension of the problem and some but not all of the contributors pursue the proposal that the civic mediates between public and private, or public and audience. In preparing this volume, we have found that the tension between these complex debates allows us to pursue a series of research questions about the (plural) relations among publics and audiences that are pertinent to contemporary discussions of the changing media environment.

## Notes

1. *Alice's Adventures in Wonderland*, by Lewis Carroll, first published in 1865 (various publishers since then). Quotation from Chapter 1, 'Down the Rabbit-Hole'.

2. The contributors would like to express their considerable gratitude to the European Science Foundation, through the auspices of its *Changing Media, Changing Europe* Programme, for making such meetings – and hence this volume – possible.

Sonia Livingstone

# Chapter 1: On the relation between audiences and publics[1]

## Why audience and public?

In approaching the changing relations between audiences and publics, one may draw on the long and distinguished intellectual history of the study of publics within political science, philosophy and cultural thought. Alternatively, or additionally, one may draw on the study of audiences within media, communications and cultural studies which, although more recent, has nonetheless proved creative, even provocative, in its analysis of processes of mediation, participation and influence. In setting the scene for the chapters to follow, this chapter will outline the widely held view of public and audience as mutually opposed, one in which audiences are seen to undermine the effectiveness of publics. It will then argue that the changing media and communications environment - characterised by both the mediation of publics and the participation of audiences - problematises such an opposition; the emergence of intriguingly ambiguous objects situated between public and audience is used to illustrate the argument.

The relation between audiences and publics is contested less because 'public' refers to a shared understanding or inclusion in a common forum (for 'audiences' may be similarly described) than because 'public' implies an orientation to collective and consensual action, perhaps even requires that action to be effective for a public to be valued. Although some have suggested that it may be easier to collapse the concept of public into that of audience, or *vice versa*, this chapter proposes that a more satisfactory account maintains their analytic separation. The strategy explored here interposes a mediating domain - 'civic culture', or 'civil society' perhaps positioned between 'the public' and 'the audience' or, more accurately, between the sphere of experience and identity and the sphere of collective, politically efficacious action. This, it is suggested, reframes in a more complex but more incisive manner many of the questions being asked, both within and beyond the academy, about the relation between audiences and publics.

### Audience *versus* public

The analysis of 'audience' and 'public' draws on distinctive bodies of theory, prioritising different issues. But they do not refer to wholly separate realities. In a thoroughly mediated world, audiences and publics, along with communities, nations, markets and crowds, are composed of the same people. This apparently banan observation is significant when we observe that it is commonplace to define audiences in opposition to the public. In both popular and elite discourses, audiences are denigrated as trivial, passive, individualised, while publics are valued as active, critically engaged and politically significant. Bearing in mind that the audience is generally ascribed to the private domain, consider these common associations of public versus private, each of which valorises public over private: rational versus emotional, disinterested versus biased, participatory versus withdrawn, shared versus individualised, visible versus hidden.

Adherents of this oppositional view, often from a political science or political communication approach, tend to ascribe a clear meaning to the public in terms of political citizenship and then ask how the media support or - more commonly - undermine public understanding and public participation. If objective information, informed consent, independent investigation are all prerequisites for a flourishing democracy, the questions for research are clear. And the answers, all too often, tend to suggest that the effect of media on their audience is seen to reposition what was or might be or should be, a public (knowing, thinking, influential) as a mere crowd (watching, sharing and emoting) or mass of consumers (driven by tastes, preferences and motivations) (Gandy, 2002).

This suspicion of the media has a long history that is strongly if implicitly encoded in our present-day tendency not only to oppose mediated communication with face-to-face communication, judging the former as inferior by comparison, but also in the ways that we map onto this opposition our cultural norms of reliability, authenticity, equality, trust, accountability - all of which are associated with face-to-face communication and all of which are routinely questioned in relation to the media. Hence, popular and academic discourses worry - undoubtedly often with good reason - about the extent to which 'media culture generally, with its emphasis on consumption and entertainment, has undercut the kind of public culture needed for a healthy democracy' (Dahlgren, 2003, p.151). Or, to put these worries into the much-used language of moral panics, many are concerned about 'citizens attenuated into measurable audiences and consumers; politics commodified into beauty pageant cum talent show; journalists transmogrified into masters of ceremony, celebrity judges and measurers of the public will' (Barnhurst, 1998, p. 203). The outcome, so the argument goes, is that the media undermine the public sphere (Habermas, 1969/89), transform politics into political marketing (Scammell, 2001), bias the news agenda according to commercial imperatives (McChesney, 2000) and distract citizens from civic engagement (Putnam, 2000). On this view, then, the last thing research should be doing is rethinking those processes of attenuation in potentially more positive terms through studying such denigrated formats as daytime talk shows or reality television, particularly when there remains so much to do to improve the reception of prime-time news or to defend resources for the documentary.

While recognising the force of these and related concerns, it remains problematic that they rely on a traditional and, arguably, limited conception of politics, one that opposes mass and elite culture (or public ideals and audience tastes), asserting a polarised theory of power in which 'hegemony theory has been used to analyse the struggle over dominance and consent waged through mass culture' (Ouellette, 1999, p.65). In relation to Habermas' theory of the public sphere, we have become familiar with the cry of elitism for the theory's idealisation of a public sphere that has, too often, turned out to devalue or to exclude some people (or discourses or topics) while privileging others (Calhoun, 1992; Eley, 1992; Fraser, 1990). However, alternative formulations, positing non-idealised yet egalitarian and inclusive accounts of the public sphere, remain hotly contested. For the moment, therefore, the role of the media in relation to the public, potential and actual, must surely remain an open question.

In the spirit of openness, rather than from any desire to celebrate the popular tastes of audiences for their own sake, I argue against any reductive polarisation of public and audience (or public sphere and media), agreeing with Dahlgren (2003, p.164) that it is imperative to 'see beyond the formal political system'. In this volume, we inquire into many phenomena that, at first glance, are of only ambiguous or borderline relevance to politics and the public sphere, asking whether the increasing mediation of people's engagement with their society transforms our once-contained conception of the audience into something more complex. As the apparent apathy and ignorance of publics, traditionally conceived, forces a broader conception of citizenship, and as it is recognised that participation is increasingly a matter of identity, of belonging, and of lifestyle, research must surely be asking when these spill over into matters of identity politics, social inclusion and exclusion, and new social movements? And here media researchers may be expected to have much to contribute, for if even if the media have proved only partially effective in informing citizens about political issues, they have proved far more effective in shaping identities and lifestyles.

### Audience *or* public

The temptation to oppose publics and audiences is encouraged by the many ways - economic, geographic, political - in which the media appear to be simultaneously expanding the scope of the audience and diminishing the realm of the public, leaving few if any aspects of social or personal life unaccompanied by, or independent of, the media. Yet paradoxically, this very expansion appears to be generating some ambiguous objects in today's 'mediascape' (Appadurai, 1996), which resist traditional or commonsense categorisations as matters of either audience or public. Not only are relations between audiences and publics becoming tangled conceptually, but empirical investigations of the everyday activities of audiences and publics are also revealing puzzling intersections.

As Barnhurst (1998, p.205) notes of his interviews with young people, 'these texts can be read as personal identification but also as moments within a political system'. The talk show, to take another example, portrays ordinary people discussing topical issues in public with experts - yet it refers to its audience rather than to the public; indeed it is often taken as representing the antithesis of rational public debate. The Internet chat room is a similarly ambiguous object, inviting private, individual, anonymous contributions to an - at times personal, at times political - public discussion. Again this may seem a phenomenon of the audience not the public, but witness the attempts by governments to harness such media - both talk shows and online chat - in the interests of governance, whether to bolster representative democracy or to encourage the shift to a participatory democracy. Consider, as a further case, a family discussion after watching the television news - is this an instance of public debate or (merely) a matter of audience reception, and does it make a difference if it occurs in the privacy of the living room or outside the home?

The common use of spatial metaphors to distinguish public and private only serves to exacerbate confusion.[2] Space turns out to be ambiguous or shifting depending on its use (the living room, the chat-room, the television studio, the music festival, the theatre). Even when certain spaces are conventionally associated with publicness or with privacy, people's uses of media in these spaces may contravene these conventions - for example, teenagers communicate privately in space that is conventionally public (using text-messaging in the cinema, for example) and they communicate publicly in space which is conventionally private (entering chat rooms, for example, from their bedroom). On the other hand, space is a resource frequently managed by others - hierarchically and normatively structured, rule-bound and unequally accessible - and hence it operates also as a constraint, 'preferring' some actors or some activities over others. For example, one may argue that it was the considerable constraints exerted on their behaviour in public places which led teens to seize on the mobile phone to subvert, in modest degree, the constraints upon them.

In seeking to understand these ambiguous communicative situations, many of which bridge mediated and face-to-face communication, we might usefully focus on the conditions of their existence. What are their modes of address, communicative conventions, priorities and exclusions, or hierarchies of expertise? How are these variously performed, negotiated, regulated, and transgressed? Intriguingly, where once these borderline phenomena stayed in the margins of academic and popular debate, today they take centre stage: from academic journals through parliamentary debate to the tabloid press, it seems that society is pondering the significance of talk shows or reality television, the transformative impact of mobile phones on social relations, the role of minority media in dividing a heterogeneous public into multiple public spheres, the legitimacy of public funding for elite culture or the meaning of online discussion.

## Audience *as* public

If one widely held view seeks to distinguish, even oppose, audiences and publics, an alternative view sees the changing media environment as signalling the actual or imminent collapse of such a distinction. Characteristic of media and cultural studies approaches, this prioritises the contextualisation of people's engagement with media within everyday life, arguing that the media do not provide a (biased) window on the world so much as a set of resources through which everyday meanings and practices are constituted; these in turn shape identity and difference, participation and culture. The activities of audiences, it is asserted, cannot usefully be separated from the activities of publics; the citizen-viewer (Corner, 1991) supplants the opposition of citizen and consumer. As Silverstone (1990, p.173) declares, the audience is:

> *a potentially crucial pivot for the understanding of a whole range of social and cultural processes that bear on the central questions of public communication ... [which are] essentially questions of culture.*

This approach argues further that, since the realm of the unmediated public is shrinking, if it still exists, any response to the so-called crisis of public communication (Blumler and Gurevitch, 1995) or any defence of the public sphere must surely include a role for the very media often taken to undermine that public. Instead of bemoaning the impact of media on publics, let us ask how media (and media audiences) can and do sustain publics.

Elaborating what Fiske termed the double movement of mediation (1987), Corner (1995, p.5) characterises the effect of the media in late modern societies in terms of contrasting forces. Through centrifugal forces, television seems 'to project its images, character types, catch-phrases and latest creations to the widest edges of the culture, permeating if not dominating the conduct of other cultural affairs'. This, I suggest, poses a particular challenge for audience research as, insofar as we are all always part of audiences now, the necessity for any particular theory of audiences (rather than of publics, or cultures, or consumers, etc.) seems to be increasingly questioned. Simultaneously, through a contrary centripetal force, Corner notes 'the powerful capacity of television to draw towards itself and incorporate (in the process, transforming) broader aspects of the culture'. This poses a challenge to political communications research as publics are drawn onto the media stage on which public and private life is displayed, while anything not on the media stage is marginalised, rendered invisible. In response, the analytic criteria for evaluating deliberation, participation or inclusiveness in terms of a valorisation of face-to-face communication must now surely be rethought.

Yet, simply eliding our key terms by redefining audiences as publics does not resolve problems other than those of semantics. And, insofar as this perspective has sometimes overreached itself, overstating or celebrating the perhaps - tangential political importance of everyday activities, one could even argue that the problems have become obscured. Starting with questions of audience, it seems, tends to lead one to see all aspects of audience as a matter of public or citizenship significance, leaving unresolved the bounding or contextualising of such claims (Livingstone, 1998). The relationship of audiences to media contents is always mediated by culture or cultural identity, but does that make all audience activity a matter of identity politics?

## An exercise in keywords

Since both 'audience' and 'public' are terms central to conceptual debates as well as being in common and variable usage in everyday discourse, some attention to definitions may prove helpful in working out a relationship between them that neither opposes nor elides them. Not forgetting the claim by Williams (1961, p. 289) that there are no masses, 'only ways of seeing people as masses', a claim one might repeat also for audiences, markets and even publics, let us consider how our key terms are anchored through their relations with other terms (see Appendix, where we consider further how these are linguistically and culturally specific). And let us not be put off by a notable absence: the standard reference work, Raymond Williams' *Keywords*, lists neither public nor audience, but he does discuss 'public' in relation to 'private', and 'audience' in relation to 'masses'.

### Public and private

In *Keywords*, Williams (1983) identifies the origin of 'private' in negative terms, through the contrast with public (as 'withdrawn from public life', from the Latin root *privare*, to bereave or deprive - hence private soldier, private parts). In the sixteenth century, the limited access implied by 'private' came to mean privileged (private property, private view, private education) and was then, in the $17^{th}$-$18^{th}$ centuries, supplemented by the meanings of autonomy and intimacy (the privacy of the family, private life, private enterprise). But what then is this public life from which the private represents a withdrawal? Hartley (2002, p.189) offers a positive definition of term 'public', noting that since classical times:

> *the people comprising the public could gather in a single space within sight of each other (in Greek: agora, in Roman: forum). It was here that free citizens argued, legislated and adjudicated, both in their own interests and on behalf of others who were not free - slaves, women, foreigners, children. With the growth of polities to many times the size of these classical antecedents, the public was 'abstracted' or virtualised - it was either an imagined community or could gather together only by representative means.*

Here we have an abstracted, modern version of 'public', which is frequently characterised in normative terms precisely to distinguish 'fully fledged' publics (Dayan, 2001, p.769) from proto- or quasi- or pseudo-publics as well as from other social groupings such as audiences, communities, fans, crowds and masses.

Allowing for some debate, these features typically include a relatively stable social group, a shared symbolic world-view, a commitment to internal debate, the generation of a political agenda, performative self-presentation to itself and to other publics[3] and a reflexive specification of criteria for belonging.

Furthermore, again unlike other social groupings, this normative, abstracted public - widely theorised today in the terms of Habermas' theory of the public sphere - requires a visible and open space in which to engage in rational-critical discussion in order to build consensus and legitimate democratic government. As Habermas (1984, p.49) puts it:

> By 'the public sphere' we mean first of all a realm of our social life in which something approaching public opinion can be formed. Access is guaranteed to all citizens. A portion of the public sphere comes into being in every conversation in which private individuals assemble to form a public body.

Far from opposing public and private according to any simple polarity, then, the Bourgeois public sphere is precisely composed of the activities of private individuals (rather than the activities of politicians, officials or bureaucrats), but only insofar as they bracket their differences and do not act out of their private interests, as Calhoun (1992, p.13) stresses:

> the notion of common interest in truth or right policy thus undergirded the 'bracketing' of status differences [and] rational argument was the sole arbiter of any issue ... the public defined its discourse as focusing on all matters of common concern [and] the emerging public established itself as inclusive in principle.

By contrast, when private individuals, including audiences, engage in conversation, access is generally restricted, interests and status differences are far from bracketed off and truth may not be the goal.[4]

## Audience and masses

Under the keyword 'masses', Williams (1983, p.192) captures widespread ambivalence in both popular and academic discussion of the audience according to which the 'masses' is 'a term of contempt in much conservative thought, but a positive term in much socialist thought'. For the former, 'audience' is seen as 'something amorphous and indistinguishable', connoting base, low or vulgar (c.f. also the multitude, mob, rabble and crowd), as opposed to notions of eminence, rational, expert, good standing. For the latter, we see a stress on 'the people', especially 'ordinary' or 'working class' people as a positive force, associated with two other complex terms - democracy and the popular. In audience research, both meanings of audience retain some purchase.

Nonetheless, in defining the audience, Hartley (2002, p.11) draws only on the former meaning of 'mass' when he states:

> The term audience is used to describe a large number of unidentifiable people, usually united by their participation in media use. Given the varying demographics of this group, not to mention variations between nations, the concept itself is a means by which such an unknowable group can be imagined. Naming an audience usually also involves homogenising it, ascribing to it certain characteristics, needs, desires and concerns. The audience is a construction motivated by the paradigm in which it is imagined.

Hence, he follows Williams in emphasising the amorphous and indistinguishable character of the audience, but underplays work seeking to valorise audiences as plural and as contextualised within the popular. More important to Hartley is the way in which the notion of audience is co-opted by powerful institutions to further their own interests, most notably media institutions (Ang, 1990).

McQuail (1987, p.215), by contrast, eschews the 'rather simple surface meaning [of audience] as the aggregate of persons forming the readers, listeners, viewers for different media'. Instead, and more neutrally, he stresses the 'fundamentally dual character' of the audience as:

> a collectivity which is formed either in response to media (channels and content) or out of independently existing social forces (when it corresponds to an existing social group or category or the result of activities by a social group to provide itself with its own channels of communication media). Often it is inextricably both at the same time.

This second meaning of audience intersects with that of public, for 'the key element in this version of the audience is the pre-existence of an active, interactive and largely autonomous social group which is served by particular media, but does not depend on the media for its existence' (p.219). In other words, a pre-existing social group may be both part of an audience and part of a public; clearly, in the analysis of each, much rests on the viability of the distinction between being served by and being dependent on the media.

## Contested concepts

This keyword analysis of 'audience' and 'public' reveals some points of connection and contrast between them. Far from asserting any grand resolution or prescriptive definitions of terms, the remainder of this chapter will attempt to clarify the consequences of particular conceptual choices, particularly seeking to identify which of these provide constructive if contestable opportunities for analysing the changing media environment.

Those who wish to prefer publics over audiences argue that 'audience' is descriptive while 'public', although sometimes used descriptively (as in public opinion, the general public), is essentially normative (as in public service, public sphere), encoding consensual, strongly-held values (of inclusivity, rationality, disinterestedness, etc). Hence, only certain groups, certain forms of communication, certain channels of participation meet the demanding criteria for 'the public' or 'publicness'; others fail to qualify. Intriguingly, not only does this appear to exclude groupings that we may wish to call publics, on some grounds at least, it may also include some less than ideal groupings. If we pluralize 'the public' as 'publics', then one public must represent the out-group for another, becoming not 'we' but 'them', leading Dayan (2001) to ask if some publics can be irrational, even hateful. For although ideally a public should strive for a common and inclusive discourse, bracketing interests and investing in efforts to translate across experiences, in practice many social groupings commonly labelled as publics operate irrationally at times, or in a prejudiced or competitive manner.

Not only are publics held to encode consensual, and positive, values but they are also held to be collectivities, more than the sum of their parts, while audiences by contrast are merely aggregates of individuals (Harré, 1984). However, as with the broader distinction between public and private, this distinction works better in the abstract than when applied to any particular situation. What can one claim empirically for 'publics' that cannot also be applied to audiences - who know of each other, are reflexively aware of their membership of a larger group, who may even meet and discuss their viewing or listening, sometimes sending feedback to broadcasters, and certainly sharing in national media events?[5]

Given the difficulties of sustaining both collective and normative claims for 'the public', one might more modestly claim to seek an account of when and under what conditions people - qua publics or audiences -constitute a collectivity. According to which values might this be characterised, when is this mediated, and with what consequences? This is to consider 'public' as an adjective rather than a noun: doing or saying things publicly, making things public, conducting relations in public - these distinguish 'public' from 'private' but they set less stringent requirements for identifying 'the public'. Moreover, they suggest some obvious ways in which the media could enhance publicness, through publicising, making actions visible on the media stage, promoting reflexivity, bringing matters into the open, and so forth.

However, while adjectival use of the term need activate only one of the multiple criteria for 'the public' identified in more idealistic definitions, it postpones the question of when these variously public deliberations, actions or interests merit the attention, the weight and seriousness, traditionally accorded to 'the public'. Often, as noted earlier, such weight is reserved only for public deliberation that has political consequences, although this in turn begs the question of whether political institutions are receptive towards their various publics.

For those who prefer to prioritise 'the public' as a noun, something is lost by applying the term loosely - sloppily some would suggest - to any public discussion, any community-based activity or any forum for mass-mediated gossip or chat merely because it is visible or popular. For others, setting such demanding standards for 'the public' brings its own problems. First, too stringent a definition includes little and excludes most of human activity, resulting in the pessimistic conclusion that public life is dead. Second, it has generally proved that those activities which meet these high standards are characteristic of elites, excluding from view the heterogeneous if conflicting activities of the majority. Third, and perhaps least explored but most interesting, is the suggestion that it is precisely these broader, diverse forms of social activity - which are 'public' but not yet 'the public' - that demand a rethinking of the relation between public and private, state and civil society, for this new, and heavily mediated century (Beck, 1992; Giddens, 1991).

## Mediated publics, diffused audiences

How should these themes be explored in the context of changing media and changing Europe? We begin by observing that one cannot now imagine how the public can be constituted, can express itself, can be seen to participate, can have an effect, without the mediation of various forms of mass communication. Making something public today means representing it in the media, especially on the scale required in a globalised society; keeping something out of the media spotlight is to symbolically annihilate it (Tuchman, 1972). Can publics retain, or even gain in, vigour and integrity once they are no longer simply served by but rather dependent on the media? Crucially, the media mediate: they select, prioritise, shape, and so on, in accordance with the institutions, technologies and discursive conventions of the media industry. To make something public is to transform it in ways that media theory and, especially, audience research, has long sought to analyse.

Not only is the public changing, so too are audiences (see Butsch, 2000). There have been several attempts to periodise the history of audiences. Abercrombie and Longhurst (1998), to take but one, identify three broad phases of the audience: first, the simple co-located face-to-face audience; second, the mass audience - lasting throughout modern history - aligned to the boundaries of the nation state and so most readily identified both with public service and with the needs of citizens; and third, the diffused audience, no longer containable in particular places and times, but rather part and parcel of all aspects of daily life, certainly in industrialised nations and increasingly globally. As they put it, today 'the qualities and experiences of being a member of an audience have begun to leak out from specific performance events which previously contained them, into the wider realms of everyday life' (Abercrombie and Longhurst, 1998, p.36-7). Hence, a stress on the process of mediation, rather than on discrete media influences on the audience or public, is called for.[6]

The mediation of the public is widely regarded with pessimism - as a refeudalisation of the public sphere by which public discussion is downgraded into publicity: 'the deprivatized province of interiority was hollowed out by the mass media; a pseudo-public sphere of a no longer literary public was patched together to create a sort of superfamilial zone of familiarity' (Habermas, 1989, p.162). By contrast with face-to-face communication, where one can check whether communication is trustworthy, authentic and reliable, the increasing mediation of the public opens the door to inauthentic, motivated and divided discussion (Curran, 1991; Dahlgren, 1995). Yet this is too simple an account of the media, as Habermas himself acknowledges. In his essay on *The Critical Society* (in Outhwaite, 1996, p.320-1), Habermas critiques Adorno and Horkheimer for positing (commercial) media as displacing (authentic, public) face-to-face communication:

> *According to Horkheimer and Adorno, the communication flows steered via mass media* take the place of *those communication structures that had once made possible public discussion and self-understanding by citizens and private individuals. [...] On the one hand [the electronic media] transforms the authentic content of modern culture into the sterilized and ideologically effective stereotypes of a mass culture that merely replicates what exists; on the other hand, it uses up a culture cleansed of all subversive and transcending elements for an encompassing system of social controls, which is spread over individuals, in part reinforcing their weakened internal behavioural controls, in part replacing them.*

Here Habermas draws on contemporary media research, including audience research, to identify a series of problems with the 'stylising oversimplification' of Horkheimer and Adorno. These include the competing interests which influence broadcasting institutions (economic, political, aesthetic, ideological, professional); competing obligations guiding content producers (especially, tension between commercial imperatives and professional journalistic codes of conduct); the polysemic character of media texts, even the most popular or trashy (for texts incorporate both dominant and critical messages); the lack of simple mapping between textual content and audience reception (because encoding and decoding contexts differ systematically); and a tension in technological development between tendency towards centralisation/standardisation and diversification /innovation.

These complexities suggest lapses or failures in the 'encompassing system of social controls' that, more optimistically, open up opportunities for authentic and diverse dialogue between government and citizens. Notably, in the face of the rise of voter apathy and the decline of civic society, we are witnessing considerable efforts and initiatives to engage audiences in civic or political fora, these being aided - or so many hope - by new forms of interactive and participatory media. Thus, governments are regarding the potential civic or political participation of what were once 'merely' audiences with some optimism, spawning a series of mediated initiatives in cultural citizenship, political socialisation, participatory deliberation, e-democracy, citizen engagement, and so forth (Scammell, 2001; Bentivegna, 2002).

As publics extend their scope, encompassing greater heterogeneity, they seem to lose power, fragmenting under internal dissent or the dissipation of shared values. Consequently, government-sponsored initiatives to enhance participation find they need the media if they are to manage communication within and across ever-larger publics. Unlike publics, as audiences extend their scope, even beyond national boundaries, they do not necessarily lose power, thereby rendering audience participation potentially a source of strength rather than threat to the interests of publics.

Initiatives to enhance public participation not only question the assumption that the media have undermined politics, seeking instead to harness the power of the media to democratic ends, but they assume more fundamentally that politics has been undermined by other, deeper causes. In other words, rather than treating the public and the political as synonymous, which as Warner (2002) points out is a commonplace confusion which leads to the marginalisation or neglect of any public discourse or activities for which no direct political consequences can be traced, we might even propose instead that 'the public' embodies higher ideals, worthier practices and values than are often evident in the messy world of politics.

Warner returns to Kant's enlightenment philosophy to explain how, for Habermas, it is precisely those discourses and activities of the public which do have direct political consequences that should be regarded critically, rather than those which do not. Thus:

> *Kant recognises that there are publics, such as the reading world, that do not corre-spond to any kind of polity. They enable a way of being public through critical dis-course that is not limited by the duties and constraints of office or by loyalties to a commonwealth or nation. These critical publics may, however, be political in another or higher sense. They may set a higher standard of reason, opinion and freedom - hence the subversive potential in his picture of enlightenment.*

*(Warner, 2002, p. 45-6)*

### The private in the public

Implicit in this more optimistic reading lies a view of the public as dependent on the private (rather than politics or the state). The resources, the competences, the motivations which lead people to participate in public draw - in a manner little understood - on the lived experiences and activities, the conditions and constraints, the identities and relationships of people in their status as private individuals. In other words, rather than denigrating certain kinds of sociality as 'less than public' - as pre- or proto- or quasi-public - we could ask, what does it take for people to participate in public, what does the public require, what are its preconditions? We need an account of the formation of public opinion and of citizens - early expressions of interest, exploration of experience, tentative trying out of viewpoints. This may not happen in the public sphere but the public sphere depends on its happening. Again Habermas leads the way, suggesting that, 'the subjectivity the family nurtured was "audience-oriented" because it was played out in dramas staged for the other members of the family' (quoted in Calhoun, 1992, p. 10-11), 'audience' here taking on its traditional meaning as 'an audience with the King', rather than referring to the mass media.

This subjectivity, for Habermas, sustains the Bourgeois public sphere: 'The public's understanding of the public use of reason was guided specifically by such private experiences as grew out of the audience-oriented subjectivity of the conjugal family's intimate domain' (Habermas, 1969/1989, p. 28). Calhoun (1992, p. 35) takes Habermas to task here for treating 'identities and interests as settled within the private world and then brought fully formed into the public sphere'. However, such an assumption is not necessary in considering whether our family arguing about the news at home has an element of publicness to their apparently private discussion, particularly insofar as they reproduce (or co-produce) their identities, relations of in/equality, tactics of in/exclusion, motives for participation, and so on. As Hermes and Stello (2000, p. 219) argue from their reception study of reading detective fiction, this 'may not in itself be a political act, but as a cultural practice it is ... the domain in which we deploy a sense of self and of identity, of our place in society, the obligations we have and the rights that are due to us'. Since people not only discuss media at home - news, soaps, talk shows etc - but also use the media as an occasion, even a cover for discussion of relationships, politics, values, and so forth, arguably the domestic stage is as important for the public sphere as the media stage, albeit in different ways. Van Zoonen (2004, p. 39) extends a similar argument in relation to emotion (c.f. Madianou, this volume), pointing to the parallels between participating in a private leisure-based group - the fan community and participating in a public group - the political constituency, and arguing that:

> *The analogy between the two is structural to begin with: both come into being as a result of performance. Second, fan communities and political constituencies resemble each other in terms of activity: both are concerned with knowledge, discussion, participation, imagination of alternatives, and implementation. Finally, both rest on distinct emotional processes that range from habituation to excitement and anxiety. These emotions are differently but intrinsically linked to rationality, and lead - in concert - to 'affective intelligence'. The representation of politics on television, while generally thought to be dismally and destructively entertaining, can be seen as provoking the 'affective intelligence' that is vital to keep political involvement and activity going.*

Undoubtedly, attempts to eliminate the private (identity, lifestyle, interest, emotion, difference, etc) from the public have proved doomed to failure. This stubborn persistence of the private has stimulated proposals for an oppositional or alternative or pluralised public sphere, even including an emotional public sphere (Lunt and Stenner, in press). In any case, the public agenda is today occupied by issues once considered private, 'such as affirmative action, abortion, and the rights of sexual minorities ...issues about which large publics are either disinterested or unalterably divided. Either way, the impossibility of compromise has undermined support for many institutional remedies' (Bennett, 1998, p. 749). Fraser (1990) argues therefore that a sustainable public sphere need not, or should not, fit Habermas' ideal model of a rational-critical debate leading to a consensus among a large public ('the public'), but should instead facilitate a debate tolerant of diverse discursive modes, leading to a compromise among a range of interested rather than disinterested publics (plural). Media scholars have argued, in turn, that the media can and should play a key role in facilitating such debate. Through innovative formats, the media can promote diverse discursive modes. Through their unprecedented scope and reach, the media can bring together a range of publics. And while an argued consensus may lie beyond the conventions of most audiovisual genres, these same genres are fit for purpose for expressing heated contestations and, on occasion, for reaching a workable compromise (Curran, 1991; Dahlgren, 1995).

## The public in the private

If private activities have public consequences, if audiences are not to be opposed to publics, how far should the normative expectations of publics be required of audiences? To be sure, audience research has shown that people are, in their everyday reception of television and other media contents, often participatory seekers after meaning, not always accepting but sometimes negotiating or even resisting textual meanings. But do they have a moral responsibility to question and resist the problematic (biased, stereotyped, prejudiced or conservative) yet taken-for-granted assumptions of media messages? Are they culpable if they accept media messages with uncritical passivity? Silverstone (2002, p. 762) poses the challenge thus:

> *insofar as the persisting representational characteristics of contemporary media, above all in our media's representation of the other, remain unchallenged - as for the most part they are - then those who receive and accept them are neither mere prisoners of a dominant ideology nor innocents in a world of false consciousness; rather they are willing participants, that is, complicit, or even actively engaged, that is, collusive, in a mediated culture that fails to deliver its promises of communication and connection, with enduring, powerful and largely negative consequences for our status as human beings.*

It seems that, in countering the conception of audience as victim (commodified, passivised, institutionally managed through the use of publicity, statistics and marketing; Ang, 1990) or role, audience research has made audiences too vulnerable to the charge of villain, accountable for their activities, failing to sustain the public and therefore acting to undermine it. For often audiences do not contest mediated representations, accepting the preferred reading with little re-negotiation. And as Dayan (2001) points out in his critique of Morley's *Nationwide Audience*, those audiences who do make oppositional readings are those who are simultaneously organised as active publics.

Some defence of audiences' claims to publicness without taking on the full burden of public responsibility may be offered. First, while reception studies find only a minority who whole-heartedly counter the dominant reading of media texts, it finds many who seek to negotiate with it (Liebes and Katz, 1990; Livingstone and Lunt, 1994). In each case, this renegotiation is stimulated not by formal membership of an *a priori* public but by a conflict between the cultural claims of the text and the lived experiences of the audience, this requiring face-work at a minimum or, more ambitiously, some more active identity work through dialogic engagement (Billig, 1991).

Second, as audience research has also demonstrated, audiences act in response to their circumstances - that structured array of opportunities and constraints that is, for the most part, beyond their control, a matter of social stratification and which, undeniably, operate to make contestation or opposition difficult. Third, audiences surely encompass more than the raw material required for an effective democracy: unless we collapse the private into the public, there must be legitimate opportunity for such private pleasures as enjoyment, personal interest, relaxation and domesticity free from the glare of 'the public'. In another context - that in which educational ambitions are being institutionalised through policies for informal learning, accompanied by a moral discourse to evaluate 'well-spent' or 'beneficial' leisure time - Buckingham develops a Foucauldian critique of the 'curricularisation' of leisure (2001). A similar critique might be developed in relation to citizenship, as private leisure is scrutinised and judged - as successful or failing - for its potential or actual contribution to the public sphere, leaving no realm of public or private life free from official regimes of governance.

## Between public and audience: civic culture and the citizen-viewer

Audiences are, generally, neither so passive and accepting as traditionally supposed by those who denigrate them nor generally so organised and effective as to meet the high standards of those defining public participation. Rather, they sustain a modest and often ambivalent level of critical interpretation, drawing upon - and thereby reproducing - a somewhat ill-specified, at times inchoate or even contradictory sense of identity or belonging which motivates them towards but does not wholly enable the kinds of collective and direct action expected of a public. That, after all, is the point: it is precisely such context-dependent yet under-determined, plural and hybrid identities, understandings, practices and relationships that must and do shape people's engagement with others, in private and in public. This gives rise to the complex and ambiguous relations between audiences and publics and that we address in this volume.

Lest the evidence of mediated publics and diffused audiences seems to argue for a collapsing of publics into audiences, and vice versa, and in order to identify an alternative proposal, I conclude by asking whether between public and audience lies an intermediate realm. As several scholars have argued, this may usefully be understood in terms of the 'civic'. The introduction of a third term usefully allows us to avoid the woolly expansion of the normative public sphere concept to encompass all forms of (arguably or ambivalently) public discourse and participation, while recognising the importance of those fuzzy or ambiguous phenomena, grounded in the civil society and the lifeworld, that fascinate empirical researchers - the row over gender politics in the living room, the heated conversation in the talk show, the incipient new social movements mobilising online, and so on. Two strands of thought can be discerned in relation to the civic, paralleling the above review of ideas on publics and audiences: one concerns the decline of civil society and the growing evidence of citizen disengagement, cynicism and apathy; the other seeks to reconceptualise audiences as 'citizen-viewers' (Corner, 1995) so as to recognise the civic significance of audience activities.[7]

Dahlgren (2003, p. 155) suggests that instead of analysing media for their direct influence on publics, resulting in the decrying audiences for their apathy or the media for their refeudalisation of the public sphere:

> 'civic' should ...be understood as a prerequisite for the (democratically) political, a reservoir of the pre-or non-political that becomes actualised at particular moments when politics arises ... The key here is to underscore the processual and contextual dimension; the political and politics are not simply given, but are constructed via word and deed.

It becomes our task, then, to recognise the significance of particular words and deeds, mediated or otherwise, as they occur at particular moments when politics does or does not arise.

From a political science perspective, and hence motivated to address the challenge of an apparently increasingly apathetic and depoliticized public, Bennett (1998) also tackles the relation between audiences and publics. He is particularly concerned to critique one recent, headline-grabbing claim that denigrates audiences, that of Putnam's *Bowling Alone* (2000). While Putnam blames television for the decline in civic participation, Bennett's critique is not motivated by the desire to rescue audiences from attack but rather in order to seek a more satisfactory account of why the public has withdrawn into the privacy of the home, away from the local community activities that generate the social capital necessary to sustain political engagement. Although both theorists postulate civic culture as mediating between the private realm of individualised domesticity and leisure and the public realm of societal debate and politics, Bennett (1998, p. 744) argues for a more fundamental economic and cultural shift over the past half century, rendering television viewing merely a consequence rather than the cause of the problem:[8]

> *What is changing about politics is not a decline in citizen engagement, but a shift away from old forms that is complemented by the emergence of new forms of political interest and engagement... civic culture is not dead; it has merely taken new identities, and can be found living in other communities.*

Although Bennett (1998, p. 745) perhaps confusingly labels these new forms of culture 'uncivic' (to discriminate them from hostile or anti-public sentiments), he invites a debate over those new forms of public activity which could be supported by new forms of media, although how this may work - how far lifestyle and identity really translate into identity politics and new social movements - remains to be seen. Intriguingly, in the face of new possibilities for an expanded, even global public, it seems that the grounding of face-to-face, daily experience comes increasingly to the fore: perhaps in response to doubts regarding the trustworthiness or exploitability of globalised, mediated publics, 'the new concerns of lifestyle politics are more personal and local than national and governmental in scope and relevance' (Bennett; 1998, p. 748).

Dahlgren (2003, p. 154) similarly turns to the lifeworld, the realm of experience, for a source of renewal for the public sphere, stressing that 'such dimensions as meaning, identity and subjectivity are important elements of political communication' and so central to explaining how people become citizens and how they participate in public. Conceptually he argues:

> *If the more familiar concept of the public sphere points to the politically relevant communicative spaces in daily life and in the media, civic culture points to those features of the socio-cultural world - dispositions, practices, processes - that constitute preconditions for people's actual participation in the public sphere, in civil and political society.*

This leads him to the empirical question (2003, p.152), 'what are the *cultural* factors that can impinge on the actions and communication of people in their roles as (multifarious) citizens?' To address this, Dahlgren sketches an analysis of civic culture that combines questions of formal membership and consequential action with the subject dimensions of citizenship, identifying a range of distinct dimensions, each of which is acted on or influenced by the media, and each of which may work to support or undermine democracy.[9]

A diversity of projects may be located under this umbrella agenda for empirical research on audiences, civic culture and publics. For example, Barnhurst listens out for the intervention of both personal and media influence through a series of life history narratives, in trying to understand how young people become citizens when their main resources for decoding the world come from the mass media. Where Liebes (1992), some years before, revealed the reflexive difficulties of parents in attempting to mediate between the reductionist 'us' and 'them' framework of television news and their often right-wing teenagers, Barnhurst (1998, p. 215) suggests that young people themselves recognise that they cannot escape the media's framing of political events; indeed they seek and puzzle over 'primary experiences', touchstones for their own reflexive political judgement:

> *The stories young adults tell are intensely personal and local. They respond to media content in the context of a television set at home with parents, or at the bar with friends. They discuss their emerging selves, in reference to the media, with peers. They find more sources and expose themselves more widely to alternative media because of teachers. They are what can be described as active citizens in the interstices of power/knowledge, even if not in the modes and regions prescribed by democratic theory.*

In pursing this agenda, it must be as important to ask about the limits as the scope of these and similar claims. So, one wonders about the limits to Barnhurst's claim: are there ways of discussing the media in everyday life that do not constitute an incipient or actual citizenship? If 'understanding an issue comes scattershot, as in the case of the famine essay, from pop songs, TV commercials, documentary films and - most importantly - personal discussions more than from journalists' (Barnhurst, 1998, p. 216), then do any and all media contribute to informed citizens, to public opinion and public discussion? And, are all audiences ready and willing to participate thus? Perhaps, as he concludes, 'these young people, far from being dummies, are deeply committed to finding the truth about the political worlds they inhabit' (p 216). But if this is the case they do not appear to act on this commitment in conventionally recognised ways (Bennett, 1998).

Barnhurst and Liebes were concerned with the role of the news. But if we interpose civic culture - the locus of identities, values and cultural understandings - between the audience and the public, then other media forms and contents may surely also contribute. Hermes and Stello (2000) consider how far participating in an audience, in a complexly mediated late-modern world, means participating in a public. They ask whether 'reading a mass-marketed genre such as crime fiction be construed as a form of cultural citizenship (p219)?' Again, this frames citizenship in terms of experience rather than formal participation in political structures: 'citizenship is first of all the ways in which we feel connected to the different communities we are part of, ranging from formally organised communities such as the nation state to virtual communities such as feminism' (Hermes and Stello, 2000, p. 219). Their conclusions, however, are equivocal - unsurprising for a reception study, since audiences rarely speak with one voice, their views being as polysemic as any media text. As Livingstone and Lunt also argued (1994), such text-reception research provides stronger evidence for cultural citizenship as a questioning of belonging, positioning or equality than as a means of mobilising active participation or radical critique. According to Hermes and Stello (2000, p. 230):

> *Cultural citizenship is about confusion and near-irresolvable dualities, but also about a particular type of pleasure and reflection on those dualities and identities that will by and large keep conservative and progressive forces in balance ... it is structured as a domain of pre-political consideration, of unease with states of being, rather than as a monument to specific rights, duties or identities.*

Finally, I note that in my current research project, conducted with Nick Couldry and Tim Markham at LSE, we are exploring whether and in what ways the media offer a means by which people seek to participate in a shared public, a means by which the public sphere reaches out to the people and invites them to participate. Or, perhaps, the media close doors instead, excluding or distracting people from public connection or inviting escape into a more private world. Through detailed qualitative work with a diverse group of respondents, we are examining two common assumptions about democracy: first, that most people share an orientation to a public world where matters of common concern are, or should be, discussed (we call this orientation 'public connection'); and second, that public connection today centres on mediated versions of the public world (i.e. that public connection is increasingly sustained by a convergence in what media people consume). Hence, we hope to discover not just people's political values and their cultural attachments, but also their views on what are appropriate topics for political discussion and action, the range of people they regard as legitimate political actors, and the spaces or sites that they feel appropriate for political discussion and action.[10]

## Conclusion

In setting the scene for the chapters to follow, this chapter has argued that, in the late modern societies of Europe and elsewhere, the distinction between audience and public is increasingly hard to draw, as the media become ever more deeply embedded in all aspects of society. Telling the story of audiences means telling a story of changing forms of media and hence of changing forms of communication among peoples. The analysis of publics, by contrast, centres on an attempt to understand the significance and consequences of public - by contrast with private - forms of activity or spaces for activity. While historically sensitive, this also foregrounds the normative by seeking to understand how publics not only do but also should act, for the benefit of democratic society. The analysis of audiences and publics is becoming entangled insofar as it can be said that audiences are on the rise while publics are in retreat, but also that the two are linked. Such questions are not solely theoretical: there is ample justification for the careful empirical analysis of those diverse circumstances in which claims are made regarding either or both 'public' and 'audience'. Research must address whether, when and how the activities of particular, located audiences constitute a form of cultural engagement that matters to the public sphere and, as diverse media become integrated into public and civic processes, whether the media might transform - for better or for worse - the activities of publics as they ever more closely overlap with audiences.

Contemporary dilemmas regarding the relation between public and audience may be encapsulated in the following case study. Ouellette, influenced by Tony Bennett's (1995) Foucauldian analysis of the museum as a governmental apparatus, critiques the attempt to use public service media to socialise or engage otherwise apathetic audiences by focusing on the policy debates leading to the introduction of the public broadcasting service channel (PBS) in 1960s America. These, she shows, were motivated by an explicit policy of 'transforming television viewers into active citizens', proposed as a deliberate alternative to the 'consumer sovereignty promoted by commercial television' (Ouellette, 1999, p. 63). This vision informed Lyndon Johnson's State of the Union address announcing PBS in 1967, where he promised to 'make our nation a replica of the old Greek marketplace, where public affairs took place in view of all the citizens' (Ouellette, 1999, p. 67, from Miller, 1993, p. 136). However, PBS was highly controlled, materially and discursively. Never permitted to threaten the dominance of commercial broadcasting, instead it socialised audiences into 'good citizens' according to familiar Enlightenment ideals, embodied in the forms of rational-critical dialogue that characterises public service television. For Ouellette, this extension of governance to the once ill-disciplined audience has resulted in a normative and self-disciplining 'public' that reproduces middle-class standards of order and good taste, hence undermining rather than furthering the radical ideals of an enlightened and empowered public.

This chapter has similarly argued for a transcendence of the audience/public opposition for, as a growing body of literature makes clear, such binary thinking no longer fits either the subtleties of media texts or the complexities of media power in late modern societies. However, I part company with the Foucauldian critique, as asserted by Ouellette, Bennett and others against the Habermasian position, instead ending with a question. Undoubtedly, the now-familiar critique of the public sphere is fair, for through its rigorous, perhaps even rigid, norms of access, discourse, topic, and consensus-seeking, the Bourgeois public sphere legitimates only a narrow portion of the population as 'the public', excluding others. But does this make Lyndon Johnson's ambition fatally flawed in principle or only flawed in its implementation? Surely there can be mediated spaces, which invite and valorise participation from more diverse publics? And surely these can not only encompass debate on minority or alternative topics but also contest the very norms of rational-critical debate or consensus politics themselves? After all, the media are not so successful in managing their complex institutions, texts and audiences so as to exclude deliberation, contestation, even transgression. Perhaps the media can, under certain conditions, play a role in exploring or challenging the limits of governmentality rather than merely serving as the instrument of its ever-more efficient control. Where else, after all, could such contestation occur if not in mediated spaces? These, then, are the issues to be pursued in the chapters to follow.

## Notes

1. Many thanks to the colleagues with whom these ideas have been discussed: Nick Couldry, Daniel Dayan, Kirsten Drotner, Angela Livingstone, Peter Lunt, Mirca Madianou, Tim Markham, Dominique Mehl, Ulrike Meinhof, Dominique Pasquier, Roberta Pearson.

2. As Warner (2002, p. 47) comments acidly in relation to Habermas' Structural Transformation of the Public Sphere, 'the "sphere" of the title is a misleading effect of English translation; the German Öffentlichkeit lacks the spatializing metaphor and suggests something more like "openness" or "publicness". The French translation, L'Espace Public, is worse.'

3. Habermas explains the performative thus: 'the concept of *dramaturgical action* refers primarily neither to the solitary actor nor to the member of a social group, but to participants in interaction constituting a public for one another, before whom they present themselves' (*Aspects of Rationality*, in Outhwaite, 1996, p. 135).

4. Does this provide a clear means to divide publics from audiences? Unfortunately, as Habermas' critics have made clear, differences are rarely bracketed in practice and, as some argue further, nor should they be. Notably, those developing discourse norms for alternative or oppositional formulations of the public sphere find they must begin by unpacking any categorical boundary between public and private.

5. Indeed, under reflexive modernity, the claim that the audience has no representation of itself *qua* audience (e.g. Hartley, 2002), being a statistical aggregate described by others, seems untenable. Today, all category memberships are reflexively discussed. As Dayan (2001) observes, a member of the audience - alone in the living room or otherwise - is always aware of the wider collectivity sharing the experience with them, and so is only one step away from the way in which 'a public both knows itself to be - and wishes to be - seen' (Dayan, 2001, p. 752).

6. Silverstone (2002, p. 762) defines mediation as 'the fundamentally, but unevenly, dialectical process in which institutionalised media of communication are involved in the general circulation of symbols of social life. That circulation no longer requires face-to-face communication, though it does not exclude it.'

7. Two terms are often conflated here: 'civil society' refers to the realm of social order, of common or shared understandings, norms and values; 'civic culture' refers more to the realm of collective interest and mobilisation, the values, institutions and practices geared towards social and political outcomes that enhance democracy. The opposite of the former is uncivil, the opposite of the latter is disengaged. As used by Bennett, Dahlgren and others, civic culture

seems to refer to something less political than politics and something less ideal than the public.

8. Bennett identifies a third cause, one that accounts both for growing individualisation and for declining political engagement, namely the dramatic shifts in the labour market and the economy in the post-war period. Guided by accounts of late modernity developed by Giddens, Beck and others, Bennett amasses evidence that questions simplistic accounts of a decline in trust, interest or participation among the public, instead demonstrating the more complex links among growing economic insecurity, gendered division of labour, career uncertainty, and labour market instability on the one hand, and changing group structure, loss of tradition, growth in risk and altered sense of belonging or loyalty on the other. The result is that 'replacing traditional civil society is a less conformist social world ... characterised by the rise of networks, issue associations, and lifestyle coalitions facilitated by the revolution in personalized, point-to-point communication' (1998, p. 745).

9. These are: values, anchored in the everyday, formally articulated as the basis of democratic principles; affinity, the minimal sense of commonality and trust required for collective or community action; knowledge, the literacy required to make sense of the world so as to select among competing directions; practices, the traditions, habits and performances that mobilise meanings and bring about democratic society; identities, the reflexive sense of social belonging and subjective efficacy required to mobilise people as a public or citizenry; and discussion, the means of communicative interaction that embodies principles of inclusiveness, visibility and problem-resolution.

10. The project is entitled 'Media Consumption and the Future of Public Connection', with funding from the Economic and Social Research Council ('Cultures of Consumption' Programme, grant number RES 143-25-001); see www.publicconnection.org.

## References

Abercrombie, N., & Longhurst, B. (1998). *Audiences: A Sociological Theory of Performance and Imagination*. London: Sage.

Ang, I. (1990). *Desperately seeking the audience*. London: Routledge.

Appadurai, A. (1996). *Modernity at Large: Cultural Dimensions of Globalization*. Minneapolis: University of Minnesota Press.

Barnhurst, K. G. (1998). 'Politics in the fine meshes: Young citizens, power and media.' *Media, Culture & Society, 20*, 201-218.

Beck, U. (1992). *Risk society: Towards a new modernity*. London: Sage.

Bennett, L. (1998). '1998 Ithiel De Sola Pool lecture: The uncivic culture: Communication, identity, and the rise of lifestyle politics.' *Political Science and Politics, 31*(4), 740-761.

Bennett, T. (1995). *The birth of the museum*. London: Routledge.

Bentivegna, S. (2002). 'Politics and new media.' In L. Lievrouw & S. Livingstone (Eds.), *The Handbook of New Media* (pp. 50-61). London: Sage.

Billig, M. (1991). *Talking of the Royal family*. London: Routledge.

Blumler, J. G., & Gurevitch, M. (1995). *The crisis of public communication*. London/New York: Routledge.

Buckingham, D., Scanlon, M., and Sefton-Green, J. (2001). 'Selling the Digital Dream: Marketing Educational Technology to Teachers and Parents.' In A. Loveless, and Ellis, V. (Ed.), *Subject to Change: Literacy and Digital Technology* (pp. 20-40). London: Routledge.

Butsch, R. (2000). *The Making of American Audiences: From Stage to Television 1750-1990*. Cambridge: Cambridge University Press.

Calhoun, C. (Ed.). (1992). *Habermas and the public sphere*. Cambridge, Mass.: MIT Press.

Corner, J. (1991). 'Meaning, genre and context: the problematics of 'public knowledge' in the new audience studies.' In J. Curran & M. Gurevitch (Eds.), *Mass Media and Society*. London: Methuen.

Corner, J. (1995). *Television form and public address*. London: Edward Arnold.

Curran, J. (1991). 'Rethinking the media as a public sphere.' In P. Dahlgren & C. Sparks (Eds.), *Communication and citizenship: Journalism and the public sphere in the new media age*. London: Routledge.

Dahlgren, P. (1995). *Television and the public sphere: citizenship, democracy and the media*. London: Sage.

Dahlgren, P. (2003). 'Reconfiguring civic culture in the new media milieu'. In J. Corner & D. Pels (Eds.), *Media and the Restyling of Politics* (pp. 151-170). London: Sage.

Dayan, D. (2001). The peculiar public of television. *Media, Culture & Society, 23*, 751-773.

Eley, G. (1992). 'Nations, publics and political cultures: Placing Habermas in the Nineteenth Century.' In C. Calhoun (Ed.), *Habermas and the public sphere*. Cambridge, Mass.: MIT Press.

Fiske, J. (1987). *Television culture*. London: Methuen.

Fraser, N. (1990). 'Rethinking the public sphere: a contribution to the critique of actually existing democracy.' *Social Text, 25/26*, 56-80.

Gandy, O. H. (2002). 'The real digital divide: Citizens versus consumers.' In L. Lievrouw & S. Livingstone (Eds.), *The Handbook of New Media* (pp. 448-460). London: Sage.

Giddens, A. (1991). *Modernity and Self-Identity: Self and Society in the Late Modern Age.* Cambridge: Polity Press.

Habermas, J. (1969/89). *The structural transformation of the public sphere: an inquiry into a category of Bourgeois society.* Cambridge, M. A.: M.I.T. Press.

Habermas, J. (1984). 'The public sphere: an encyclopedia article (1964).' *New German Critique, Autumn*, 49-55.

Hartley, J. (2002). *Communication, Cultural and Media Studies: The Key Concepts.* London: Routledge.

Hermes, J., & Stello, C. (2000). 'Cultural citizenship and crime fiction: Politics and the interpretive community.' *Cultural Studies, 3*(2), 215-232.

Liebes, T. (1992). 'Decoding Television News: The Political Discourse of Israeli Hawks and Doves.' *Theory and Society, 21*(3), 357-381.

Liebes, T., & Katz, E. (1990). *The Export of Meaning: Cross-Cultural Readings of DALLAS.* New York: Oxford University Press.

Livingstone, S. (1998). 'Audience research at the crossroads: the 'implied audience' in media theory'. *European Journal of Cultural Studies, 1*(2), 193-217.

Livingstone, S. M., & Lunt, P. K. (1994). *Talk on Television: Audience participation and public debate.* London: Routledge.

Lunt, P., & Stenner, P. (in press). 'The Jerry Springer Show as an Emotional Public Sphere.' *Media, Culture & Society.*

McChesney, R. W. (2000). *Rich Media, Poor Democracy: Communication Politics in Dubious Times.* New York: The New Press.

McQuail, D. (1987). *Mass Communication Theory: An Introduction* (Second ed.). London: Sage.

Miller, T. (1993). *The Well-Tempered Self: Citizenship, culture and the postmodern subject.* Baltimore, MD.: Johns Hopkins University Press.

Morley, D. (1980). *The Nationwide Audience: Structure and Decoding.* London: British Film Institute.

Ouellette, L. (1999). 'TV viewing as good citizenship? Political rationality, enlightened democracy and PBS.' *Cultural Studies, 13*(1), 62-90.

Outhwaite, W. (Ed.). (1996). *The Habermas reader*. Oxford: Polity.

Putnam, R. D. (2000). *Bowling Alone: The collapse and revival of American community*. New York: Simon & Schuster.

Scammell, M. (2001). 'The Media and Media Management.' In A. Seldon (Ed.), *The Blair Effect - the Blair government 1997-2001* (pp. Chapter 23). London: Little, Brown and Co.

Silverstone, R. (1990). 'Television and everyday life: towards an anthropology of the television audience.' In M. Ferguson (Ed.), *Public communication: the new imperatives* (pp. 173-189). London: Sage.

Silverstone, R. (2002). 'Complicity and collusion in the mediation of everyday life.' *New Literary History, 33*, 761-780.

Warner, M. (2002). *Publics and Counterpublics*. New York: Zone Books.

Williams, R. (1961). *Culture and Society*. London: Fontana.

Williams, R. (1983). *Keywords: A vocabulary of culture and society*. London: Fontana.

Zoonen, L. van (2004). 'Imagining the fan democracy.' *European Journal of Communication, 19(1)*, 39-52.

Daniel Dayan

# Chapter 2: Mothers, midwives and abortionists: genealogy, obstetrics, audiences & publics[1]

## Lunch in Leipzig

'The genealogical side of analysis,' writes Michel Foucault, 'deals with series of effective formations of discourse. It attempts to grasp ... the power of constituting a domain of objects... Let us call these domains of objects positivities...' (quoted in Dreyfus & Rabinow, 1982, p. 105). This paper is concerned with 'positivities', with social realities such as *audiences* and *publics*, and with the speech acts or observational practices that produce them. These practices do not have to be lofty, nor do they necessarily manifest a "lowly origin', a *pudenda origo*: 'catty fights, minor crudeness, ceaseless and nasty clashing of wills...' (Dreyfus & Rabinow, 1982). Yet, they can only be detached from their result at the price of reifying these results. 'Many people write of the public as if it were someone whom they had just met for lunch ... at the fair in Leipzig", writes Schlegel (Merlin 1984, p.1). 'But who is that public? It is not a thing but a thought, a postulate, like church.' A similar awareness of reification is very much on the mind of the literary historian Hélène Merlin for whom the question is one of finding out - the period after the French wars of religion had exploded any unitary conception of the political body - 'how a *persona ficta*, the literary public progressively emerged, both indebted to the political body and disentangled from it" (Merlin, 1984, p.1). In both cases the notion of a 'public' is characterised by a profound hesitation on the part of the writer. Merlin's 'public' is a fictive being, a '*persona ficta*', the literary substitute of a disintegrated political body, but it progressively 'disentangles' itself, and presumably acquires some degree of autonomous existence. Schlegel wittily insists that the public is 'not a thing but a thought'. Yet, he concludes, 'it is a postulate, like church.' The church - or, more precisely, the unity of the church - is certainly a postulate. But any sociologist would point out that the church is also an organised body, a political power, a landowner, an economic institution. The hesitation or ambivalence concerning the real status of publics, or as it was put recently, ' the real world of audiences,' lingers to this day. It seems clear that - simultaneously, or at different times - publics belong in all three universes identified by Popper. First, publics are notions, ideations, or - as Schlegel puts it - 'postulates'. Second, publics are also sociological realities that one can observe, visit or measure. Three, publics finally allow for specific kinds of subjective experiences (Hartley, 1988). The purpose of this paper is to define the public as a process combining a *persona ficta*, the enactment of that fiction, and the experience involved in such an enactment. All this at a moment when the notion of a universal public, while still held as a norm, gives way to a multiplicity of publics whose encounters, debates and contests invite recasting the public sphere in terms of a 'sphere of publics' (Fraser 1992).

Publics differ, of course, in terms of the values they invoke and the issues they put forward. However, beyond content and values they are also distinguishable by their very structure, by the nature of what one might call their constitutive features. The focusing of collective attention generates a variety of attentive, reactive or responsive 'bodies'. In a way this chapter is about the social production of shared attention, and about the different entities ('*personae fictae*'), collective or not, that emerge in the role of enacting that attention through reaction and response - publics, audiences, witnesses, activists, bystanders and many others.

The first task is to acknowledge the diversity of this heterogeneous *ensemble*. A series of comparisons of various contrasting entities will enable the drawing of a first sketch, a delineation of the *'persona ficta'* called 'public'. The second exploration will narrow the focus to take a closer look at the various *'personae fictae'* involved in the reception of television. The key distinction made here is that between publics and audiences, or more precisely, between publics and different sorts of audiences.

## Paying attention to attention

If audiences vary, publics do so as well. The notion of public is too often subsumed by the dominant model of political publics. This conflation is misleading. Publics are far from constituting a monolithic *ensemble*, an obedient army marching in good order under the banner of political publics. Issue publics are flanked by identity-seeking publics and text-oriented publics (Dayan, 2003). Publics also have careers. They go through different stages including birth, growth, fatigue, ageing, death and sometimes resuscitation, not to mention hiding. Maurice Agulhon (1968) offers a beautiful example of rebirth in his study of penitent brotherhoods in eighteenth-century southern France. Disbanded in the aftermath of the French Revolution, these brotherhoods re-emerged some years later in a new atheistic garb. Penitents had become Freemasons. In other words, values had changed but not a certain voluntarism, nor a certain style of sociability, nor a definite penchant for secrecy. This penchant prevents, of course, brotherhoods or Freemasons from becoming fully-fledged publics. This point introduces the third area to be explored in this chapter . It has to do with publics and their visibility.

The *'persona ficta'* called 'public' requires visibility. However, the question of visibility is linked directly to an uneasy balance between the fictional dimension of publics and their sociological dimension. Publics are both intellectual constructions and social realities. The extent to which they are one or the other depends largely on how they are observed, how the observation is reported, and what sort of discourse is fed. It is therefore essential to closely watch those who watch publics. Publics often start their careers as a glint in their eye. More often than not, the gaze of such observers is performative. But it can perform in various registers. Depending on the case, those who watch publics (those who pay attention to attention) can be 'just looking', or they can be the true genitors of the observed entities, or their foster parents, or at least, their midwives. Sometimes there is little to observe, because publics have panicked and turned into 'marrano' publics donning, like Harry Potter, a mantle of invisibility (Noelle-Neuman, 1984). Sometimes there is nothing to observe at all because midwives have turned abortionists and potential publics went down the drain of unrealised destinies.

## A French accent

A last point. It concerns my own *linguistic habitus*. Raised as a French speaker, I do not conceive of 'audience' as a generic word to be contrasted with a narrow, normative notion called, ' public'. On the contrary. The generic word in French is 'public' and 'audience' is that particular version of 'public' that is defined by quantitative measurements. One of our shared findings in this volume is that the existence of different understandings of the same words often turns comparative research into a game of hide-and-seek. (See Meinhof in this volume.) Thus, for me, when English-speaking researchers discuss 'active' audiences, or analyse the speech of audiences, they are already dealing with a reality I would intuitively call 'public'. 'Public', taken in this French generic sense is no longer a normative ideal, but a whole range of sociological possibilities, one of which is the observational artifact called 'audience', one of which illustrates an ideal norm, but most of which are still in need of being characterised. Should I stick to the French terminology? No. This chapter is precisely about exploring the entities that different languages designate with deceptively similar words. Should I propose a new vocabulary right away? Once again, the answer is, no. I am not able to do so. Producing - or endorsing - a terminology can come only as a result of discussion, not as its prerequisite. I, therefore, have little choice but to work with a double understanding of the word 'public' and a double understanding of the word 'audience'. My discussion will therefore address four simultaneous notions. When speaking of publics, I shall, in most cases, be referring to a discrete, often mythologised, type of collective actor involved in political and cultural processes; but I shall also on occasion use 'public' in a generic sense. When speaking of 'audiences', I shall discuss the audiences of quantitative research, but I also intend to consider those put forward by reception studies. I hope the context will dispel the ambiguity surrounding each term.

## Public as persona - portrait in five comparisons

### Spectators

Most of the difficulties encountered with (quantitative) audience studies stem from the fact that concerned individuals generally do not know they are part of audiences. They are part of audiences in the sense that Molière's Monsieur

Jourdain speaks in 'prose'. That is, they are immersed in 'audiences' without realising that they are anything more than simple spectators. They have excellent reasons to be unaware of their audience status. This status is bestowed on them from the outside. 'Audiences'- as opposed to publics - exist only on paper. They involve no sociability, no performing, no feeling of identity, no ritual where belonging is affirmed or reinforced. They are spectators added to other spectators - spectators in the plural. If such spectators are said to be representative, their representativeness has nothing autonomous about it. It, too, is bestowed on them from the outside. This is why audiences do not and should not speak, unless animated by ventriloquists. Symptoms do not speak on behalf of an illness. It is the doctor that speaks. John Hartley puts it brilliantly (1987, 1988) when he writes that audiences belong in the world of discursive creations. As such, they are not fit for empirical study. Their study belongs in discourse analysis, says Hartley. It therefore makes little sense to compare such audiences with publics, to describe them as more or less active, as more or less involved or committed. Publics may be sociological realities. Audiences of this sort are observational aggregates. This is why I propose to start from the individual spectator. What are the features that distinguish this spectator from a public?

The difference is not a matter of numbers. A public is not simply a spectator in the plural, a sum of spectators, an addition. It is a coherent entity whose nature is collective; an *ensemble* characterised by shared sociability, shared identity and a sense of that identity.

The difference between plural and collective finds an echo in the matter of styles of attention. The attention of an individual spectator is somehow 'floating', (like that of a psychoanalyst). Even when focused it remains undirected, open, ready for the unexpected, ready to enjoy the unexpected. The attention of publics is more than focused: it is issue driven. Through various attempts at co-ordination, it is meant to be convergent. Members of a public are not blind to the unexpected; yet, they know in advance what to look for. This distinction is true of television spectators, but it can be confirmed in other contexts. In their study of the triumphant return of General MacArthur to America, after his involvement in the Korean War, G & K Lang stress the somehow unfocused nature of the attention the military parade elicits among spectators in the streets of Chicago. By contrast, the directive attention of television crews never misses an opportunity to aggrandise the event or increase its charismatic appeal. In contrast to spectators in the street, these crews seem to know exactly what to look for. They behave like a partisan public (Katz & Dayan, 2003).

The third distinction concerns styles of behaviour and the issue of performance. A spectator is characterised by involvement with the text, film or programme attended, an involvement whose intensity may trigger identification, or lead to 'para-social interaction'. A public rather seeks social manifestations of its pleasure, displeasure, approval or disapproval. Spectators expect involvement. Publics engage in collective performances. There are situations in which involvement and performance can take place simultaneously (a rock concert, a football match). Yet, they may also exclude each other. More often than not, there is a time for involvement and there is a time for response; and one of the characteristics of the visual media is perhaps their extended postponement of the moment of response. This distinction is not merely chronological. In the course of a study on the *Sundance* film festival (Dayan, 2000), I noticed that some participants had come to watch films. Others had come to be the publics of the festival. The two activities turned out to be much less complementary than expected. Those who became engrossed with films tended to forget they were a public. Others kept ready to jump, poised for performance, wary of any intense (distracting) involvement with the movies.

The fourth distinction concerns the very process of watching. Typically the television spectator enters the process of 'audiencing' (Fiske, 1992) - or what I called 'audienciation' (1998) - by accepting the participative frame (Livingstone & Lunt, 1992) handed over by the programme , and by becoming, at least fictionally, part of the 'imagined community' of spectators that this participative frame offers as a promise (or as a lure). This is how the experience of the spectator becomes a social experience, an experience of 'watching with', no matter how lonely the spectator may in fact be (Cavell, 1982). Thus, during the sixties, the spectator of Norwegian news programmes could join an imagined community of 'rational-legal' spectators (Ytreberg, 2000). Thus, in the France of today, the spectator of the political puppet-show, *les guignols de l'info* (*Canal Plus*), joins an imagined community whose professed anarchism curiously blends into a form of gallows humour reminiscent of Louis-Ferdinand Céline's smirking contempt for democracy. In such situations, a spectator has two options. One is to accept the offered frame and join the imagined community that comes with it. The other is to reject the frame and become a non-spectator.

Publics have other options. In particular, they can construct an alternative frame of reception, a counter-frame. By so doing, they transform the proposed 'imagined community' into an object of investigation, a theme for reflection. By so doing, they question the values incorporated in the frame, and raise the Brechtian question of how such values could ever be defended, if at all. The imagined community of rational-legal viewers can be denounced as a pious lie; the 'rebel' community of *les guignols de l'info* as another (less innocent). Thus, like Morley's 'oppositional' readers (1980), the members of publics are able to join in viewership without accepting the proposed frame; they are capable of establishing their own viewing contract. In other words, publics display a collective autonomy not afforded to individual spectators. They may enter audiences, but on their own terms.

## Crowds

The notion of 'public' and the notion of 'crowd' are usually perceived as antithetic. Publics embody normative rationality. Crowds, on the contrary, exemplify irrational behaviour and have generated sociological anxieties since the end of the nineteenth century. Despite such anxieties, we know from various ethnographies that crowds can be neither violent nor irrational. Kurt and Gladys Lang point to their conversational sociability (1968); Timothy Garton Ash stresses the quiet, yet determined character of the crowds that peacefully achieved the Velvet Revolution in Prague (1990). I have also shown that crowds can perform in a distanced, parodic, reflexive style (Dayan and Katz, 1992). Le Bon's rejection of crowds as mindless often expresses his own fears. Even Tarde's more nuanced approach, requires a caveat. The existence of crowds involves not only imitation, but conversation as well, even though, of course, not all conversations involve a deliberative dimension.

Despite their proposed symmetry, crowds and publics are not exclusive entities. Some crowds behave like publics. Some publics take the form of crowds. The difference is a matter of space, of locality. It is ultimately one that involves skin, the sense of touch. Publics can belong in the public sphere and in a public space. Crowds are to be found in public spaces only. Is there a difference? Yes. A public sphere involves a circulation of discourses. A public space involves a circulation of bodies. In the public sphere, violence is exclusively symbolic. In a public space, violence may be physical as well. Thus, some publics are congregative, but in general, they do not need to be. Crowds must be congregative, or they stop being crowds.

A public, therefore, differs from a crowd, in that its existence is not predicated on sharing a certain physical location. I propose that a public is by nature dispersed throughout the population, I would say, 'diasporic'. It can take the form of a crowd, but it is never co-terminous with any crowd. It can take a congregative form, but it can also disperse without dissolving. Belonging to a public is not a matter of breathing the same air.

The emergence of print media makes contiguous publics obsolete or occasional (provided that our notions of 'publics' were relevant before their emergence). People who applaud in the theatre, or shout 'Bravo' in opera houses are not publics, but metonomies of publics. They are not illustrations of what a 'public' is, but only of what a *contiguous* public is. They are not the necessary point of departure of any reflection on 'publics'. They are, on the contrary, an avatar, which requires explanation. It is necessary to start by defining publics, and then explain what it means for publics to gather.

Yet, if contiguity stops being a defining feature of publics, we must then define publics in some other way. In the absence of an actual gathering, we have to turn towards some construction of a collective identity. The nature of such a construction will be explored in the rest of this chapter . However, two points can already be made. First, the construction of collectives usually involves a process of imagination, an imagining of community, a map of belonging. Publics therefore involve fictions of publics. Second, such fictions have authors. The construction of collectives involves architects. It is therefore important to look at how publics are born. It is also important to look at how they die - or survive. Some of the key issues concerning publics concern their transient - or resilient - nature: their fleeting, amorphous character - or institutionalisation. Crowds gather, then disperse. Publics exist without gathering and they survive dispersion.

## Communities

A public has much in common with a community and for a simple reason. A public is a community. Like any community, a public involves a dimension of shared (and imagined) identity, a certain style of sociability, a degree of persistence through time. A public is of course a dispersed community - as most communities of today are - and the study of diasporic media (Naficy, 1993) shows that the survival of communities often depends on the ability to form publics.

But, there is a difference between the communities called 'publics' and those to which one is attached by birth. This difference is already evident in Weber's distinction between 'communalization' and 'sociation'. Grounded in affect and tradition, 'communalization' is based on the subjective feeling of belonging to a given community. (It is traditional.) Linked to rational action and conceived in view of a given finality, 'sociation' is organised in contractual manner (it is rational and legal). An example of a sociation is a 'conviction based association, in relation with defending a cause' (Weber, 1971; Faveri, 2004). All this means that joining a public, as opposed to being part of a community, involves a political, ethical or aesthetic decision. This decision should be discrete, individual, reflexive and free. But, belonging to a community may precede, or even preclude choice. With regard to a community, acting freely may consist in choosing *not* to belong. Freedom may then be construed as betrayal.

The difference between public and community is therefore a normative one. It is linked to the distinction between 'public' and '*oikos*', between the public sphere and other spheres ruled by interests that are not generalizable.[2] In other words, a public is defined in reference to values that are actually or potentially universal; that are construed as universalisable. The 'universality' criterion excludes any intermediary body between the individual and a public. A public is a collective made of individual responses. Such responses cannot be pre-formatted or pre-determined by membership in a community, since a community harbours interests that are not always universalisable. This is why any (traditional) community, in order to become or join a public, must undertake a process of translation, of reformulation of the values it advocates (Dayan, 1999).

The normative distinction of public and community may sound very theoretical. In fact, it has direct repercussions on the political arena. It is an essential part of the media justification when it comes to opening or closing the agenda; when it comes to letting-in or bouncing-off an issue or a public; when it comes to gate-keeping.

## Activists, militants

Publics are often opposed to audiences, which are the somehow leisurely, idle versions of publics. But publics can also be opposed to militant groups, or 'activists', the latter word being particularly useful when it comes to blurring the limits between support (for a cause or an opinion) and involvement in violent activities. A current euphemism transforms 'terrorists' into 'activists'. This euphemism is not altogether incorrect, since terrorists are activists. Yet, it does not take much expertise to realise that terrorism involves a few extra dimensions.[3] The distinction between militant groups and publics is no less difficult, yet it is equally manageable. Thus, it is possible to speak of a 'militant public', which presumes that not all of them are. What are, then, the differences between militant groups and publics?

They seem to concern organisational styles and registers of action. In terms of organisation, an activist is affiliated to a specific group. A public, on the contrary, perceives itself as potentially infinite. An activist is part of an institutionalised entity, with hierarchies, rules and levels of decision-making. Publics are characterised by blindness to hierarchies, by blissful anarchy, by organisational innocence. In terms of action, activists do engage in tactics, and routinely practice a ranking of ends and means. Publics only engage in actions wholeheartedly embraced. Sartre-type dilemmas are not theirs. Activists may accept having 'dirty hands'. Publics display 'pure' motives. In a way, purity is their business. The actions of a public are aiming, not at expediency, but at exemplarity. Such actions are rhetorical in nature. They are meant to persuade, to invite imitation.

In sum, while activists engage in instrumental action, the members of a public operate on a gestural register. Their distinctive mode of action is conveyed through signs and it aims at convincing the (yet) unconvinced. The publics' mode of action is fundamentally dramaturgic and it can best be defined as a performance.

## Witnesses

It is highly unusual to use 'witness' to speak of someone who watches a film, work of art or television programme, although it may happen in specific cases. Yet, many events and situations tend to involve witnesses as well as publics. Both notions stress an orientation towards a given focus of attention. Both stress dimensions of publicity, performance and commitment. Such dimensions, I believe, are always found in the case of publics. Such dimensions characterise the act of witnessing as well. A testimony is a public performance whose author is committed (and liable to the risk of perjury). Yet, publics and witnesses differ in significant ways.

First, a witness is typically an individual. Such a figure can exist in the plural (it takes many witnesses to confirm a fact). Yet, each testimony has to remain singular. In other words, witnessing is never collective. A collective witness would be highly unreliable, or the meaning of being a witness would be altogether changed. 'Jehovah's Witnesses' are not 'witnesses' in the usual (judicial) sense of the word.

Second, and in line with the first feature, a testimony must refer to a particular, singular occurrence. When a testimony no longer bears on an individual occurrence, and concerns itself instead with general issues or principles, its abstraction makes it no longer a testimony. For example, *apostles* are witnesses of the passion of Jesus. They are indeed recounting a chain of specific events. But, martyrs are offering a testimony of their commitment to a doctrinal body (rather than the relation of a singular occurrence). *Martyr*, in Greek, means witness, but clearly, the notion of witnessing has a very different meaning here. Or, to take another example, let us follow Hegel during one of his daily walks in Jena. Hegel all of a sudden sees Napoleon riding on horseback. On that day, recounts the philosopher, I saw 'History'. As a philosopher, may be so. As a witness, Hegel only saw a stout man, with a triangular hat, riding a horse (Lilla, 2001, p. 131).

A third difference concerns temporal orientation. The temporality of witnessing is typically retrospective. Like Barthes' photographs, a witness always says, 'This has occurred'. When witnesses no longer commit themselves to affirm, 'this has occurred' and start assenting 'this should occur', they no longer act as witnesses, but as members of a public.

The last dimension has to do with the semantic field of 'attention'. A witness reports on an event/situation that he/she has attended. A public is a group made of those who react to an event or situation to which they have decided to pay attention. It should by now be clear that, given the diasporic nature of publics, attention does not presuppose attendance. We also know from scores of social psychology experiments and courtroom interrogations, that attendance does not always entail attention. A major function of contemporary media is to organise the large-scale management of public attention. As to attendance, it has progressively changed status, in order to become, as Benjamin famously put it, an aesthetic provider of 'aura'.

This brief analysis confirms a few things we already know about publics. Publics are collective and not plural. Publics are concerned with issues and not with particular situations. This brief analysis also helps us clarifying two new dimensions: (1) The experience of publics is characterised by a prospective temporality (rather than with the retrospective one of - say - meaning making audiences, always running the risk of turning into 'salt pillars'). (2) Publics are crucial performers of a social process technically known as 'agenda-setting' and which I would define in general terms as the 'directing of public attention'. As agenda setters (and as trendsetters), publics find themselves in competition with the media. In a way, publics and media are contenders. In a way they are also colleagues. Depending on the situation, publics will be hailed by the media, celebrated as vanguards, used as vantage points; or they will be banished and shouted down, treated as unwelcome intruders in a well-choreographed game.[4]

### Summing up defining features

A few specific dimensions emerge from the comparisons made so far:

1. In contrast to that of *crowd*s, the interaction of publics can be devoid of any local or tactile dimension, and be exclusively conveyed through signs.

2. As opposed to spectator, a public is not simply many spectators. It is not a plural, but a collective; and like any other collectivity, the collectivity called public depends on a process of imagination. It is a realised fiction.

3. As opposed to a *militant organisation* a public is defined by actions that take the form of a visible performance. Directed towards other publics and taking place in the public sphere, this performance involves a large-scale dramaturgy, a Goffmanian exercise in self-presentation. Publics must be exemplary; they are proposing collective role models.

4. Unlike witnesses, publics do not relate to particular situations but to the principles or issues that these situations exemplify, and to the values involved.

5. As opposed to *communities*, publics are submitted to the normative requirements of the general public sphere. They must offer a discourse directed towards the common good, a discourse that is potentially universal.

These various elements of definition need to be further specified; they presuppose additional features. Let me therefore propose six brief explorations. Three concern features I have already addressed (sociability, performance, issues). Three have not been explicitly mentioned so far (commitment, reflexivity, stability).

*Performance* links the notion of public to that of a public sphere. A public not only offers attention, it calls for attention. Any public requires another public watching it perform. The performance may be polemic or consensual. It cannot be invisible. A public must 'go public' or it is not a public. A public is eager to be watched. It always strikes a pose.

Registers of sociability, *styles* of interaction, differentiate given publics from other publics. Thus, there are ' manners of publics' in the same way one would speak of 'table manners'. Dispersed publics rely on epistolary or argumentative rhetorics. Dramaturgical conventions better suit situations when publics are gathered. Theatregoers applaud or boo. Concertgoers respect an absolute silence, or engage in noisy cheering, whistling or dancing. Festival participants politely ask questions. Operagoers don tuxedos or jeans. Demonstrators lie on the pavement, or chant, or fly to faraway destinations to become 'human shields'.

A public can only exist in *reflexive* form. Either it knows it exists or it does not exist. A public is a collective subject that emerges in response to mirror images of itself. The seventeenth century public emerges through reading and discussing newspapers where the notion of ' public' is being discussed (Peters, 1992). In other words, 'public' belongs to the category of collective subjects that are imagined in first person, by a 'we'.

Publics require loyalty on the part of their members, an implicit *commitment* emanating from those who wish to join. Once committed, the members of publics cannot just change their minds. No Frenchman could be pro-Dreyfus and pro-Zola on Monday and against Dreyfus and Zola on Tuesday. Parting company from a public is something that must be explained, argued, justified.

The question of commitment is connected to the equation of stability. A public cannot be too transient. It requires a minimal stability. But issues might come and go, triggering different publics. One way of endowing publics with some amount of persistence consists in linking issues to each other, in connecting the same public to different and successive issues. 'If you supported position A, then you must support position B.' This amounts to organising clusters of kindred issues, that is, to elaborating an ideology. This also amounts to institutionalising publics. Thus some publics turn into associations, social movements or parties. How institutionalised can different forms of publics manage to be?

The last dimension concerns *issues* Quite often publics are not constituted in response to works, texts, events or media, but in response to issues, even when such issues are linked to specific works, texts, events or media. For example, in nineteenth-century France, the battle between literary publics triggered by Victor Hugo' play, *Hernani,* was less about the merits of the play itself, than about the legitimacy of a theatre that dared trample the aesthetic rules of classical tragedy. With reference to Dewey, one can therefore suggest an interactive link between issues (or problems) and publics. Problems and publics generate each other. Is this always the case? Does a concern with issues characterise all forms of publics?[5]

The portrait I have just offered is the portrait of a *'persona ficta'*, the portrait of a myth, a subjunctive fiction. Yet, no matter how subjunctive, this fiction serves as a model. Fiction turns into a political force by providing scripts for action. The real problem with this model is therefore less its fictional status than the nature of the fiction proposed. This fiction is essentially political. Not all publics are political. Publics come in many shapes. Even if they display a core of common features they cannot be reduced to a single model.

## Audiences & publics - Stages, backstages and curtains

### A preference for issue publics

Publics must be specified, both by origin and by object. Stressing the social origins of a public does not at all consist in proposing that a public must be equated with the group it comes from. For example, members of a class or an ethnic group do not automatically join the same publics. Defining a public is done, first of all, by pointing to the object on which attention is focused. The notion of public is relational. There are no publics in general for the same reason that words - Austin tells us - make little sense outside of sentences. Whether conceptualised in terms of interpretation, in terms of evaluation, or in terms of response, publics are always the publics-of-something. The nature of the something in question determines the nature of what 'public' must be compared to. Sometimes 'public' must be compared to crowd, sometimes to spectator, sometimes to community, sometimes to 'citizen', and the list goes on. Each of these oppositions can be profitably explored, but in the course of any given study, not all of them are simultaneously necessary and only a handful is crucial. The social construction of publics is context dependent. Their focus provides specific analytic criteria.

In the field of media studies, 'public' is generally opposed to 'audience'. The audience is the public's other, an unfortunate 'doppelganger', characterised by a series of lacks. Until recently it was said to have no sociability; stability was precluded by the rhythms of consumption; commitment was rendered impossible by trendiness; performance was pointless in the restricted confines of the private sphere. Was this binary characterisation (this character assassination) useful? Are there only two collective actors involved in the social process of attention-reception-response to media? Do we find the same collective actors in front of a fiction programme and in front of a football match? Even if we restrict our investigation to television we can easily point out that there are many sorts of audiences and at least three ideal types of publics.

1   'Taste publics' are generally focused on works, texts, or programmes; the performance of these publics is 'verdictive' (evaluative).

2.  'Issue publics' are generally but not always - as we have seen with the *Hernani* example - linked to the political. They specialise in the production of public problems. Their performance is largely 'expositive' (definitional) and is aimed at determining certain courses of action.

3. 'Identity publics' (such as those of music, games or sports fans) display their response to games or performances in order to endow themselves with a visible identity. Their performance is made of 'behabitives'.

Of course, in actual situations, the three ideal types tend to overlap and the corresponding performances are never discrete. Yet, in each case, one type may be said to dominate. In this section, and in this chapter in general, I have chosen to stress 'issue' publics. I did so because they are better known, and because focusing on one type of public simplifies comparison with the equally complex world of audiences.

Let us turn, then, towards publics and audiences in the context of television news events, knowing that even the crudest of quantitative audiences share at least two characteristics with publics.

1. Like that of publics, the experience of audiences involves a dimension of imagination, concerning the others who share with them a given participative frame (Livingstone & Lunt, 1992) or whom they join in 'audiencing' ( Fiske, 1992).

2. Like that of publics, audiences embody a fundamental dimension of social experience: collective attention, 'watching with' (Dayan, 1998).

### A fable

Here is a fable. It is a fable about a small minority in an imaginary European democracy where this minority has been present for one thousand years, for the oldest families, and about half a century for the most recent. In this large country, there has been a recent series of debates between spokespersons of the minority and the major newspapers, editors, journalists. These debates start as dispersed expressions of dismay at the content of editorials, talk shows, newspapers or newscasts. Readers and viewers from the minority are amazed at what they see as the inadequate reporting, sloppiness, and systematic partiality in a number of stories that concern them indirectly or directly. They try to explain that a daily diet of consistently hostile representations in the form of news, documentaries, fiction texts, and debates might lead to regrettable consequences, such as physical violence and the casting out of the group as a whole. Their warning is ignored but, perhaps, proved correct by the gravest wave of violence directed against that minority since World War II. For about a year the violence goes largely ignored by an embarrassed government and largely unreported by ambivalent media.

At that point audience members in the minority start systematically watching news, recording them on tape, looking for examples of misreporting; comparing coverage of similar events in different countries; comparing experiences with other readers or viewers; documenting local acts of violence through photographs, witness accounts and medical reports; also documenting the failure by the media to report on them. When they have gathered (what they believe is) an impressive amount of evidence, they go public with this evidence and send it not only to the media, but also to political officials and parliament. The pattern of over-reporting, non-reporting, or misreporting whenever the minority is collectively concerned is denounced as an incitement to hatred and as a repeated breach of the deontological norms of professional journalism.

Whether or not the issues are accurately framed and their authors correct in linking the outbursts of violence to the emergence of a new form of xenophobic discourse, it is clear that a public is emerging. This public is making general, universalisable claims: protesting against discrimination; condemning the breach of journalistic standards. This public is also ready to perform in public. Finally this public proves itself as one by generating 'counter-publics'.

Such counter-publics, (some of them speaking in the name of the same minority), and largely represented in op eds, and letters to the editor (a) deny any justification to the claims made (b) reject the representativeness of those making those claims, and (c) present the question of a specific violence exerted against that given minority, as a sectarian issue, unfit for generalisation and unworthy of the public sphere.

For a long time the minority public finds little support or media endorsement. Counter-publics are supported by various columnists and, in particular, by those who ignored the outbursts of violence in the first place. These columnists explain that the burning of specific religious buildings, the desecration of identified cemeteries, the beating of selected pupils in schools and the updating of an old vocabulary of ethnic insult are not directed at any particular group. They stem, on the contrary, from a general climate of violence, the causes of which are too deep to warrant action given the facts at hand. That the vast majority of attacks should concentrate on about 1% of the population (the minority in question) is deemed irrelevant.

There is undoubtedly a definitional battle going on, concerning the framing of the mistreatment issue and whether it should enter the public agenda. Whether correct or not, minority members who engage in this definitional battle form publics. My point here is that the members of this new public have not ceased being part of audiences. They need to be audiences if only to check whether patterns have changed, whether misrepresentation is over, whether on the contrary new discriminatory narratives have been invented. Is there, then, a lesson to my fable? [6]

There are in fact three lessons, besides a basic one that suggested (until recently) that hate campaigns are best avoided. (a) The same minority can generate different publics. (b) What starts as conversations held in the private sphere leads to opinions defended in the public sphere. (c) There is a reversibility between the status of public and that of audience: publics and audiences can - and do - turn into each other.

## Publics and audiences: reversibility

Publics must always have been audiences. In the political domain, they stop being audiences when their concern for an issue prevails over their engagement with the narrative that calls for it. It is this concern for - and focusing on - an issue that constitutes an audience into a public. According to Dewey, the emergence of a public and the investigation of a given issue, leading to the statement of a public problem, are two aspects of the same process.

Once constituted, publics need nevertheless to remain audiences in order to check the progression of 'their' problem on the political agenda. As audiences, they have to find out what is being narrated. As publics they try to point out how it is narrated, and why. In a word, audiences and publics are not separate continents.

This does not mean that there is a flawless continuity between audiences and publics. I believe that decisive thresholds separate them. In the introduction to this volume, Sonia Livingstone poses two excellent questions. 'When is a public not an audience?', and 'when is an audience not a public?' A possible answer is, 'never, really'. My own answer would be: 'in most cases'.

Can a public not be an audience? In my view, certainly. Yet, most publics start their careers as audiences and intermittently revert to the status of audiences. They need to be audiences for three reasons. (1) When publics mobilise around issues, they respond to situations that are generally mediated, situations to which they are first exposed as audiences (Boltanski, 1993). (2) Once issues are constructed, publics need media to reach their members. New members will typically be recruited from audiences. (3) As Kirsten Drotner puts it, the literacy skills required by publics to emerge, connect and organise are, in most cases, never taught at schools, or taught *post facto*, when people have already mastered them. So, how then, are they learned? They are picked-up, acquired in the familiarity with media output that characterises audiences.

Can an audience not be a public? It seems to me, that the answer is once again, 'yes'. Most audiences are not publics. To put it in very simple terms, a public is born when members of an audience decide to join and go public. Going public involves on their part the construction of a problem, a reflexive decision to join, commit, perform, etc. Most audience members do not feel the urge to enter that process. This does not mean that they hide. Audiences are not especially bashful and the private sphere is not a closet. Yet, it does not offer the type of visibility sought for by publics.

But is the distinction between audiences and publics equally relevant for all varieties of audiences? Is it still relevant when it comes to 'meaning-making audiences'; when it comes to 'audiences that speak'?

## Talk - formal and informal

This is, in a way, the question raised by Peter Dahlgren when he discusses various forms of 'political talk' and describes 'civic culture' as the site of a continuity between the pre-political and the political. Thus, writes Dahlgren, 'we cannot know in advance just what talk of a pre-political nature will, within the context of ongoing interaction, turn, perhaps indirectly towards the political' (Dahlgren, 2003, p. 151-169). Dahlgren emphasises the 'permeability of contexts', the 'messiness and unpredictability of everyday talk', the fact that what is political or not is never *a priori* given.[7] Yet, concedes Dahlgren, 'not all the communicative interaction of the everyday life should be treated as a civic discussion'.

> *There has recently been some argument as to whether political talk among citizens is best understood as grounded in the informal flowing character of everyday speech or should rather be seen as a separate and distinct mode of activity. Schudson (1997) has made the controversial case that 'conversation is not the soul of democracy'. His point is that conversation is basically about sociability. Political discussion, on the other hand, is about solving problems, finding solutions to conflicts It is purposive, and goal-oriented. Democratic deliberation is not 'spontaneous'. Rather it is civil, public, and not necessarily egalitarian. It opens up the door for social discomfort, seemingly the opposite of what is usually intended with conversation.*

> *(Dahlgren, 2003)*

Michael Schudson (1997, 1998) proposes a sharp distinction within the domain of what Bill Gamson would call 'political talk'. On the one hand, conversation is characterised by informality, sociability and - presumably - pleasure. On the other hand, debate is characterised by purposiveness, connection to issues, publicness and the risk of conflict. While aimed at distinguishing between forms of talk, this opposition is very similar to that between audiences and publics. As Dahlgren concludes, 'Schudson and others are operating with an understanding of political discussion that is rather bounded, indeed, one might call it 'formal'. Political discussion is associated with a specific kind of context. It becomes situationally distinct from other modes of talk.'

Dahlgren is correct in pointing out that this understanding of political discussion is rather bounded, situationally distinct (and formally distinct as well) from other forms of talk. Yet, this should not mean it is endowed with a totally independent mode of existence. There can be porousness between different forms of political talk just as there can be porousness between any two linguistic registers. While acknowledged, (and I believe it should be) this porousness does not preclude forms of talk and linguistic registers from having distinct existences, identifiable features and definable statuses. I believe that forms of talk are relevant to the distinction between audiences and publics; that in the matter of political talk, as well as in other matters, publics and audiences differ.

## Thresholds, backdrops and iron curtains

Dahlgren makes us aware that there are politically relevant exchanges outside institutional politics. But must we believe that there is a binary opposition between 'institutional politics', on the one hand, and 'the rest', on the other hand? 'The rest' is not institutional but it can be more or less formal, more or less public, more or less dramaturgic. 'The rest' does not simply consist of informal exchanges taking place in the life world. What is missing from Dahlgren's essentially continuist position is the notion of a threshold *within* the sphere of non-institutional politics; a threshold between what I would call 'audience-talk' and 'public-talk', a threshold between - roughly - conversation and debate.

'Café" conversations, writes political philosopher Jean Marc Ferry, 'are not strictly private and they are part of the dynamics through which public opinion is constructed' (Ferry, 1989, p. 22). Ferry agrees here with Dahlgren. But he seems to agree also with Schudson.

> *When a given group engages in political discussion, the expressed opinions must fulfil a specific condition. Even if they are conducted in public, and even if they concern matters of public interest, these opinions must reach a potentially infinite audience (via the media) in order to enter the public sphere. (Ferry, 1989, my translation)*

Like Schudson, Ferry stresses the existence of a situational threshold between forms of talk. As I indicated earlier, I believe this threshold to be porous but to exist nonetheless. It is a threshold, not an iron curtain. If a curtain at all, it would be closer to the backdrop that isolates stage from backstage in a theatre. Actors are not locked up on stage. They circulate back and forth. As any Stanislavsky student knows, they bring on stage the rich variety of their daily experiences. Yet, they do not act in the same way, nor speak the same words, when they are on stage as when they are at rest.

In other words, one cannot speak of just two possibilities. Political discourse is not condemned to being either formal or conversational. One should take account of three possibilities. The first is 'formal politics', but there are two others. There are people that chat and there are people who chant in the streets. And the latter, people that chant in the streets, are engaged in politics, but not in 'formal' politics.

1. Formal political debate is the moment when the talk of publics is invited into the discourse of politicians or journalists. Turned into an argumentative

resource, this talk is now offered in quotes, excerpts or paraphrases that are supposedly expressive of the will of the public, and serve as a justification or legitimation for given courses of action within the political system.

2. But before being excerpted and quoted and used as a legitimation for formal political programme s, the talk of publics is chanted, heard in talk-shows, read in op eds or letters to the editor. At this point the talk is public, commits its authors and obeys given rules, but these rules are not yet those of formal politics.

3. And, even before this crystallisation into identifiable public positions, the themes addressed are born in informal exchanges and conversations, which may be explicitly political, or not, or not yet.

Formal politics does not concern us here because it does not involve performance or talk by either publics or audiences. As to informal politics, I believe it involves, not only the elaboration of common opinions, but also their confrontation in various public contexts. Private conversations allow for the elaboration of opinions. Public confrontations turn such opinions into politically-relevant themes. The latter may then be recruited or not by those who decide on agendas.

Are audiences an ideal site for the emergence of a 'civic culture'? For Peter Dahlgren, they are. For Zygmunt Bauman (Bauman, 2002, p. 171) the situation is exactly the opposite and the dynamics of audiences leads to uncivic culture, to privatising the social, to translating the collective into individual terms. I feel, in fact, much closer to Dahlgren. I believe that audiences can indeed foster the emergence of a civic culture. This is what I tried to express in *'Le double corps du spectateur'* (1998) when I noted that reception studies were curiously prone to adopting the retrospective temporality of textual regurgitation, instead of choosing a prospective orientation, one that would have allowed for a highlighting of the role of media-reception in the emergence of new meanings and the formation of public opinion. I was stressing the necessary connection between audiences and publics. I was stressing, in other terms, that elaborating public opinion and expressing it are two related activities. I still think they are related. But I insist they are distinct. The distinction points to Goffman. It is one between dramaturgic registers. It is also one between writing practices[8].

## Genealogy and the observers' gaze

### Obvious, obtuse

Debates about the nature of publics run a risk of turning into exchanges of non-sequiturs. This happens because the argumentative registers in which they are being discussed are in fact heterogeneous. Discussing 'publics' is, sometimes, reminiscent of Borges' 'Chinese Encyclopedia' (Foucault, 1973) in which every entry involves *sui generi* principles of relevance. Thus cats may be divided into Siamese cats; angry cats; black cats; cats that are painted with ink and a brush, yawning cats, etc. not to mention of course, Cheshire cats, smiling cats and virtual cats. There is no limit to the diversity of cats, nor is there any to the diversity of publics, unless some principle of relevance is proposed. The principle of relevance I would adopt here points to how our notions were constructed, for which purposes and by whom.

In a way this leads to a philological - or to use Nietzsche's vocabulary, a genealogical - investigation. Thus, if we look, for example, at the pedigree and birth circumstances of 'publics' and 'audiences' it seems that being constructed from outside would characterise 'audiences' while 'autonomous' construction would characterise publics. Of course, audiences are not always waiting for Prince Charming to offer them the kiss of life, and publics are never totally autonomous in their self-construction. Publics need co-producers to help them exist and to advertise their claims.

Still, the amount and nature of mediation required when it comes to granting existence are quite different. Notions such as 'audiences' and 'publics' can be referred to the professional bodies that produce them and to the professional or lay organisations that use them. Such notions are also tokens, objects in circulation between institutions. They tend to be pliable to the semantics of these institutions. Thus, I would suggest that a demographers' audience and a semiotician's audience are quite different from each other; that an empirical object that consists in being counted is not quite the same as one that consists in being listened to. In a way the different varieties of what I generically call *publics* are born in the eyes of their beholders.

The question of birth - or construction - is linked here to the question of observation. Thus, if I keep using 'public' as a generic term, and if I choose observation as the relevant criterion, there are two sorts of publics. The first sort is performing out in the open. It is a collectivity whose nature consists in being *obvious*. (But, of course, even obvious publics are only partly obvious. What is obvious is not the whole of the public. Only a part of it shows.) The second sort is not performing; it remains private. If a collective at all, it is an *obtuse* one (Barthes, 1970). But obtuse publics are not necessarily collective. They can be actually collective (meaning-making audiences) or they can be just plural (consumers).

It is useful, then, to find out who is interested in obvious 'publics' and who is interested in obtuse ones. The question of *who* immediately translates into the question of *why*. Why should this or that notion be conceived of at all? What purposes does it serve? What was the conceiver's intention when producing it, constructing it, uttering it? How does the semantic range of the notion (that is, its definitional content) relate to the question that led to inventing it in the first place?

### Demographers, semioticians, journalists

Quantitative audiences could be described as demographers' 'publics'. They are the version of 'publics' that demographers construct for the sake of advertisers. Meaning-making audiences could similarly be described as semioticians' 'publics'. They are produced by reception scholars, either for academic purposes (extending to the speech of readers a know-how or '*savoir faire*' gained in the analysis of texts) or, for ideological purposes (rebutting Adorno's 'great divide', redeeming the popular). When demographers look at 'publics', they see age groups. When semioticians look at 'publics', they see interpretive communities.

The third type of 'public', the type I have described so far as 'performing' or as 'obvious', seems to be produced by the members of the public themselves, and, up to a point, it is. But of course this sort of public is also a raw material for journalism. Whether political or cultural, it is an intrinsic part of what the discourse of journalism is about. Day in and day out, this sort of public is written up and handed over by journalists to politicians, historians, political scientists, and also to other publics. Obvious publics are crucial to all news stories that are neither 'happenings' (train crashes) nor human-interest stories, but manifestations of collective opinion. Thus, and beyond publishing polls, a large part of the journalistic production consists in what I would call, 'publi-graphy', the chronicling of *obvious* publics.

This constructionist approach explains why various types of generic publics are not only described by different words, but also inserted in different types of sentences. Thus, in French, audiences tend to *be*; publics tend to *do*[9]. The sentences that include audiences tend to simply point to their existence, size or qualities. The sentences that include publics do not stop when they have designated them. Once designated, publics are meant to do something. This is understandable. Obvious publics are already known to exist. Stressing their existence is a tautology. Obtuse publics on the contrary are not assumed to exist. Pointing to their existence becomes a worthy finding, sometimes a scoop. Thus, an important question to ask is: how heavily does a public's existence depend on the writer's intervention?

Obvious publics keep gesturing at you. They want you to notice. Demographers' 'publics' (consumer audiences) depend for their existence on the demographer's god-like pronouncement. They can also be called 'pronounced publics'. (And on the seventh day, the demographer rested.) Semioticians' publics (meaning-making audiences) need some boosting, some triggering, a smaller but definite degree of professional mediation. They can also be called 'catalysed publics'. The professionalism of the observer (or lack thereof) becomes an important variable. 'Obvious' publics are visible with a naked eye, available to the type of untrained attention that any of us is able of providing; identifiable by the most superficial journalistic observation. 'Obtuse' publics, on the other hand, need the trained eye of a specialist in order to be identified, singled out, gathered or made visible. They become visible only if you come equipped with goggles, with the *'camera obscura'* of methodology.

All this points to the crucial function of the observer's gaze and what it does. All this points to the fact that this gaze is rarely 'constative'. On the contrary, it is endowed with all sorts of illocutionary and perlocutionary powers. Is it so too for *obvious* publics? Are they delivered to us by specific gazes? Handed over to us by specific forms of discourse? I believe that each type of public is indissociable from a certain type of utterance. What is then the utterance that speaks obvious publics? In order to find out let us look at these obvious publics and how they are born.

### Obvious publics as co-production

'Obvious' publics should be directly visible, available to the naked eye, dispensed from being constructed by a mediating discourse. Yet the media have the power of 'carving' the public sphere (the sphere of publics), and that of 'casting' the publics of which (at the level of pre-institutional politics, at the level of the elaboration of public opinion as *agon*) this public sphere is made. They can establish how many publics there are, how legitimate they are, and who they are. The publics come into existence via this casting. Does this mean that I am abandoning the idea of an autonomous presentation performed by the publics themselves, for the sake of an external presentation performed instead by the media? Does this mean - in other words - that I am renouncing the dimension of 'obviousness'? No.

But 'obvious' publics emerge in fact through a co-production. This co-production does not cancel the publics' dimension of obviousness. It assists it. It is, in fact, unavoidable. It is unavoidable, because, without it, (without the media) the publics of complex societies could never reach their constituencies. To go public in our societies means going on the air, or in print, more often than taking to the streets. But going on the air (and in print) involves being allowed or encouraged to do so.

In the political domain, there exist at least two sorts of publics. Publics of the first sort try to address the problems they face by turning them into shared issues. In a way such publics emerge because they are confronted by problems that no one else takes charge of. I would follow Michel Callon in calling these publics 'orphan publics' (Callon, 2002). Publics of the second sort choose to endorse someone else's problem or cause. I would call them 'advocacy publics'. Thus, in the example I gave earlier, minority publics in a western country, are 'advocacy publics' when they mobilise against war in Iraq. But they also become 'orphan publics' when they protest the torching of their own schools. Whether orphan or advocate, all publics require a further advocacy, a meta-advocacy of sorts: that of the media.

The first style of media performance consists in acknowledging would-be publics, and in directly conveying their claims. The more direct the relay, the more obvious the public. Thus, would-be publics are allowed to become publics, and distinguished from other - unfortunate — candidates that are not acknowledged and for which I have forged the name of 'unpublics'. In the case of the latter, the media intervention is that of an abortionist. In happy cases it is rather that of a midwife. Op eds and letters to the editor act as recruiting agencies.

## Letters and op eds

A recent study of the rhetoric of letters to the editor (Soulez, 2002) points to the fact that letter-writers usually start by stressing the representative dimension of their positions. Almost always, they claim to be speaking - not simply in their own name - but in the name of a wider constituency. This claim is often incorrect. Yet, it may become true. By placing the formulation of an issue in the public domain, by presenting a potential constituency with an explicit position to rally around, an empty claim may turn into a fuller one, and finally into a self-fulfilling prophecy. This is true of letters to the editor. It is even truer of 'op eds' or invited articles. And the role of the media in recruiting constituencies is far from limited to politics. Let me propose a cultural (literary) example. It concerns A S Byatt's op-eds (reprinted in *Le Monde*) about the Harry Potter novels (Byatt 2003).

Besides scolding J K Rowling for a technological reductionism that turns magic into gimmickry, and for treating the magical world as a development agency for commercial products (Sony dreamt it, Harry did it)[10], Byatt interestingly categorises four types of readers: (a) children who love the *familienromanz* dimension of the Potter novels, a dimension akin to daydreaming, which allows them to reinvent themselves; (b) adult amateurs, who are sternly rebuked for clinging to the unsexed world of the period of latency, and for their aggressive-regressive enjoyment of paranoid fears; (c) literati who are also connoisseurs of children's literature, aware of the true mystery of the world, and unwilling to accept that this mystery be enclosed inside some fantasy park or parallel world. This is the group in the name of which A.S.Byatt writes. (d) Her writing berates a fourth group, which consists of academics involved in cultural studies. Much more than regressive adults and daydreaming children, these are the targets of Byatt's attacks. For them, the differences proposed by Byatt between regression and reflexivity or enchantment and fantasy, etc. may be true but irrelevant. They reject distinctions between high and low culture. They define culture not by contents, but the ways it is used. They replace evaluation by ethnography and aesthetics by sociology. It is this group that Byatt picks as her opponents. It is them she makes responsible for success of the Potter books. Why them?

Because they are a worthy target. Because they form a clearly identified group, are perfectly capable of performing in public and because, finally, they provide an issue. All this explains why, after having scanned the horizon, it is with them that Byatt decides to pick a quarrel (as carefully as one picks a flower). With the other groups, a debate would have looked like an adult scolding a bunch of children or a teacher berating retarded grown-ups. With the cultural studies crowd, on the contrary, the matter of 'quality' can provide an extensively debatable issue. It can enter a deliberative agenda. By bringing cultural studies into the picture, A.S.Byatt has simultaneously constructed three related entities: (a) a public (the one she claims to represent and tries to recruit); (b) a counter-public (the crowd of cultural studies, perhaps led by Stuart Hall as Voldemort?) (c) an issue: 'Is success a substitute for evaluation?' The stage is set. Arguments and adrenalin can start flowing. A few distinguished media have relayed Byatt's recruiting ad. A public might be born. If this public survives, they will deserve credit. They acted as its midwives.[11]

## Midwives, abortionists and tender parents

But the media can also function as a screening agency, becoming no longer midwives, but 'bouncers' of publics, or worse, abortionists. They can easily do so by rejecting op eds, by returning letters to the editor, by closing the gates of talk shows, by selecting for publication poorly-written letters with unconvincing claims, by conceding access to figures that are too famous to be silenced and then neutralising that access through character assassination. In a word, there are numerous situations in which publics-in-the-making are either prevented from performing and thus made unable to attract members, unable to access their possible constituency; reduced to the status of embryos, or denied any legitimacy - that is, presented as lobbies, interest groups, particularistic communities.

The dividing line is obviously linked to the ideological preferences of the opinion-shaping media rather than to any identifiable criteria. Thus, when the ombudsman of a respected French daily is asked to comment on the criteria he is using to select publishable letters, he replies that too few letters on a given subject mean that the issue is not serious. But too many mean that the issue could be artificially created or inflated. One is to be cautious when letters are too few and even more cautious when they are too many. What then, I wonder, is the right amount? Is such a 'quantitative' assessment, anything but a smokescreen for arbitrary decisions? [12]

When they have aborted some publics and allowed others into existence, the media can adopt towards the latter the role of tender, nurturing parents. They can abstain from a minimal gate-keeping by knowingly putting pseudo-events on the air. (Think, for example, of a live funeral whose corpse would jump out of the coffin, pick up his shroud and run away.) They can also offer to some publics the sweet niches of what Dominique Mehl describes as a 'private-public sphere'. Once installed in such niches, the representatives of given publics become deliciously safe from any risk of debate. They are no longer spokespersons. They are witnesses and no one can debate what they present as their 'experience'. Thus, the wife (and lawyer) of the 'activist' Carlos finds herself invited to a talk show on the theme of 'impossible loves'. The man she loves is in prison. She suffers. She discusses the anguish of separation, and the reasons why she loves and admires Carlos. At that point the lawyer replaces the lover and delivers a powerful harangue on the evils of the world and why Carlos is right in his decision to confront them. No less than A. S. Byatt in my earlier example, Madame Carlos is in the business of recruiting. She is addressing a potential constituency. Yet, her performance radically differs from Byatt's. The latter wants to elicit a debate. Madame Carlos speaks about her love life. No one - not even her analyst - can question what she says. This is no place to point out that Carlos is a mass killer and that slaughtering civilians is, perhaps, not the only remedy to the evils of the world.[13] Similarly, when the mother of a kamikaze is explaining why her son or daughter is a good son or good daughter, and why he or she acted with virtue, she is actively recruiting support. How can anyone confront the red-eyed mother and ask her, 'do you know how many people your child killed? Do you know how old they were?

In contrast to directly relaying performances that aim at creating publics or keeping them mobilised, the nurturing role of media can also offer indirect relays. Such relays first consist of adopting a given public's agenda (a practice that typically characterises what the French call ' *journalisme d'opinion*'). They also consist in being around when a public needs its performance to be seen. (During the demonstrations against economic globalisation, local television stations in Geneva managed to be present wherever the RAI did not send crews, in order to make sure that no performance or event would go unrecorded. (Villa, 2002) Media relays further consist in highlighting the themes that support a public's claim. Thus, 'distant sufferings' can be instrumentalised, harnessed and made into rallying signs for advocacy publics. As John Durham Peters concisely put it, pity is less a feeling than an argument (Boltanski, 1993; Peters, 2004, in press). But the most interesting ways of indirectly conveying the claims of a public concern language.

### The arts of publi-graphy

They consist in two symmetrical phenomena. In the first case, a medium adopts the language of a given public. It endorses not only its agenda, but also the very wording of that agenda, the way a situation is linguistically structured, the 'primary definers' used. In the second case, the media substitute their own language for that of their adopted publics: They speak in their name, offer a curious performance, one reminiscent of *karaoke*. Publics are moving their lips. But it is the media that sing.

The indirect presentation of the discourse of a public leads to a number of excesses I have denounced elsewhere (Dayan, 2003). Such a critique, while necessary, is not my point here. Indirect presentation is often unavoidable. In most cases, the existence of a public reaches us in a discourse that is initiated by that public, but not directly spoken by its members. Indeed, in my earlier example, no one spoke in the name of A.S.Byatt or tried to rephrase what she had said (myself excepted). But in a majority of cases we attend a fascinating and - I believe - rarely discussed phenomenon. Performing publics lend themselves to an unacknowledged polyphony, to a dialogism that transforms the practice of journalism. Statements made by publics are embedded within those of journalists. Statements made by journalists are presented as those made by publics. Citations blur into the surrounding text. Titles are disowned by recourse to quote marks. A persisting ambiguity surrounds the question of who really speaks.

This situational osmosis between media and publics forces me to accept that in most cases obvious publics are less autonomous than I made them out to be. Like children whose mother answers too often in their stead, even *obvious* publics may have difficulty growing and finding out who they really are. In other words, the primal link between midwife and public is not easy to break.

Quantitative audiences result from a pronouncement. They are not to be heard, only to be heard about. Meaning-making audiences can be heard, but something is missing from what we hear. They were cajoled into speaking by actual voices, but these voices have often been erased from final reports.

What about our obvious publics? It should be clear that their 'obviousness' comes hand-in-hand with a specific form of dialogism.[14] They always reach us through some narrative. Another voice has grafted itself upon theirs. As Victor Turner (1974) brilliantly puts it, we know of 'social dramas' through 'stories about them'. As a result, obvious publics are a chimera, a tale told by two heads, a speech that conveys two voices.

Thus, like demographers' publics and ethnographers' publics, obvious publics are engendered, produced by a given corporation of '-graphers', of 'sociographers', of observers that write. They are media children.

## Conclusion

My three purposes in this chapter were: (1) To portray a notion called 'public', a myth that becomes a sociological reality in virtue of its performative dimension. (2) To observe the interplay of 'publics' and 'audiences'. (3) To observe the posture of those who observe publics in order to propose a genealogy of the observed entities, in order to link 'positivities' to the intellectual gestures that produced them.

Thus, focusing on three of the notions perceived as essential for the study of television by both myself and many authors of this book ('publics', 'consumer audiences', 'meaning-making audiences') and using the term 'public' in the French generic way, I noticed that some publics were there for anyone to see, and that other publics required professional mediation in order to become visible. I called the former 'obvious publics' and the latter 'obtuse publics'. Then, among obtuse publics, I noticed that some were triggered into existence and that others were just pronounced to exist. I called the former 'catalysed publics' and the latter 'pronounced publics'.

Clearly, obvious publics have been of particular interest to me. Leaning on Austin's theory of performatives, I have tried to emphasize three of their key dimensions: visibility, dramaturgy and performance. In a word, obvious publics belong in a theatrical model of the public sphere. Lastly, the adoption of a genealogic perspective made visible other dimensions of my three entities. Perhaps the most important concerns imagination.

All three entities considered here - obvious publics, catalysed publics, pronounced publics, or if one prefers, publics, meaning-making audiences, consumer audiences - rely on fictions, on processes of imagination. Publics, being collective formations, rely on processes of imagination for their very existence. They are based on collective fictions and have no other choice than that of being "imagined communities". In fact the "imagined communities" which Benedict Anderson describes started their careers as reading publics. Consumer audiences also rely on such processes as provided to them by "participative frames", which tell them who are the others they are watching with. This is how each individual spectator enters the process of "audiencing" (Livingstone & Lunt, 1992; Fiske, 1992).

It is clear, however, that, while consumer audiences and publics both rely on processes of imagination, they very much differ in the way they use collective fictions. For publics, the fiction is a condition of existence. Publics are enacted fictions. For consumers the fiction is no condition of existence, since they do not know or care for the collectivity they are claimed to form. The fiction of a collective becomes then one of the pleasures (and meanings) offered by the programme. It is not an *enacted fiction*, but an *entertained fiction*.

What then about meaning-making audiences? Do they also rely on fictional self-perception? On imagining themselves as community? My answer is that they may individually do so (when, as spectators, they enter the process of *audienciation*), but collectively they do not need to. They do not need a fiction to imagine themselves as a group because they have been selected - or identified - as a group by someone else. Thus if a fiction is needed at all, it is needed not by them, but by those who conceived of them as a group; by those who assigned limits to that group; by those who, in other words, imagined them.

### Afterword

To conclude this brief exploration of the institutional pedigree of the three key notions used in our branch of media studies, I propose a brief summary of the dimensions that show why and how these notions have been used. Table 1 identifies the six main dimensions in terms of type of activity; place in communicative chain; nature of engagement; focus of orientation; nature of construction (beyond the individual); and the need for imagining community. Table 2 summarises the responses to the following five questions asked of each conceptualisation, each 'persona ficta' (obvious publics, consumer audiences, meaning–making audiences): Is visibility inherent or bestowed? How autonomous/heteronymous is the construction? What sort of discourse constructs each category? What dimension does each discourse stress? What is the reason for observation?

*Table 1: Observed dimensions of consumer audiences, meaning-making audiences and publics*

| 1. Type of Activity | |
| --- | --- |
| Consumer audience | Consumption |
| Meaning-making audience | Interaction, sociability |
| Public | Action as performance |
| **2. Place in communicative chain** | |
| Consumer audience | Receiver end of communicative chain |
| Meaning-making audience | Receiver end of communicative chain |
| Public | Both sender and receiver |
| **3. Nature of engagement** | |
| Consumer audience | Entertainment |
| Meaning-making audience | Involvement |
| Public | Commitment |
| **4. Focus of orientation** | |
| Consumer audience | Segment of Raymond William's flow |
| Meaning-making audience | Message or text |
| Public | Issue |
| **5. Nature of construction: beyond individual means** | |
| Consumer audience | Plural |
| Meaning-making audience | Collective |
| Public | Collective |
| **6. Need for imagining community** | |
| Consumer audience | Yes, as access to audiencing |
| Meaning-making audience | Yes, for the observer |
| Public | Yes, for self constitution |

*Table 2: Observing the observers of consumer audiences, meaning-making audiences and publics*

| 1. Visibility | |
|---|---|
| Consumer audience | Obtuse, blunt, invisible |
| Meaning-making audience | Obtuse, blunt, (made visible) |
| Performing public | Obvious |
| **2. Autonomous/heteronomous construction** | |
| Consumer audience | Totally heteronomous |
| Meaning-making audience | Largely heteronomous (catalysed) |
| Performing public | Largely autonomous (co-produced) |
| **3. Discursive Filiation** | |
| Consumer audience | Statistical discourse |
| Meaning-making audience | Academic discourse (semiotics |
| Performing public | Journalistic discourse |
| **4. Observed dimension: what** | |
| Consumer audience | Demographics |
| Meaning-making audience | Interpretive resources, cognitive categories |
| Performing public | Action |
| **5. Reason for observation** | |
| Consumer audience | Consumption, advertising |
| Meaning-making audience | Redemption of the popular; ethnography of the nearby |
| Performing public | Democratic process (in politics and culture) |

## Notes

1. I have progressively developed many of the ideas proposed in this chapter throughout a series of papers on publics, and in particular, *Le Double Corps du spectateur*, (1998). I must thank the colleagues and friends who discussed my successive formulations: (1) at the seminar on Publics of *L'Ecole des Hautes Etudes*; (2) at the *Arrabida* seminar on Publics and Television in Lisbon; (3) at the *Rockefeller foundation*, Bellagio. Among them: Todd Gitlin, Dominique Pasquier, Sabine Chalvon, Roger Chartier, Guillaume Soulez, John Fiske, Jose Carlos Abrantes, Mario Mesquita, Susan Neiman, Hélène Merlin, Louis Quéré, Serge Proulx. But above all, I must thank the co-authors of this book: Kirsten Drotner, Sonia Livingstone, Mirca Madianou, Ulrike Meinhof, Dominique Mehl and Roberta Pearson for long hours of wonderful discussions during which friends occasionally joined us: Ib Bondebjerg, Peter Golding, Elihu Katz, Lewis Carroll. A shortened version of this chapter has appeared in *Journal of Media Practice*, Volume 6:1.

2. French journalist Antoine Perraud suggests that my series of comparisons fail to include a crucial one between *public*s and *lobbies*. But *lobbies,* while sometimes exerting their influence in the public sphere, tend also to seek the secrecy of 'arcana'.

3. On March 26, 2004, two French television channels (fr 3, LCI) reported on the death of three men they called 'activists'. All three called themselves warriors, and all three were killed in combat. One wonders, then, how to call those activists that do not kill or maim people, but just chant in demonstrations or fix posters on city-walls. Minstrels? Street singers? Urban decorators? Some 60 years ago, Victor Klemperer took over the Orwellian task of analysing semantic pathologies. The job is now available.

4. Agenda-setting research is fundamentally concerned with the framing of issues and who determines the frame. Do issues emerge from publics and are then relayed by media? Are issues constructed by media, and then adopted by publics? There are inevitable controversies on the circuits of causation. Two notions can clarify such controversies. The notion of a 'sphere of publics' in which publics are competing for the selection of public issues, and for the framing of such issues, establishes the media in a powerful position of arbitrating between claims. The notion of an 'osmosis' between certain media and certain publics cuts through many chicken-and-egg debates by stressing that issues (and publics) are co-produced.

5. 'Commitment', 'stability', 'issues', raise questions about the life-span of publics. Publics are born, may die, try to expand their life beyond the circumstances that saw them emerge. They look quite different depending on whether they are observed in a moribund state, or in '*statu nascendi*'.

6. This fable could also be told as an actual story, identifying a country, a minority, specific media, and specific dates. I chose not to do so, for two reasons. (1) I have tried to propose a vignette that is general enough to highlight the reversibility of audiences and publics. (2) It does not matter who is the minority or where the story takes place. Universal principles are at stake.

7. This is in the context of a discussion of the neo-republican perspective.

8. This formulation is indebted to a text that Barthes hated and which he once described to me as a package ('ficelage'). In this 'ficelage', Barthes described the 'Fashion System' as a two-level-system, in which written fashion as opposed to enacted fashion plays the leading part.

9. This point was whispered to me by Dominique Mehl, in French, in the course of a general discussion in English. Thanks, Dominique.

10. The formulation is mine as is the summary of Byatt's argument.

11. One reason for Byatt's decision of taking 'issue' with 'cultural studies' is that a debate involving cultural studies might enlist a larger constituency than taking sides on Auden's view of enchantment. Auden readers are likely to be less vocal.

12. This took place during a seminar I co-organized with IsabelleVeyrat-Masson at *Institut d'Etudes Politiques de Paris*. 'Les Médiateurs face au Public'. *Temps media & société*. May 3, 2002.

13. The talk show is Mireille Dumas' *'Public/Privé'* whose title seems inspired by D. Mehl's analysis. When she appeared on another type of show, Maitre Béatrice Coutant-Peyre, was actually challenged.

14. This dialogism is improvised in a number of ways. Each journalist in front of a new situation has to invent his or her own polyphonic mix. However, as pointed out to me by journalist Jean François Fogel, the mix may become institutionalised and certain polyphonic combinations emerge as trade marks for newspapers. Translated into guidelines, they are discussed in manuals of style. Yet, as far as I can judge, *manuals of style* are not really concerned with dialogism, polyphony, or the pragmatics of speech acts. Deontologies are often based on linguistic approaches that require some updating.

## References

Agulhon, M. (1968) *Pénitents et francs-maçons*. Paris: Fayard.

Ash, T. G. (1990) *The magic lantern. The revolutions of 1989 witnessed in Warsaw, Budapest, Berlin and Prague*. New York: Random House.

Austin, J. L. (1962) *How to do things with words*. Cambridge: Harvard.

Barthes, R. (1970) *'le Troisiéme Sens. Reflexion sur quelques photogrammes d' Eisenstein, Cahiers du du Cinéma*. Juillet. 1970.

Barthes, R. (1983). *Fashion system*. New York: Hill & Wang.

Bauman, S. (2002) *Society under siege*. Cambridge: Polity Press. 167-170.

Benjamin, W. (1936) 'The work of Art in the Age of Mechanical Reproduction' in W. Benjamin, *Illuminations*, New York: Shocken Books. 217-250.

Boltanski, L. (1993) *la souffrance à distance*. Paris: Métailé.

Byatt, A. S. (2003) 'Harry Potter, pour immatures de tous ages'. (tr) by J. Vaché. *Le Monde Horizons/débats*. Dec 2. 15

Callon, M. (2002) 'Lay scientists and medical publics'. *Oral communication*. U. of Paris X: Nanterre.

Cefai, D & D. Pasquier. (2003) *les sens du public*. Paris: Presses Universitaires de France.

Cavell, S. (1982) 'The fact of Television'. *Daedalus*. Fall. 75, 92.

Dahlgren, P. (2003) 'Reconfiguring Civic culture in the new media milieu' in J. Corner & D. Pels (eds.) *Media and the restyling of politics*. London: Sage.

Dayan, D. (1992) "Les Mystéres de la Réception" *Le Débat*. n° 17. Paris. Gallimard 144: 162.

Dayan, D. (1998) 'Le Double corps du Spectateur: Vers une définition processuelle de la notion de public' in S. Proulx (ed.) *Accusé de Réception: Le Téléspectateur construit par les Sciences Sociales*. Québec: Presses de l'Université de Laval.

Dayan, D. (1999) 'Maintaining Identities, Constructing Identities: Medias & Diasporas', in J. Gripsrud (ed.) *Television and Common Knowledge*. London: Routledge.

Dayan, D. (2000) 'The Social Construction of a Film Festival'. *Moving Images, Culture & the Mind*. Ib. Bondebjerg (ed.) Luton: University of Luton Press. 43: 55.

Dayan, D. (2001) 'The peculiar public of television'. *Media, Culture & Society* London: Sage vol 23, (6). November. 743-765.

Dayan, D. (2002) 'Cui Bono' in D. Dayan. (ed.) *A chacun son 11 septembre*. Paris: INA. Documentation Française.

Dayan, D. (2002) 'Untimely information. Tales of victims in the French media', *Partisan Review* N°1, Winter. 10:19.

Dayan, D. (2003) *Debate with D. Pasquier, J-P. Soulages & M. Lits. Conference: la recherche en communications dans les pays francophone*s. University of Bucarest. July.

Dayan, D. & E. Katz. (1985) 'Electronic Ceremonies Television Performs a Royal Wedding". M. Blonsky, (ed) *On Signs*. Oxford. Basil Blackwell.

Dayan, D., & Katz, E. (1992). *Media Events: The Live Broadcasting of History*. Cambridge: Harvard University Press.

Dayan, D., E. Katz & M. Mesquita (2003) *Televisao, Publicos*. Coimbra. Minerva.

Dreyfus H. & P. Rabinow. (1982) *Michel Foucault: Beyond hermeneutics and structuralism*. Chicago University Press.

De Faveri, M. (2004). *Télévision et lien social. Unpublished DEA Thesis. Department of Sociology*, University of Geneva.

Ferry, J-M. (1989) 'Les transformations de la publicité politique' in D. Dayan, J-M. Ferry & D. Wolton. (eds) *Le nouvel espace public*. Paris Hermés IV, 15:27.

Fiske, J. (1992) 'Audiencing: A cultural studies approach to watching television'. *Poetics*. 21: 345-35.

Fraser, N. (1992). "Rethinking the public sphere". In C. Calhoun (Ed.), *Habermas and the Public* Sphere. Cambridge, Mass.: MIT Press (pp. 109-142).

Foucault, M. (1973) 'Introduction' to *The order of things: An archeology of the Human Sciences*. New York. Random House.

Gamson, W. (1992) *Talking Politics*. Cambridge. Cambridge University Press.

Goffman, E. (1959) *The presentation of self in everyday life*. Garden City, New York. Doubleday.

Hartley, J. (1987) 'Invisible Fictions, Paedocracy, Pleasure'. *Textual Practice*. 1:2, 121-138.

Hartley, J. (1988) 'The Real World of Audiences' *Critical Studies in Mass Communications*, Sept. 234-238.

Katz, E. & D. Dayan. (2003) 'The public is a crowd, the crowd is a public. Latter day notes on Lang and Lang's 'MacArthur in Chicago', in Katz, Orloff, Liebes & Peters (eds) *Canonic Texts in Media Research*. Cambridge. Polity Press. 121:136.

Lang, K. & Lang, G. E. (1968). *Television and Politics*. Chicago: Quadrangle Books.

Lilla, M. (2001) *The Reckless mind: Intellectuals in Politics*. New York. NYRB.

Livingstone, S. & P. Lunt (1992) 'Un public Critique, Un spectateur actif' Dayan, D. *A la Recherche du public*. Hermès 11-1, Paris, Presses du CNRS. 145-157.

Mehl, D. (2003). 'Le Témoin, figure emblématique de l'espace public-privé' in Cefai, D. & D. Pasquier (eds). *Les Sens du Public*. Paris, PUF.

Merlin, H. (1984) *Public et litterature en france au XVII° siécle*. Paris, les Belles lettres.

Morley, D. (1980) *The Nationwide Audience, Structure and Decoding*. Television monograph. London, BFI.

Naficy, H. (1993) *The Making of an Exile Culture*. Minneapolis University of Minnesota Press.

Noelle-Neuman, E. (1984) *The Spiral of Silence: Public opinion, our social skin*. Chicago. University of Chicago Press.

Peters, J.D. (1992) 'Distrust of representation. Habermas and the public sphere'. *Media, culture and Society*. 15 (4).

Peters, J.D. (2004) 'L'enigme du Tueur Vertueux' in D. Dayan, *La Terreur-Spectacle*. Paris. INA. 2004 (in press).

Schudson, M. (1997) 'Why Conversation is not the soul of democracy' *Critical studies in Mass Communication*. 14(4): 297-309.

Schudson, M. (1998) *The Good Citizen*. New York. The Free Press.

Soulez, G. ( 2002) 'Choc en retour. les téléspectateurs et le II septembre 2001'. In Dayan, D.(2002) (ed) *A chacun son 11 septembre. Dossiers de l' Audiovisuel*; Paris, INA, 104, 39:44.

Turner, V. (1974) *Drama fields and metaphors*, NY, Cornell University Press.

Villa, M. (2002) 'Carlo Giuliani; chronique d'une mort par dispositif'. *Interview with Daniel Dayan*. Milano, IULM University (in press).

Weber, M. (1971) *Economie et société*. Paris, Plon: 411.

Ytreberg, E. (2000) 'Communicating Authority in Public Service Televison: Paternalists and Bureaucrats, Charismatics and Avant-gardists'. *Oral Presentation. Research Seminar in Media Anthropology*. University of Oslo. February.

Dominique Mehl

# Chapter 3: The public on the television screen: towards a public sphere of exhibition[1]

## Media and life-styles: the French scene

This chapter deals with programmes on French television where the words of ordinary citizens, invited to recount or demonstrate their personal life, constitute the crux of the show, irrespective of what genre (talk-show, reality show, reality television) directors of the channels assign to the programme. The focus, therefore, in this chapter is on programmes which, whether they are for entertainment or devoted to societal discussions, train their spotlights on the private life of people from civil society and dedicate their microphones to collecting the words of lay people.

The pioneering programme in this vein, *Psy show* (1983), presented couples in crisis that together recounted their marriage problems and were questioned by a psychoanalyst. This media innovation gave rise to intense controversy because of its extreme brazenness as, for instance, in the first programme the husband admitted to being impotent while the wife admitted to being unfaithful.

In the mid-80s a wave of programmes described as 'reality shows' burst onto the scene, all of which were based on the same type of idea: 'unknown' people were invited to talk about their private life quite unreservedly, often under the gaze of a psychologist. A feature, specific to these programmes, was the openly stated goal of doing something about the problems aired on the screen. The first "official" reality show, *Perdu de vue* ('Lost from sight') brought together, under the sympathetic eye of the *compere*, families in tears after the disappearance of a loved one, often an adolescent, whom the police had not been able to find. The assistants on the programme carried out an inquiry and sometimes found the runaways. Each week the television host orchestrated live reunions, after having copiously sounded out the hearts and minds of the relatives or close friends in search of their loved ones.

*Témoin numéro un* ('Witness number one') struck the pose of active, efficient television assisting the institutions of society but this time in relation to the judicial apparatus. Here the presenters worked with those leading the investigation, the police or the examining magistrate, through calls for witnesses, transmitted live during the programme, in order to make headway in judicial inquiries that had reached an impasse. Once again, the misfortune of the families and close friends affected by a murder, an attack or a presumed kidnapping provided material for both the television programme and the report on the investigation being carried out.

A programme that plays on feelings can hold the attention of the public for several months. *L'amour en danger* ('Love under Threat') attempted to do this by bringing out as-yet unarticulated or implicit marital arguments. A psychologist then puts forward a quasi-psychoanalytical interpretation of the causes of disagreement. The explicit intention was, thanks to this psychological support, to help the couples become reconciled. Once again, the couple's quarrelling spared no details of their private life, from their sex lives, which in many cases had collapsed, to the sharing of toothbrushes.

*Mea culpa* aimed at pacifying a village, a local area or a collective living space torn by serious neighbourhood disputes. While the presenter called on both sides to listen and understand each other, the stories spared no details about the everyday life of the victims (an HIV-positive child not allowed into school, a gay concierge subjected to the fury of the tenants, etc).

During the same period, these social programmes on television also underwent a considerable transformation. Initially, they adopted a very classical model of discussion and confrontation between actors in the field and specialists, based on polite and reasoned discussion. (The prototype of this genre is *La marche du siècle* in which the demonstrative and educational intention is clearly stated.) Then a more polemical format emerged in which the *sine qua non* was to orchestrate extreme differences of opinion that would be broadcast live, with the presenter adopting an extremely aggressive tone *(Ciel mon mardi* is the best illustration).

At the time of writing, a more peaceful breeze blows over French screens. The current model of discussion owes more to the confessional than to conversation. Two programmes are symbolic in this respect: *Bas les masques* and *Ca se discute*. The *Bas les masques* series, now ended, showed a few anonymous people who, in a face-to-face discussion looked the host straight in the eyes and, hand on heart, spoke about their personal suffering (incest, alcoholism, disability, etc). Most of the themes these types of programmes cover are linked to personal morals and to health, while themes related to social issues (housing, work, unemployment, etc) remain virtually unmentioned. Staging gives the impression of speaking in confidence, with the presenter prompting along the lines of a psychoanalyst and tears tend to be welcome. There is never a single expert present.

*Ca se discute* has been developed in a similar vein but the staging is rather different. The themes cover concerns that are almost entirely centred on morals and health - sexuality, education, childhood, adolescence, kinship, family, illnesses, disabilities, psychological problems, mental illness, etc. Several witnesses sit opposite the presenter and, at his bidding; reel off their life history. The presenter prompts them, encouraging confidences and introspection before turning to another guest. Some participants have a preferential status and are called on in the course of the programme to speak from a platform that faces the public. But they always speak about their private life in the first person. Occasionally experts are invited to this platform and complete these individual life histories but do not take part in discussions, either with the anonymous participants or with the presenter. For their part, the participants sit next to each other but it is extremely rare for them to speak to one another. The presenter is always the compulsory intermediary who sees to it that no polemical discussion disturbs the show. His or her favourite phrase, the *leitmotiv* of all the programmes, is: 'we are here to understand and not to judge'.

More recently, and rather later in comparison with other countries, the so-called 'reality-television' programmes have reached the French screens and this new trend was inaugurated by *Loft Story*, the French adaptation of *Big Brother*. However, the French version differs from the initial format because of the desire of programme makers to attenuate conflicts, competitiveness and the harshness of human relationships. Thus, individual competition for personal gain is replaced here by the intention of forming a couple by the end of the programme. Sex is banished from the screen and the focus of evening prime time viewing is largely concentrated on family life.

By now, all the different formats designated by the term 'reality-television' are shown on French screens: programmes dealing with survival in extreme conditions, recruiting and training show-business *wannabees*, as well as those that stage a love affair. This chapter is based on programmes that, whatever the label their makers may use, show intimacy under the heading of revealing private lives, feelings and interpersonal relations. They attract the public onto a terrain that had previously appeared to be taboo.

Programmes copied from models tried and tested in other countries always come to France later and in attenuated mode. Reality shows and the adaptation of *Big Brother* only reached France months or even years later than other countries. Talk shows in France were conceived of in a very non-conflictual mode and are only now beginning to launch formats that are more polemical or more aggressive from a psychological point of view. Reality-television made its first faltering attempts with *Loft Story*, a completely sentimental adaptation of *Big Brother*. These new developments have nothing to do with the 'specificity' of French mass culture, for this is as aggressive and violent as those beyond our frontiers. Even so, they have sparked a reaction from the weight of intellectuals who are still not yet converted to mass culture and who periodically orchestrate powerful campaigns against the French audiovisual scene evolving in this direction (see Mehl, 2002a). These accusations do not prevent French television from following international trends but, for the time being, the version is always softer.

The present study has been based on an analysis of both the production and the reception of these programmes, as the history of these programmes is also the history of the consecration of the ordinary audience as actors in the public discussion of mores and social values, as well as their evolution as those audiences. These programmes thus appear as the spearhead of a transformation of the public voice, enabling the public and private spheres to be articulated along new lines. At the same time, they mark a climax in the construction of an active, involved, reactive audience, one that is an actor in these new televised scenes. These television programmes based on private lives thus appear as illustrations and symbols of the way in which the public sphere is evolving in contemporary society and the implications this has for transforming the audience into a new public actor.

Today, on televisions all over the world, the audience has become as big a star as the presenter on the small screen. No longer can a studio discussion be envisaged without an invited audience, the visibility of which varies but is always stressed. In the mid-80s the television confession programmes (reality shows and intimate talk shows) made the audience a central character in productions focused on personal experience, private life and talking about oneself. In reality, the television audience becomes the main actor in a recreational show - they play their own role, change the emphasis in the scenario written by the directors at the outset and maintain suspense about the outcome of the challenge. The audience really steals the show from the presenter who, at least in French programmes, remains extremely discreet about the daily lives of the candidates on trial.

As well as transformations in the relation of the audience to the screen, there have also been changes in the ways in which discussions of public issues are orchestrated by the media. The public sphere, shaped by the confrontation between the discourse of experts, administrators and intellectuals has undergone a deep change, influenced by a new focus on the discourse of the uninitiated and the account of personal experiences.

These two changes are linked. On the one hand, the public on screen promotes a public sphere that is in symbiosis with the private sphere. On the other hand, from the societal point of view, the blurring of the frontiers between the personal and the community spheres is based on the valorising of self-representation. This movement is captured and amplified by the mass media. The public and the private intertwine in the social sphere, as they do on screen. In addition, the witness who emerges from the ranks of the audience represents the symbolic figure of this interaction.

In fact, the new forms of television presentation invite us to question the public both as a noun and as an adjective. Who, what sort of profile, what sort of utterance, what sort of link with society, what type of group and interests are embodied in these new characters on the media stage? Who looks at and listens to them, what sorts of bonds does the spectator create with them and what interaction is set up between those present in the auditorium? In addition, what type of advertisement, of circulation of discourse, ideas, feelings, and emotions are enhanced by shows based on the celebration of the discourse of the ordinary citizen? What sort of public sphere is thus formatted?

## From the public as spectator to the public as actor

The history of television is synonymous with the history of the rise in salience of the public. This begins with the public's every greater visibility but extends to its growing activity. From the outset, television has been concerned with building a vast audience. The first programmes, whether they be documentaries, news programmes or dramas adapted from classical literary works, made no secret of their desire to be within reach of all. A concern to be educational and the endeavour to popularise guided the first steps of directors, sponsors and producers. Whether it is the screening of a classical work or the camera exploring social terrains, the institutions or places frequented by the public, they always attempted to attract a wide audience aroused by curiosity, rather than by a desire for culture. The early directors of television dramas and documentaries have said they had in mind an image of a public which conformed to an idea and a representation of the average citizen or the broad mass of ordinary French people, and they adjusted their remarks and their editing to non-elitist ears. Yet, this broad mass of the ordinary audience remained at a distance. Sitting at home or sometimes in collective viewing situations, they received the image, took possession of it, reacted to it, and discussed it or fell asleep. This reception remained restricted to private homes or back rooms in cafés. It was not shown on screen or in any way integrated into the show.

The audience discretely but very rapidly - starting with games, followed by the development of big entertainment shows and then the growth of studio discussions - began to come closer to the studios, then to move in comfortably in ever-increasing numbers. Gradually, the literary programmes began to line up a few guests quietly seated on chairs behind the authors being questioned about their work. From time to time, the camera would turn on them and enable the tele-spectator to contemplate this respectful and silent audience, one that also constituted the backdrop to the programme. The happy few admitted to the studio embodied the posture, which at that time was expected of the audience, more typically seen at school where speech is received calmly and deferentially. However, their discrete presence also pointed the way to the media signing an agreement with the flesh-and-blood audience now visible on screen.

With the expansion of discussion programmes (political, social, cultural) the space open to the presence of the public broadened out. Tiered seating was installed all round the central stage where the verbal sparring started and where the arguments, which the topic on the agenda aroused, developed. The cameras frequently probed the ranks of this public, capturing looks, expressions, smiles and approval, or signs of disagreement or of impatience. The public became numerous and meaningful.

On big variety programmes and games, the public became noisy. They were encouraged to clap by a master of ceremonies; they did not yet have the right to speak but it was legitimate to express their reactions, to show these and to make themselves heard. The public, hitherto passive, became a public that reacted. It emerged from the shadows and silence into the light of day, with the right to speak under supervision. Increasingly numerous, visible and audible, the public nevertheless retained a status of spectator.

A qualitative change took place when the public was called on to do more than demonstrate a stance of contemplation or participation, when they were called to play an active role in the foreground. This gradual evolution over the years increased in scale with the invention of talk shows portraying unknown citizens and reality shows that starred anonymous people. Mr Average Man was now front stage. People who had nothing special to commend them either in terms of knowledge or of responsibilities became the active protagonists of programmes. Ordinary people were promoted to the ranks of star. People who knew nothing were all over the media. The audience had become the actor on television.

This incorporation of the audience into the programmes was not a trivial event, the outcome of the gratuitous invention of professionals to vary the pleasures and to enliven their shows. In reality, it indicates a deeper transformation. It is symbolic of the communication contract, specific to what many authors, in the wake of Umberto Eco, have attributed to the arrival of neo-television. This is a television in which the messages and the links established with the public fall within the province of a pact of participation, which replaces a pact of the educational type, characteristic of paleo-television (Eco, 1990).

Without subscribing to the idea of an irreversible historical movement which would see paleo-television disappearing and collapsing under the attack of the new media order, it is nevertheless appropriate to recognise that two types of contractualisation co-habit, personifying different forms of appropriation. The first is founded on the pre-eminence of the message, on the logic of the offer, in which authors, directors, and actors are in the majority. In this configuration, the public is invited to gain access to information, to culture and to entertainment in an attitude of expectation, and of apprenticeship. Their implication in the programme is imaginary and virtual. The second is based on prioritising the bond, the relation with the spectator, and on the problem of demand. Here the audience is encouraged to become involved, to interact and to behave as a component of the programme. This is a flesh and blood relationship (Mehl, 1992).

From the outset, television for mass audiences has always endeavoured to put civil society on stage: entrusting roles to ordinary citizens, including in their programmes people who personified the public and showing images of the reactions of the tele-spectators. However, since about the 1990s, this tendency has increased and been extended to all sorts of programmes, becoming highly symbolical of the flow of communication which streams out of the screen. In other words, the contract which neo-television has signed with the public does not mean that the educational type of contract is doomed to disappear. On the contrary, the latter is being redeployed to some extent, given the multiplication of channels that ensures that television can supply a considerable variety of programmes. But the main programmes on the major channels today tend to be characterised by a concern to involve the audience and by the constant celebration of their proximity. Now, at the beginning of the twenty-first century, the two communication contracts cohabit on the television screens but it is neo-television, which sets the tone.

## The voice of the witness

The arrival of reality shows and programmes about 'private life' (Mehl, 1996) signalled the advent of the witness, the figurehead of neo-television. Ordinary people flock into the studios to recount their private life in public. They present fragments of their personal history, relate childhood events, tell stories about their marital and family life and wonder what to do about their feelings, their failures and their frustrations - all of which goes out live on television. Remarks that, until then, were made in confidence within the family, between friends or to a psychotherapist, are made in public. They are not invited to give their own opinions or to share their learning or transmit some form of knowledge that they have. They are commandeered to speak about their experience and real life. They may even discuss it all in public under the guidance of a *compère* who does not mind adopting the stance of the psychologist and whose way of speaking and asking questions encourages self-exploration. The evolution of the family, of problems in married life and of sexual relations is analysed in the light of personal story of each individual. This individual and psychological interpretation is the trademark of these programmes, which enable the public to ponder about contemporary ways of life.

Despite the extreme individualisation of what is said, there is nevertheless a social bond and communication in what could sound like something of a commotion. While each story is individual, they are related in public and are therefore modelled by a concern to be potentially appropriated by others. The witness on these television programmes is not a confidant inviting the public to visit his or her secret garden, but an actor speaking to the public with a simple proposition:

> *This is what I am like, this is how I live - you who are in the audience or watching tel-evision at home, is there anything in my story which rings a bell with you?*

Thus, if the features in the story of the witness are to be operational and are to be audible to a large and heterogeneous audience, there has to be a procedure of representation that, from the casting to the construction of the story under the guidance of the host, endeavours to ensure that the performance does not stand out too much from the crowd. Individual aspects are promoted as far as they, to some extent, personify what is general or, at least, could become so. In this respect, the speech of the witness becomes symbolic of a social experience that goes beyond the strict framework of personal experience. To this extent also, the narrative of the witness appears as a co-construction, in which the witness remains in control of the authenticity of his story but of a story chosen, evoked and framed by the choices of the host, the aim being to make it into a model.

The witness, who comes from civil society, recruited because he belongs to the world of ordinary people, is sometimes chosen for his representativeness. He is the successful candidate because he seems to personify 'Mr Average . He is not too original, too outstanding, too rare or too extreme; he may appear to mirror the average audience in which the average television viewer is supposed to recognise him or herself. The anonymity that often is the trademark of his performance stresses this affiliation with the social corpus as a whole. In the last resort he is a personification of public opinion: a public opinion in 'flesh and blood' distinct from the abstract version in public opinion polls or outlined by mediators. This is public opinion clothed in reality, a production with which the average audience is tempted to identify. Sometimes, on the contrary, the witness is an unconventional character: a victim of prejudice, attached to modes of life which are considered marginal, paralysed with unhealed wounds, an enthusiast of practices which are neither widespread nor approved of, and the originality of his story attracts attention as well as a sympathetic ear. Nevertheless, this marginal character is produced in a way that ensures he does not appear as eccentric. His special case is as if he represents a situation that is shared by others who live the same problems and the same choices silently, far from the public gaze.  On the horizon of the story of the drinker we have the experience of alcoholism; in the wake of the confession of someone who is HIV-positive, a glance at the psychological weight of the illness; in the coming-out of a gay person the shared suffering of all those who have had to hide for such a long time. The cameras turned on to the margins attract attention towards the centre. The confession of the drinker poses the question of how to deal socially with forms of dependence. The story of the HIV-positive person reveals the deficiencies of society in dealing with the Aids epidemic. The declaration of the gay person lifts the corner of the veil on contemporary forms of intolerance.

Implementing the move from the particular to the general is a trick, which implies tacit collaboration between producer and guest. However, the symbolic nature of the testifying is only really accomplished in the act of reception. It is through the intervention of the reader, the listener, the television spectator that the move from 'me' to 'us' is brought about. Private evidence accedes to debate in the public sphere when the spectator can say:

> *I have experienced, am experiencing or perhaps will experience, or those close to me have experienced, experience or will experience the same thing. And this is why this interests me.*

Thus, the individual testimony acquires the status of public speech through a process of identification (Mehl, 1994) which is made possible by the symbolic nature of the person and of his story - a process effected by the spectator and which the producer expects to take place.

The publicity granted to testimonies by people from civil society is not an invention of neo-television. Programmes, documentaries, news reports and newspapers have always preferred to stress their proximity with 'real people'. But in neo-television, the status of testimony has changed. It is not a story that has been solicited as an example to illustrate an opinion, a piece of knowledge, testifying to the truth of the stories of other people, journalists, judges and historians. Here, the testimony is of intrinsic value and has the status of an argument. The witness is not sought out to accredit the story of someone else, to say: 'What this reporter or this intellectual says is true because I have experienced it'. It is encouraged to back up a conviction and a declaration: 'What I say is true, because I have experienced it'. This change in the status of testifying is fundamentally important because it induces, as we shall see, a different form of societal deliberation and a very different shaping of the public arena from those linked to stories used to back up other discourses.

The reception of these programmes is characterised by the seal of compassionate identification or of the projection of identity. The reception of these television confessions turns out to be fairly contrasted. On one hand, there are those who totally reject these shows, saying that are revolted by their exhibitionism and that they refuse to become peeping toms. On the other hand, there are the faithful enthusiasts who identify with the programmes, the people, the suffering on show and the choices set out. Thus the relationship of the spectator to this type of programme is one in which he or she is highly involved, and comes to sympathise with the misfortunes on display and to question his or her own existence by appropriating other life experiences to build their own. The television-of-the-witness appeals to a public steeped in psychological culture, which symbolises the questions which society is asking itself, and which plunges the viewer/auditor into a stance of empathy.

## The public as actor on the screen in a game of relationships

The so-called 'reality television programmes' (examples in France in particular include the two series of *Loft Story*, as well as the media castings orchestrated by television: *Pop Star* on M6, *Star Academy* on TF1), offer a new version of involvement of the public on-screen. French commentators have seen these programmes, perhaps over-readily, as the direct heirs to the reality shows and confessional programmes. However, there are far more differences between them than similarities.

The relationship of the television viewer to 'telly-reality' programmes is, in fact, very special. This is because the prime dimension of all these programmes is now entertainment. This is what characterises the show and its reception, enabling the audience to enter the world of play. In the first instance, this playful dimension shapes the broadcast itself. In the private-life television programmes, the confession is formatted, constructed and controlled by the actors in the show. Here it is not a flow of words that invades the screen but a flow of attitudes, personal interactions and relations between individuals. Thus, in the two Loft series, we learn less about the private life of the participants, their childhood, their personal difficulties, their life-apprenticeship experiences and their psyche, than we do about the life-styles and patterns of living of a whole generation (Mehl, 2002b). The indiscreet remarks about the private life of the 'lofters' tended to be revealed by the press, rather than whispered in the loft. At the same time, the scenes shown to television viewers every day demonstrated approaches, forms of seduction, how to pick up girls, arguments and reconciliations, and discussions about friendship, love and sexuality between teenagers. The public was viewing young people as they opened up and demonstrated their modes of entry into the age of affective maturity - not in terms of conviction but in terms of individual relationships, not in terms of existential choices but in terms of their modes of relating to each other. The cameras gave vent to this aspect, relentlessly filming the quarrels, the reconciliations, the gossip and the conspiracies. As far as the corporal physical and sexual intimacy of these small groups was concerned, strictly nothing was ever shown - on the French screens at least. The cameras always acted with the utmost propriety, even when they cultivated the suspense of a possible relationship.

The programmes in which candidates were trained to accede to the world of show business were even less focused on private life. The scenarios of the prime-time sequences focused uniquely on their musical and choreographic performances, while the daily episodes focused increasingly on their relationships with each other in these pre-professional apprenticeship sessions rather than on their communal life. Their evaluations of the teachers, the doubts or hopes which the session led to, the calculations about the chances of each, mattered more and more in the show while the bathroom or dormitory scenes became less frequent. The cameras focused on other types of interpersonal relationships: those which show the competition for jobs, and particularly in the audiovisual world, between individuals who are called upon to demonstrate their capacity for expression, their personal skills and their capacity to socialise, irrespective of their diplomas or professional aptitudes (Macé, 2003).

Another dimension of this new television resides in the fact that it is no longer restricted to the role of spokesperson, intermediary and mediator between actors. Television becomes a genuine actor in social life. This dimension already existed in the reality shows when television offered to find people who had disappeared (*Perdu de vue* (Lost from sight); to intervene in criminal investigations which had run to ground (*Témoin n(1*, Witness Number One); to reconcile couples who were breaking up (*L'amour en danger,* or Love in danger) or to restore peace to villages which had been disrupted by some form of drama (*Mea Culpa*). We should also include the huge development of charity television, from *Telethons* to *Sidactions*, which regularly appeals to public generosity. The so-called 'reality-television' opens up another sphere of competence for television as actor in that it can demonstrate its contribution to social life by effecting, showing, coaching the professional recruitment of apprentice singers. Television shows the training, the pedagogical relationships, competitions, evaluations and the eliminations that mark the stages on the road to recruitment. The spectacle of the competition for jobs, the consecration of television as a distributor of jobs and the revelation of the mysteries of the star system constitute the core of these programmes.

The entertainment dimension permits a more ambivalent attitude from the audience members, who find themselves allowed sometimes to join in, sometimes to remain at a distance, sometimes to sympathise and sometimes to be ironical. The study carried out in France on the reception to the first Loft series was a good indication of the way in which the entertainment dimension implied, for the spectator, an involvement which fluctuated and swung from one extreme to the other. The suspense, which kept the audience of the Loft series riveted to the screen, had several dimensions. Reactions to the programme ranged from detachment to complicity, sometimes in the same person. On the one hand, sophisticated spectators who could decode the staging and the artifice, claimed to remain at a distance and stressed the role-play but did not adhere to the ideology of authenticity underlying the programme. On the other hand, those who identified with these ephemeral heroes recognised themselves in their language, their way of dressing and their favourite subjects for discussion, their love affairs, and their discussions adopted an attitude of complicity [2].

The fans of *Loft Story*, especially the younger generation, recognised themselves in the modes of expression and co-habitation of the people in the loft. They were also seduced by the tone of the words used in front of the cameras. The attention given to sexuality, seduction, fidelity and loyalty; conversely the quarrels, arguments and reconciliations that punctuated the daily life of the people shut up in the loft reminded them of their own concerns during their entry into adulthood. The adolescent culture and ways of socialising which was exhibited daily on the screen aroused strong feelings of identification, which one participant in a viewers' group summed up as, 'they are us'.

At the other extreme, the attachment to the programme was based on the mystery surrounding the relationship between reality and fiction, between the authenticity of the characters and the construction, or even the manipulation, by the producers. This question of the relationship between reality and fiction was the main theme of the lively discussions between secondary school pupils, family disagreements round the evening dinner table, conversations heard in the workplace or the chats and fora which flourished on the net. Were the candidates acting or were they directed? If they were acting, were they acting themselves or a role that they had been given by the producer? Are the events scripted or are they linked to the internal dynamics of the group? These discussions, nurtured by countless rumours, kept the public highly involved in the evaluation of the programme.

Lastly another dimension, valid for all the new broadcasts, is the interactive element, and this had never before been seen on French screens. The daily voting of the public was an outstanding success, while some of the eliminations mobilised several million television viewers. The feeling of being able to influence a programme was not, in the French experience, uniquely imaginary and an illusion. In the first Loft series, the voters thwarted the scenario planned by the channel. The intention was that the game would end with a couple in love who would win their dream house when they left the Loft. The daily and weekly stories broadcast focused on this hypothetical fairy-tale couple. But at the end of the game, the public voted for the unhappiest and the poorest, exchanging the sentimental romance for a social romance. In the first *Star Academy*, the public on several occasions saved and sent into the finals a candidate who was cheeky but totally devoid of talent, whom the jury of teachers regularly voted out every week. The public insisted on supporting this character, despite his mediocre performances, thus giving another meaning to the game. The setting for the final, solely determined by the producers, was almost a failure.

The reality television programmes thus present themselves as authentic consecrations of a palpable interactivity and of an influence of the public on a programme, which can be evaluated. With reality-television the public is on screen, since ordinary citizens are involved with the same ambitions as many of the young people: to gain access to the world of show business. The public is also on screen, because its telephone calls and messages have a visible impact on the programme. The public has not written the scenario but it does have the power to influence it. It has not participated in the original casting but has the power to rectify it by means of its weekly votes.

## The public/private sphere shaped by the voice of the non-initiates

The promotion of the witness and the consecration of the public as an actor on the programmes have led to in-depth changes in the public sphere. In the first instance, the relations between the public and the private have appreciably changed. It is true that, historically, the frontiers between the two have fluctuated. At any given moment, there are some questions about a confrontation between individuals and others that relate to social questions. At other times, questions, which were part of the public domain yesterday, are relegated to the private while new issues, which used to be restricted to the private sphere, emerge in collective discussion.

However, until recently, spheres have always been defined by social rules. It was the community that decided which questions deserved to become public and decreed that others could not be open to the public gaze. Mixing genres, confusing words, represented an infringement of the rules of the game that, while unwritten, were nevertheless agreed to by the social body. Moralists, ideologists and teachers defined the boundaries of modesty, discretion and the strictly private. Similarly, the contours of community discussion were socially coded. The limitsthat mark the public sphere have constantly moved but, in each period, in each conjuncture, societies have forearmed themselves against the confusion of genres. The separation between the public and the private, which is historically and culturally variable, remained an organising principle of public discussion, validated in various periods by the community of the time (Ariès & Duby, 1987).

Today this distinction is wavering, the frontiers are becoming blurred and territories are overlapping. Nowadays there are no private questions protected from public indiscretion. In discussions on the social stage, private passions are in no way repressed. The media gather and garner private information which, previously was whispered in the secret of secular and religious confessionals. The private worlds of ordinary citizens, but also of members of the establishment, are exposed for all to see and hear. Even the political class has been won over by this craze for self-revelation. At the sight of these changes, some deplore the 'tyranny of intimacy' (Sennett, 1977) that threatens to destroy private spaces, which have been dissolved into a vast magma, as well as public space, which has been turned into jelly by the priority accorded to speaking about oneself.

However, it does seem that the distinction between the private and the public has not vanished; some things are still kept to oneself and this does constitute an essential dimension of social life. But this distinction has been transformed because of the thriving of individualism and the development of the psychological culture of the masses. The articulation agreed between the speakable and the unspeakable, between the communicable and the secret, between the inside and the outside world, between what is for the self and what is for the public, is no longer socially instituted but does remain subjectively elaborated (Mehl, 2001). Each person defines the limits of his or her private world. For some, to disclose one's sex life in public is inconceivable, but if this self-display comes from a third party it is nevertheless audible. For others, to reveal marital disagreements on a studio platform amounts to an unhealthy form of exhibitionism, but to refer to one's childhood difficulties seems completely legitimate. For some, decoding parental feelings in front of a studio audience seems obscene while confessing to psychological difficulties is a form of group catharsis. For others, speaking about the smallest details of a personal daily life adds to society's thinking about itself, while revealing personal political opinions are an invasion of one's judgement. As we can see, the distinction between the public and the private has not been abolished but it has become subjective and individual and is no longer the outcome of social elaboration.

We can draw two consequences as a result. First, it is now becoming difficult to talk about a separation between the public and the private sphere. It is more appropriate to speak about their articulation and overlapping. I propose to refer to this new public sphere in which private questions accede to visibility and debate as the private/public sphere. Second, it seems inappropriate to argue in terms of territories and boundaries. It is preferable to break with this vocabulary, borrowed from geo-politics, to speak in terms of processes. Thus, we can speak of changing processes which vary according to the periods, the cultures and the individuals and which do not eliminate the distinction between the public and the private, between intimacy and openness but which confer considerable variability.

## A public sphere of exhibition

One of the consequences of this subjectivation of the public sphere and of the acquired prominence of the discourse of the uninitiated is the decline of the expert. As the television studios conducting discussions on society fill up with people recruited to talk about their everyday lives, the role of those who devote their time to making presentations of their knowledge, involving their expertise, defending their ideas and making the case for their positions, becomes increasingly secondary. The expert who is invited to these discussions is increasingly reduced to the role of assistant to the witness and may even disappear entirely from the scene. The hierarchy of discourse is reversed. Whereas the 'classical' witness was required to authenticate the credibility of the discourse of the expert, now the expert is invited to give general weight to the words of the individuals being examined. The programmes are evidence of this. Now the expert is often seated amongst the audience and is appealed to in order to punctuate a story and less and less frequently to draw conclusions or lessons. The type of invited expertise also illustrates this eclipse. The only experts who survive this general loss of status are the psychologists, who are close to the experience of the lay-people and capable of speaking about private lives and real life from the inside (Mehl, 2003). On the other hand, the more socially based expertise of lawyers, sociologists and social anthropologists is fading from the scene of public discussion. The centre of gravity of the discourse expected from psychologists is itself affected by this change in status. The psychologist is invited to accompany the witness, to relay the discourse that emerges from civil society, but is encouraged to avoid stigmatising the situations or the individual cases that are presented, not to evaluate the experience recounted on a scale ranging from the normal to the pathological nor to make any kind of diagnosis of the cases recounted. He or she therefore tends to be relegated to a role of accrediting what the witness says, without offering any judgement, of illustrating the individual situation with the help of similar cases encountered in clinical practice, but they are not encouraged to venture further with more proactive remarks, nor to deduce from the existential problem presented a more global approach to the malaise of civilisation.

The promotion of the witness and the decline of the expert contribute to a profound transformation in the public sphere. Private discussion has not taken public deliberation by storm, as was predicted by certain authors obsessed with the narcissism of contemporary societies (.Lash, 1979), but it is no longer modelled on rational discussion, based on reasoned knowledge, learning, options and ideologies as Jurgen Habermas (1962; 1987) described it. It tends to be presented in the form of a confrontation, a comparison, an evaluation of expressions, feelings, inclinations and preferences, judged in the light of the plausibility of certain choices and forms of behaviour, rather than in the light of the intellectual or normative relevance of a point of view or an engagement. Thus, diversity, which is the very basis of discussion, tends to be expressed by means of a number of experiences rather than by a number of opinions. We now have stories, narratives and displays of different experiences instead of intellectual arguments from opposite points of view. Demonstration is replaced by exhibition or display.

In these programmes, devoted to sexuality, couples, education, the family etc, the focus is not on ordinary situations, on everyday experience, or mainstream styles. On the contrary, the focus is on abnormal scenarios, minority habits, marginal situations, and unusual stories. Moreover, the basis of recruitment is diversity. Witnesses must not be over numerous but they must be very different. One example: *Jour après jour* (Day after day) dealt with marriage by showing four ill-assorted couples. The first, a couple of young aristocrats without much money but still faithful to the family traditions. The camera explored how they met, their recent life and their views on their wedding and the ceremony. Although they appear modern, they did not consent to any exception to the tradition. They did not have sex before the wedding; the husband saw his fiancée's dress for the first time at the door to the church; there was both a religious and a civil wedding; the family was mobilised to clean the silver and guests were invited to celebrate a wedding which seemed to belong to another era. Another couple - an older man and a young woman with several years difference in age - recounted how they fell in love at first sight and how they intended to legitimate it by getting married, although most people took them for father and daughter. The third couple - a Moroccan woman and a French man - talked about the cultural difficulties of negotiating different traditions and beliefs, with families belonging to very distant cultures. And the last couple was two gay men shown drinking champagne on a barge on the Seine to celebrate the PACS (*Pacte Civil de Solidarité*), which they had just signed. Thus, the main people absent from this wedding photo are ordinary, unexceptional couples.

Similarly, programmes about the family are devoted to totally heterogeneous, if not marginal, situations. Classical families with two parents of opposite sexes and their genetic children are not really the heroes of these shows, which are mainly populated by single parent families, reconstituted families, families with adopted children as well as gay and lesbian parents. The present state of domestic models is illustrated with examples, which include all the non-traditional pieces of the family puzzle. These ill-assorted couples, these very different if not totally opposed family configurations, are presented side by side, usually carefully avoiding any comparison, criticism, polemical discussion or confrontation. The host indicates who is to speak and invites all participants to listen to one another without passing judgement. He is the guarantor of an attentive ear in a spirit of cultural liberalism.

This mode of presentation complies with the second aspect referred to above, that is, the prioritising of testimony. Taking the witness on board has enormous consequences for the way the public debate is conducted. It moves away from a confrontation in terms of true or false, from right and wrong, in so far as the lived experience cannot be challenged. Anyone can reply to someone who stubbornly advances an idea by advancing other arguments. When comparing experience, on the other hand, the veracity of the story cannot be challenged. A witness cannot be accused of false testimony about his own life because nobody, in such a public sphere, has the right or the capacity to accuse him of not having experienced what he claims to have lived through. The story offered, by its very nature, is authentic. To doubt its fidelity to reality amounts to doubting the word of the person who speaks. Objections can only be formulated in terms of pseudo-objections, such as: 'I did not react in the same way when I had a similar experience'. A story, which acts as an argument, becomes genuinely impossible to challenge. This is why accounts are juxtaposed with an absence of confrontation.

Differences presented side by side with no comparison or evaluation, accounts which are presumed to be genuine - these two strands are interwoven to confer on the public sphere thus shaped a very different logic from that classically attributed to the public sphere which is governed by the confrontation of expertise, opinions and ideologies. The fact is that the public/private space is not polarised by the exchange of ideas. Theoretical and abstract discourse tends to be banned and replaced by a personalised discourse where ideas are expressed through the presentation of the real-life experience, the revelation of a slice of life, a glance at some misfortunes and the expression of emotions. Opinion edges its way in with the aid of the factual, 'this is what I live' takes the place of 'this is what I think ...'. Conviction is not expressed through the form of an argument but is conveyed by the involvement of the individual: the presentation of one's self to the public, the exploration of feelings and even of what has been repressed. Thus, the public/private sphere does not incite discussions about society. There is little discussion between the guests but they produce parallel stories. The programme does not orchestrate a choice of ideas but a comparison of values personified in divergent life styles. It is not an intellectual sphere in the classical meaning of the word but, instead, a sphere which experiments with life-styles. The argument of its rhetoric tends to be closer to exhibition than to demonstration. These are programmes to look at and to listen to. The public can do what it likes: appropriate, interpret, adopt or reject, discuss with the immediate entourage, or disagree over the proposed model with friends, colleagues or parents. Note that it is the public who improvises and shapes this confrontation; a confrontation that has sometimes been formulated on the screen, often has been merely suggested and sometimes even carefully avoided [3].

In this respect, these programmes contribute to the emergence of a particularly active public. The programme surveys confirm this. On the one hand, these stories, none of which conform to the norms, do not give rise to discussions, debates or confrontations *in situ*; on the other hand, they are hotly debated at home, in the workplace, in the café or at school, between friends, colleagues or family members. The divergent, contradictory and contrasting life choices that have avoided any confrontation on the screen become models, which are re-injected into discussions in the workplace that in turn are sometimes intense.

## The public and television in the age of individualism

These changes, which lead to the emphasising of the discourse of the lay persons and that of psychologists, are shaping the contours of a public sphere in which the discussion of ideas and the confrontation of opinions give way to the comparison of experiences. Yet, their dynamics are not entirely specific to the media. On the contrary, they are rooted in social features that the media have essentially harnessed, transmitted, amplified and enhanced. But which they have not invented (see Dubet, 1994).

The attention granted to private questions and to life histories is indeed in keeping with, and an echo of, the rise in individualism in our contemporary Western societies. Today, lifestyles, values, norms and points of reference are no longer inherited, univocal and imposed. There used to be institutions dedicated to setting out what was and was not acceptable, and distinguishing between what could and could not be said. They have not disappeared. But their influence has been considerably attenuated and has largely declined. They no longer reign supreme or have the monopoly as far as the definition of norms is concerned but tend to be in a situation of extreme competition. To put it more precisely, the churches have not vanished but attendance has dropped and, more than that, their discourse is no longer the discourse of the Gospel. Families, and schools continue to inculcate principles, and list the do's and don'ts, but they no longer have the same unchallenged authority as in preceding generations. Their precepts now have to compete with other models, taken from other sources at school, at work, or from friends, etc. The elaboration of norms and identities no longer comes from an official source, stamped with the seal of univocal legitimacy. On the contrary, the process involves gathering bits and pieces from here and there. The individual, who is entrusted with the task of finding his own way, is unsure and steers a delicate course between the various messages which society transmits to him. Having become the 'entrepreneur' of his own life, he turns to the community for assurance and reassurance, to locate landmarks and forge an identity. (See Ehrenberg, 1995; Kaufmann, 2001; de Singly, 2003; Giddens, 1994; and Taylor, 1998).

In this context, discussion plays a pivotal role in the search for norms. Discussion with oneself leads to the gigantic development of introspective practices; extends far beyond the privacy of one's own four walls, or of those of one's therapist; appears in public on the stage of countless television programmes; and fills the columns of magazines. But there is also discussion with one's peers, pupils on the same school benches or colleagues. The post-viewing surveys for both the confessional programmes and the relational reality-television programmes (of the Loft Story type) all show that, while discussions may not take place in the studio, intense discussions take place off screen (Boullier, 1996; Pasquier, 1999). The discussions that do not take place in the studio are to be found at home or in the workplace, in school playgrounds or in workers' canteens. In the last resort, there is public discussion when a multiplicity of programmes evaluates sexual experience, different conceptions of love, family separations, etc. In other words, the multiple facets of contemporary couples, education, parenting and the family are all minutely examined. This inter-individual and community discussion, which is apparently so necessary to the construction of identity nowadays, explains why television has appropriated these phenomena and erected a monument to testimonies. It also explains why psychologists of all hues are so well treated.

The second dimension of this contemporary era, which the media reflect with such perseverance, is due to the extension to the masses of the culture of psychology (Castel, 1984). Over the last fifty years, the status of psychological knowledge has considerably changed in our societies. In the earlier period, like all knowledge, it was a sum total of knowledge, findings, analyses, conclusions and hypotheses, all written in scientific books, and propagated in amphitheatres, colloquiums, seminars, etc. In short, it was a form of knowledge that was transmitted through teaching and acquired the status of an academic subject - a form of knowledge, which enhanced one's intellectual baggage.

Fairly rapidly, the professionals of psychology were called to the rescue of numerous institutions in the sphere of health, social welfare, education, or justice in order to bring their specific light to bear on the relations within these various instances, to help the professionals in these places to hear and to deal with suffering. From this point on, psychology extended its hold beyond individual consultations and beyond the spheres of knowledge and became a cog in the wheel of institutions, and its presence and influence grew steadily.

Finally, lay men and lay women hear and take hold of the language, of the individualised interpretation and the diagnostic approach of listening to doubts and unease. In all social categories people begin to talk like therapists. Just as every citizen has a minimal political culture enabling him or her to distinguish between democracy and totalitarianism without having read the complete works of Tocqueville, so does each individual in post-modern society know about the existence of the subconscious, or the Oedipus complex; how to identify symptoms; what is a *lapsus calami* or a 'complex' or a 'mourning period', without having read the complete works of Freud. Psychobabble as a mode of expression and interpretation has genuinely become shared culture and is no longer controlled by the specialist. And psychobabble, in the sense of examining society in the light of a psychological interpretation, goes very well with a public sphere formatted by self-revelation.

Thus, in the last analysis, the recent evolution of television, its programmes and the conquest of the television screens by a visible audience, seems to point to phenomena which go far beyond the imagination of the programme producers and directors. The latter invent sets and choose actors but they do so according to criteria and demands that are largely the outcome of the evolution of society. This type of evolution of society and the media translates into a public sphere of a new type in which the deliberation of society with itself actively implies the participation of civil society without confining it to the issue of political citizenship. One in which the viewer is turned into an active public[4] through his or her participation as an actor in these programmes, as well as through his or her propensity to discuss them with the viewing audience at home, at work or with friends. Here public discussion is sustained by private experience; learned arguments are replaced by the recounting of life histories; expression is as important as formulation; the witness takes the place of the expert; exhibition, or display rather than demonstration, takes pride.

## Notes

1. Looking for a translation of what I characterised in French as *'sphère publique de la monstration'*, Daniel Dayan, who closely followed the progress of this text, proposed: 'public sphere of exhibition', a term that means 'display' but also carries a connotation of 'exhibitionism'. A shortened version of this chapter has appeared in *Journal of Media Practice* Vol 6:1.

2. This ambivalence of the public/audience which we have observed amongst young French television viewers has also been noted in relation to the reception of Big Brother in other countries. See: *'La télé-réalité, un débat mondial: les métamorphoses de "Big Brother"'*, Médiamorphoses, Hors série, 2003.

3. At least this is the case at the moment for French programmes; after a wave of highly controversial programmes, the preference now is for magazines based on the juxtaposition of testimonies rather than their confrontation. However, whether the arguments take place in the wings or in the course of the programme, the logic remains the same: the source of the argument is subjective experience and not normative rationality.

4. In the meaning proposed by Daniel Dayan, *'Les mystères de la réception'*, Le Débat, N(71, September-October 1992, and inthe chapter in this book.

## References

Ariès, P. and G. Duby, (eds) (1987) *Histoire de la vie privée*, Vols. III, IV, V, Paris: Seuil, 1987.

Boullier, D. (1996) *La conversation télé*, Research report.

Castel, C. (1984) *La gestion des risques*, Paris: Minuit.

Dayan, D. (1992) 'Les mystères de la réception', *Le Débat*, N71, September-October.

de Singly, F. (2003) *Les uns avec les autres. Quand l'individualisme crée du lien*, Paris: Armand Colin.

Dubet, F. (1994) *Sociologie de l'expérience*, Paris: Seuil.

Eco, U. (1985) *La guerre du faux*, Paris, Grasset, 1985.

Ehrenberg, A. (1995) *L'individu incertain*, Paris: Calmann-Lévy.

Giddens, A. (1994) *Les conséquences de la modernité*, Paris: L'Harmattan.

Habermas, J. (1962) *L'espace public. Archéologie de la publicité comme dimension constitutive de la société bourgeoise*, Paris: Payot.

Habermas, J. (1987) *Théorie de l'agir communicationnel*, Paris: Fayard.

Kaufmann, J-C. (2001) *Ego*, Paris: Nathan.

Lash, C. (1979) *The culture of narcissism: American life in an age of diminishing expectations*, New York: Norton.

Macé, E. (2003), 'Loft story: un Big Brother à la française', *Médiamorphoses hors série*, 2003.

Mehl, D. (1992) *La fenêtre et le miroir. La télévision et ses programmes*, Paris: Payot.

Mehl, D. (1994) 'La télévision compassionnelle', *Réseaux* N° 63.

Mehl, D. (1996) *La télévision de l'intimité*, Paris: Seuil.

Mehl, D. (2002a) 'Loft Story: la fracture culturelle', in *SOFRES, L'état de l'opinion* 2002, Seuil.

Mehl, D. (2002b) 'La télévision relationnelle', *Cahiers Internationaux de Sociologie*, Volume CXII.

Mehl, D. (2003) *La bonne parole*, La Martinière.

Pasquier, D. (1999) *La culture des sentiments*, Editions de la Maison des Sciences de l'Homme.

Sennett, R. (1977) *The Fall of Public Man*, Cambridge: Cambridge University Press.

Taylor, C. (1998) *Les sources du moi*, Paris: Seuil.

Tisseron, S. (2001) *L'intimité surexposée*, Paris: Ramsay.

Mirca Madianou

# Chapter 4: The elusive public of television news[1]

This chapter brings together and challenges two popularly-held assumptions about publics and audiences. The first assumption concerns the audiences for the news genre. Audiences for the news have traditionally been differentiated from audiences for other television genres and other (non-news) media. When it comes to the news, audiences (probably the same people who watch soap operas and talk shows) are magically transformed into citizens, or, 'the public'. This transformation mainly takes place at a normative level, rather than at a descriptive one. By this I do not mean that the news audiences are more critical than those for other media, but rather that the concern with news audiences is seen as part of the democratic process and therefore its study is rendered legitimate. In other words, according to this approach, audiences for news should be publics, but often fail to meet this expectation (as in arguments about political cynicism, apathy, low turnout for voting and *video-malaise* - for a critique, see Norris, 2000). Such observations and concerns, of course, are understandable in that the news is probably the most common means through which people get in touch with politics. What I want to do in this chapter is to rethink the dichotomies upon which the normative assumptions for the news audience are based, that is, between public and private, rational and affective, disinterested and interested. Drawing upon empirical work with audiences, I aim to show how people's actual engagement with the news is a complex and contradictory process that transcends these categories.

The second assumption concerns the equation of publics with nations or other supposedly homogenous groups. Although it is generally recognised that it is more useful to think of publics in the plural, rather than in the singular (Fraser, 1992; Livingstone & Lunt, 1994; Robbins, 1993; Warner, 2002) when it comes to the nation and its minorities homogeneity is often taken for granted. Despite the recognition of the existence of multiple publics, or public sphericules (Gitlin, 1999) within these publics, homogeneity is assumed. This view is compelling in the sense that publics often coalesce around issues, but it should not blur our awareness that such combative moments are contextual and often temporal. The boundaries around publics are porous and their members can move in and out. Consequently, we could argue, homogeneity and consensus are often ephemeral achievements and are difficult to sustain in the long term. Nations and ethnic groups are no different: their members might be brought together around one issue, but might be dispersed or even actively challenge the dominant view on another issue. This chapter proposes that we think of nations, minorities and publics in a flux - never static, always dynamic and changing. However, this process of fluidity is not arbitrary. Taking the diversity within the publics as a starting point,

I then go on to look at the moments that catalyse participation in - or exclusion from - publics and public life in general.

The chapter is based on an ethnographic study of media consumption in Athens as part of a larger study of the relationship between media, identities and the politics of nationalism and transnationalism (Madianou, 2005a). It uses participant observation, group and in-depth interviews with 69 Greek[2], Greek Cypriot[3] and Turkish-speaking[4] people living in Athens over the course of two years (1998-2000). Through the empirical work, I became interested in both the affective dimension of news consumption as well as the diversity of the news audience. It emerged that significant issues among minority audiences in Greece were the performance and experience of diversity as well as whether an essentialised understanding of difference plays a role in processes of inclusion and exclusion. Is it possible that the news, through their ubiquity and power of representation, can play a role in processes of participation in, or withdrawal from public life in general?

What emerges from these opening paragraphs (as well as from the rest of this volume) is the multiple meanings and definitions of the word 'public' as both a noun and an adjective. In this chapter, public is used in three different yet related ways. The first meaning is very broad and signifies the citizens. This use is common among political communication scholars and political scientists who use the term 'public' as an alterative to 'citizens' or 'the people' in general. Although this usage is often relatively neutral (Norris, 2000; Schudson, 1995) it is frequently loaded with a normative dimension of how the public should perform its duties (Habermas, 1962/1989) and sometimes juxtaposed with an empirical description of how it fails to do so (Putnam, 2000). The second way in which the term 'public' is used in this chapter is one that equates the 'public' with the 'nation' (a popularly-held meaning, see Appendix to this volume). The third meaning relates to the use of 'public' as an adjective, as in the phrase, 'public life'. 'Public life' here is understood broadly as political and democratic processes, mediated and unmediated, and open to all.[5]

The ethnographic perspective adopted in this study extends beyond a methodological approach as it has informed the study in a more fundamental way. I did not take either publics or news for granted, but was instead driven by a bottom-up approach. Instead of defining public and the news in advance and then examining whether people conform to these ideal types, I investigated what meaning these terms had in the everyday engagements people had with the media. This explains why this chapter is not about publics in the sense of discreet groupings of people organised around discourse (for a definition along these lines, see Warner, 2002). In the present study no such grouping was observed, but this does not mean that they do not exist.

A final remark about theory: the present perspective on the news is influenced by the mediational or ritual approach to the news as an indispensable and dynamic component of social and cultural life (Silverstone in press, p. 17). This approach is complementary to, but also marks a step further from the studies of news reception[6] insofar as the emphasis is not only on the text and its interpretation, but also on the news as a social phenomenon. In this context, news viewing emerges as a ritual that punctuates everyday life, echoing the ritual model of communication rather than the transmission one (Carey, 1989). In the following section I will map out the different ways in which people engage with the news, thus challenging the assumption of the rational news public that only watches the news in order to make informed decisions. First, I provide some context for the Greek broadcasting system and the particular features of news programmes.

## Wall to wall news?

The context for this study is the Greek broadcasting landscape that partly shapes the consumption of news and its impact in public life. The commercialisation of the broadcasting system in 1989[7] brought sweeping changes in programming and also in the format of news broadcasts, which have been characterised for their length (sometimes reaching up to three hours) and their emphasis on 'live' reporting and studio discussions.[8] The popularity of news broadcasts in Greece is reflected in their proportion of overall television programming. This had reached 35.5% and 76.7% respectively for the two public broadcasting channels (ET-1 and NET) and 43.5% and 40% for the two leading private channels (ANTENNA, MEGA) at the time of the fieldwork (1998-2000) (AGB Hellas Yearbook, 1999, p. 37). Audience measurement studies have indicated that television is by far the dominant medium for information: 71% of the Greek population watch the news everyday compared to 17% who listen to the radio news and 16% who read the newspapers on a daily basis.[9] Given also that the Internet connection rates continue to be the lowest in the EU,[10] it is not an exaggeration to talk about the dominance of television news and even the phenomenon of wall-to-wall news on Greek television. Although there have been efforts by the private channels themselves to self-regulate this phenomenon and to set standard times and duration for news broadcasts, the situation was largely unchanged at the time of writing.

## News - beyond a source of information?

A man wakes up in the morning to the sound of the radio news. A woman takes her breakfast in front of the television screen. They both listen to the radio in their cars stuck for hours in the notorious Athens traffic. A family has dinner while watching the evening news; and a couple falls asleep while watching the late night news bulletin.

This section describes a range of activities that revolve around news programmes,[11] but extend beyond their informational dimension. In fact, it emerged that the majority of the time that my informants spent watching or listening to the news was not for purely informational purposes. Informants routinely described their daily schedule as revolving around different media habits: waking up with the news on the radio in the morning, listening to the news on the way to work, watching the news whilst having dinner, and falling asleep with the television on. Although no one followed news programmes in their entirety, almost all informants would engage with the news at some point during the day, most commonly between 19:30 – 22:00 when the evening news bulletins are scheduled.

Many informants described themselves as 'addicted to the news'. By this, they meant that if they were at home and the news was on they 'have to switch the television on'. This was often an intermittent type of viewing, as no one continually engaged with the programme for two hours or more. This 'addiction' was disrupted when people went on holidays, usually to the islands where they had no access to television or newspapers, which they described as a 'period of detoxification'. As one informant put it: 'without the news it feels strange, that you have cut yourself off'. People attributed this 'addiction' to their need to 'keep up with reality'[12], thus identifying news with reality. However, given the ubiquitous presence of the media in the everyday lives of people and the extent to which it is embedded in daily structures and practices, another interpretation is that the need to watch the news is a need to regulate one's life. Thus, the longing for the news while on holidays can be seen as the longing for the routines and organisation of everyday life.

Such observations point to an intimate dimension of news consumption that punctuates daily life, thus providing its audiences with an almost paradoxical reassurance (Silverstone, 1994). News can be the morning alarm clock, the voice that keeps company those who feel lonely, the means through which to avoid having a conversation during a family dinner, a mindless ritual, or the organisation of everyday life itself. Such uses echo Lull's 'structural uses' of the media and include the moments when television functions as an environmental source or background noise, as well as its role as a regulative source that punctuates time and activity (1990, p. 35).[13]

Researchers have long observed the plethora of parallel activities that take place in front of the television screen, what Bausinger had termed 'parergic media activity' (1984, p. 349). Although it has been well documented that the media are hardly ever used in a pure and complete way, requiring our full concentration (Gunter & Svennevig, 1987; Gauntlett & Hill, 1999; Morley, 1995), there is a need to investigate further what roles beyond the obvious ones the media play in the everyday lives of people.

Another dimension of news consumption to emerge from the empirical work was the instrumental use of the news, a facet that extends beyond the commonly documented usages. Some of the respondents, on occasion, saw television as the vehicle to voice complaints or criticisms. One informant, Yannis, told how a family acquaintance appeared on television to complain about an inflated bill he received from the water supply company. Only after he appeared on television, Yannis added, was his complaint taken seriously. Another informant, Nicos, told me that a relative of his called the local authorities with whom he had a dispute and threatened to call 'the channels'[14] to complain. This instrumental use of the media extends beyond their typical role as a medium for information. News media in Greece are used for non-media related purposes, often with successful results, confirming that mediated communication is more than a linear transmission of information.

The above viewing practices suggest that the news is a central component of everyday life that extends beyond a source of information that will 'arm people for vigilant citizenship' (Schudson, 2000, p. 194). What does this observation imply for the news audiences or publics? Although the intimate dimension of news consumption seems to belong to the private rather than the public sphere, the last example about the instrumental uses of the news cuts across the public - private divide. At one level, people are driven by their private interest when they call the television channels to voice complaints, or when they evoke 'the channels' as a threat when dealing with the, at times, unhelpful authorities. In the first case, the private interests are expressed publicly (when complaints are broadcast on live television and radio); while in the second, the threat of publicness aims to protect the private interest. Such observations are indicative of the quality of public life in Greece[15] where the news media can literally become the mediators between public institutions and private interests. Using the news media to achieve one's interests is a far cry from normative theories that presuppose a disinterested public (Habermas, 1989). Nonetheless, by enabling people to deal with the authorities the news media fulfil a role that is vacant in Greek public life thus blurring the boundaries between the private and the public. Moreover, the publicised complaints themselves did not belong to the private sphere in the first place, as they were the result of the bad practice of a public utility company. These observations are reminiscent of Canclini's argument about Mexico where people resorted to radio and television to obtain recognition, justice or reparation that traditional citizen institutions did not provide (Canclini, 2001).

## Reasoning audiences

The private and sometimes intimate aspects of news consumption are but one facet of the process. Audiences engage critically with the news in terms of both its content and genre (the form and style of the particular broadcasts). At times, the critical readings or reactions to the news were seemingly at odds with practices described in the previous section as aspects of the intimate dimension of news consumption. One such example is the critical stance towards the style and form of news programmes exemplified in the phrase: 'news programmes are no longer watchable', which was repeated by many informants. At first reading, the phrase is in stark contrast to the high viewing rates that news programmes attract and the heavy news consumption. How can one be 'addicted to the news' and then declare that it is no longer 'watchable'? This contradiction becomes less puzzling if we distinguish between two levels: 'news is no longer watchable' refers to the quality of news as information and is related to the critical stance of viewers, whereas 'news is an addiction' refers to the habitual, routine viewing of news programmes, every evening at the same time. This paradox points to a particular collision between the critical faculties of the viewers and their actual practices and the need to be able to investigate both what people say (about the media) and what they do (how they actually use them).

A similar discrepancy occurred in relation to viewing practices and attitudes towards the public service channels, ET1 and NET (also referred to as ERT which is the generic term for both). The ambivalence towards the public service channel is significant, as it is the form of broadcasting that has been associated - not uncritically - with a working model of a contemporary public sphere (Blumler, 1991). Although a large number of informants mentioned that ET-1 and NET were the most decent channels, very few actually watched them.[16] Some informants, usually the younger ones, pointed out that ET-1 and particularly NET, which largely focuses on current affairs programmes and documentaries, is the best channel. However, very few admitted to actually watching it, and in fact, during none of my visits to my informants' households were they watching the NET news. One informant said that sometimes she even forgets that ERT exists. Sophia described ERT's style as primitive compared to that of private channels, which 'have turned news into a spectacle ... It's sad, but ERT does not sell', she added. This was a phrase repeated by many informants.

On the other hand, older informants described ERT as a government mouthpiece. This is reflected in the use of the adjective 'governmental' [kyvernitiko], which was sometimes used instead of 'public' [dhimosio], or 'state' [kratiko], to describe ERT. One informant in his forties mentioned that he does not expect impartiality from the ERT channels, as their position will be inevitably biased. Vassilis was sceptical of the clientelist relationships between ERT"s administration and the government and pointed to the number of ERT"s employees: 'The state is corrupt and inept because it employs 10,000 people in ERT whom we pay as taxpayers. They do nothing; they just sit on chairs'. The age difference between those informants who expressed a positive attitude towards ERT and those who associated the channel with the government can be explained by the latter's experience of the pre-deregulation era when ERT was tightly linked to the governing party's politics.

Most informants, however, discerned a significant difference in ERT"s news programmes and overall output in comparison to previous decades. They attributed this change to the privatisation of the airwaves and the proliferation of channels that increased competition for audiences. The ending of ERT's monopoly brought about more polyphony, also within ERT"s own programme. However, many people were unconvinced about the quality of this diversity and expressed strong suspicions about the covert interests [*symferonta*] that still determine broadcast news in both public and private channels. Viewers often told me that 'all channels show the same things' and they explained this through a political economy argument, which associated media output to media (cross)-ownership and the symbiotic relationship between media companies and the government.

Conversely, three informants recognised what could be termed as an oppositional public sphere in the proliferation of channels that provide people with choice. As one informant noted: 'one can watch TILETORA, a channel well known for its far right positions, or the channel of the Communist Party'. Andreas argued that there is more diversity in the post-deregulation era and said that the particular format of the news, with its long duration and succession of invited guests, allows for a number of voices to be heard, even if this is for the sake of sensationalism and attracting viewers:

> *Do you know what I believe about the Greek channels? That the news is certainly biased, but there are talk shows and the moments when news programmes become like talk shows with all these 'windows', and there you can get indirect information about the background of the issues. This is where you can see some weirdos who tell their own story. OK? This is when you can think about the other side of the events. (Andreas, 34 years old)*

A similar argument was voiced among Turkish speaking informants about a popular talk show that resembles a form of oppositional public sphere (Fraser, 1992; Livingstone & Lunt, 1994). The talk show is called 'Jungle' [*zougla*] and tackles social issues and exposes the authorities in a rather sensationalist manner. Highly critical of the government and those in power, it perhaps resonates with the general dissatisfaction in the Turkish speaking neighbourhood over unemployment, poverty and lack of resources. Triandafyllopoulos, the journalist-presenter, voices the criticisms and concerns that people in Gazi are unable to raise themselves. Men often mentioned Triandafyllopoulos and his programme in everyday conversation: 'as Triandafyllopoulos said...' or, 'he is the only one who tells the truth'.

## Diverse audiences
The above media practices and discourses were common to most informants regardless of their ethnic background. However, there were some important differences. One is that Turkish speaking and Greek Cypriot people also had access to transnational media from Turkey and Cyprus respectively. Another important difference among the Greek Cypriot and Turkish speaking informants was that the news would not be used in instrumental ways for voicing complaints.

Furthermore, informants from all ethnic and cultural groups were equally critical about news content and form. In examining the reception of the reporting of national and international affairs through the news media, I observed that people would challenge the news and the official discourse about the nation found in the news. Critical readings were not the result of a membership in an *a priori*-defined public but a matter of positionality and the result of a 'conflict between the cultural claims of the text and the lived experiences of the audience' (Livingstone, 2004 - introduction to this volume). For example, interviewees from all ethnic groups criticised - albeit for different reasons - the reporting on the Cyprus issue, which was one of the case studies in the overall project chosen because its centrality in Greek public life for over three decades. The Cyprus problem is referred to in Greece as one of the 'national issues', a view that is prevalent in the media.[17] The history of the island is one of competing nationalisms (Greek and Turkish) and post-colonialism. A former British colony, Cyprus gained its independence in 1960. The military junta in Greece orchestrated a military coup in 1974, Turkey then invaded the north of the island and ever since, Cyprus has remained divided.

Greek Cypriot viewers thought that the reporting on Cyprus was inadequate and did not reflect their experiences of the conflict, while Turkish-speaking informants rejected the reporting as irrelevant in comparison to their own everyday problems as Greek citizens. Many Greek informants, in turn, challenged the official view that the Cyprus problem is a national issue, the view expressed in the reports in question. These interpretative frameworks were not cast in stone, as there were discrepancies within each group. Most importantly, discrepancies depended on the context in which interpretations took place and the positionality of each informant. Thus, for instance, while a Greek informant contested the Greekness of Cyprus in the context of interpreting a report on Greek-Turkish relations, he referred to Cyprus as 'ours' when discussing the conflict and NATO's intervention in Kosovo in Spring 1999. This shift results from how the informant positions himself in different contexts: he allows himself to contest the official discourse on Cyprus in the context of Greek politics, but embraces this very official discourse in the context of international affairs. News consumption seems to transcend ethnic divisions in the sense that there are similarities in media engagement patterns across ethnic groups, and there is diversity of interpretations of media content within ethnic categories.

Another aspect of the diversity of the news audiences is evident in the instances when they switch off. A small number of informants from all ethnic groups chose to abstain from watching the news, thus becoming the opposite of those 'addicted to the news'. This withdrawal is as telling as audiences' engagement with the media is. It combines both affective aspects as well as a critical evaluation of the news. Moreover, switching off is never purely a matter of choice. It depends on issues of access, contextual knowledge and trust towards the journalists and the media.

## Switching off

A few informants said that they had recently decided to stop watching television on a regular basis. Such decisions are mainly attributed to the lack of trust towards journalists and the media. Thodoris, a Greek taxi driver in his 30s said: 'It's all fake. I often feel television takes me for a fool [*vlaka*]'. Thodoris described himself as a former heavy viewer, who watched the news regularly. However, even if he denied watching the news at the time of the interview, he was well informed about current affairs. Even if he did not proactively switch on the television he found out the latest news through friends, family, clients or the other media, notably radio.

Other interviewees who did not follow the news regularly were Greek high school students and working class housewives who attributed their lack of interest in the news to their workload, but also to the lack of contextual information with which to interpret the news, particularly the news on national issues. This made them less keen to follow the news and current affairs programmes, a phenomenon related to class and age (also evident among younger Turkish speaking viewers). Such patterns seem to confirm the findings of British researchers on gendered media use (Morley, 1986; Gray, 1992). However, gender differences were only observed among working class families. In middle and upper middle class families, and generally among the more educated informants, gender differences were no longer salient.

For a couple of Cypriot viewers the catalyst for a withdrawal from watching television and current affairs was the way that the Cyprus issue was portrayed in the Greek media. This couple of middle class informants were so dissatisfied that they decided to ban the television from their home. What is different in their case is that the reasons for switching off were not gendered or class-based, but rather grounded in the dissatisfaction with the reporting of the 'national issues', particularly when Cyprus is involved. Interestingly, both these informants were well informed on current affairs as a result of rich information networks ranging from interpersonal relationships to other media.

Dissatisfaction with the quality of reporting prompted some Turkish-speaking informants to switch off their sets. What is notable in their case is that their withdrawal resulted from a number of negative personal experiences with the media and journalists. People from Gazi (the neighbourhood in Athens where many Turkish speakers live) felt that there was distortion and falsification whenever the neighbourhood or its inhabitants were represented in the media. Watching oneself or one's acquaintances on television did not invoke familiarity as it did for the Greeks, but rather exclusion. Reports on Gazi generated tension, frustration and even anger. 'We've been in magazines so many times and there hasn't been a positive article even once', Yilmaz said. 'They write whatever they feel like', noted Suleyman, and added that journalists will hardly ever tell the truth.

While Greek informants had mainly positive, direct experiences with the media to refer to,[18] Turkish-speaking informants recounted only negative ones. This is a fundamental difference between the groups (the Cypriot informants reported no direct experiences) that shapes trust in the media and the overall interpretative framework. Furthermore, the ordinariness with which Turkish-speaking informants use the Greek media is in stark contrast to the ways in which the informants see themselves represented in the media.

The next section explores the consequences of this symbolic exclusion and whether it plays a role in an exclusion from public life in general.

## When exclusion matters

One of the angles through which the audience and public relationship is explored in this chapter is that of ethnicity and diversity. This last section examines the role that media can play in including or excluding people from public life, especially when this exclusion is based on an essentialist understanding of difference. The focus here is on the instances when diversity is translated into exclusion. When does 'switching off' translate into withdrawal from public life in general? Does it have a more direct impact on people's lives and participation in the democratic process?

What emerged from the previous section is that, although many consumption patterns cut across ethnic divides, the reasons that led to the phenomenon of 'switching off' were ethnically demarcated. The other parameter affecting switching off is class (with the exception of the Greek Cypriot couple). However, none of the Greek informants gave negative personal experiences as the reason leading to switching off - an observation which brings ethnicity, or rather an essentialised understanding of difference, to the centre of this analysis. This ethnic dimension was not the expression of a primordial identity, but rather a reaction to a process of ascription and labeling which takes identity politics into a false circle. One consequence of this process and of the withdrawal it brings about is the lack of trust of journalists and the lack of confidence to voice one's complaints. While Greek informants called 'the channels' to voice their complaints about the public services, the Gaziots had no equivalent channel of communication. It was the mainstream media that they wanted to complain about. Of course, as noted earlier, some programmes such as 'Jungle' did function as an alternative public sphere among my informants. It seems, however, that such programmes did not make people feel positively represented. Following Canclini's (2001) argument about Mexico, if Greek viewers sometimes resort to the media to get what traditional citizen institutions do not provide, Turkish-speaking viewers (also Greek citizens) do not seem to have an equivalent resource, or the confidence to create one.

This lack of confidence is evident in the absence of any efforts among my informants to set up local or community media. In response to my question, as to whether they had thought of setting up a Turkish language radio station in Athens,

Orhan said: 'we haven't thought about it. And even if we plan it, I don't think we will be able to. They will probably shut us down'. This phrase exemplifies a number of points that pertain to the minority. First, the remark that they had never considered setting up their own local media is indicative of their general lack of confidence, also manifested in the projection of a negative result. Such a projection, however, is justified if one takes into account the accumulated negative experiences with journalists, the media and the authorities in Greece in general. This is an example of the mediation process, where media power (in this case, power to exclude) is located at different, although interconnected levels (Couldry, 2003; Madianou, 2005a and b). The negative experiences with the journalists affect the trust informants had in the media, which in turn shapes the decoding of the news. Moreover, as seen in the case above, the negative media experiences and the lack of trust undermine confidence to establish their own media that could make their voices heard, thereby establishing their presence in public life (Phillips, 1995). It should be noted, however, that the exclusion that the media bring about in this case is not only their responsibility. Media operate at a symbolic level that reminds informants of their exclusion at a material and other symbolic levels as well.

## Conclusions

This chapter, based on an empirical study of news consumption among Greek, Greek Cypriot and Turkish-speaking audiences, set out to challenge two assumptions about audiences and publics for news. News consumption emerged as a multi-faceted process that transcends the public - private divide. The emotional, intimate and sometimes instrumental uses of the news are deeply intertwined with the rational and critical dimensions of news consumption, rendering audiences both rational and emotional, both citizens and consumers. Indeed, it was observed that, on some occasions, the media come to fill the void that is left by traditional citizen institutions, as people turn to the television news for information, advice, justice or just attention.

This potentially empowering function of television, however, does not apply to all of its users. In examining the plurality of the audiences for Greek news, it was observed that in some cases diversity is translated into withdrawal and even exclusion from public life. More specifically, this applied to the Turkish-speaking viewers, who felt ostracised by a television discourse that systematically misrepresented them. Their negative personal experiences with the media maintained a process of exclusion that heightened their existing material and symbolic exclusion within Greek society and deepened their lack of confidence to voice their point of view, or institute their own media, which could strengthen their presence in public life. The optimistic message here is that all this can change, since exclusion and the reactions it generates are based on an essentialist understanding of difference and not on a given, primordial identity. If essentialism produces essentialism, openness can encourage inclusion and the recognition of plurality.

In this context, the concept of the public appears relevant for the study of news consumption, not in a normative way, but as it opens up the field to politics and can make arguments about the relevance of cultural engagement in the democratic process. This is particularly evident in the blending of the private and public domains and through the various ways that the media (as texts, forms, technologies, institutions) catalyse audiences' participation in, or withdrawal from, public life.

## Notes

1. Thanks to Sonia Livingstone, Daniel Dayan, Kirsten Drotner, Dominique Mehl, Danny Miller, Ulrike Meinhof and Roberta Pearson for comments on a previous draft. A shorterned version of this chapter has appeared in *Journal of Media Practice* vol 6:1.

2. 33 Greeks living in Athens were interviewed.

3. The sample consisted of 15 Greek Cypriots born in Cyprus and living in Athens.

4. Turkish speaking people are part of what Greece officially recognises as the Muslim minority, which comprises of three indigenous ethnic groups: Turkish, Pomak and Roma. My sample consisted of 21 informants of either Turkish or Roma origin living in the working class neighbourhood of Gazi and for whom I use the term 'Turkish speaking'. For a discussion of the complexities surrounding these minorities and their communicative resources see Madianou (2005b). For all groups a gender, age and class ratio was sought, although, as in all qualitative research, the sample is not statistically representative.

5. Michael Warner (2002, p. 29) distinguishes between 15 definitions of the adjective public in opposition to the word private, at least three of which can be found in this definition of 'public life', namely, 'open to everyone (as opposed to restricted to some), political (as opposed to non-political) and circulated in print and electronic media'.

6. Examples of this significant tradition include: Gamson (1992); Jensen (1988); Lewis (1991); Liebes (1997); Philo (1990); for the interpretation of a news magazine programme see Morley (1980).

7. Greece was the last country in the EU to deregulate its broadcasting system. This was a political and contingent decision rather than the product of planning and public policy as Papathanassopoulos has noted (1990, p. 387). For further analysis see Papathanassopoulos (1990) and (1999).

8. For a more in depth analysis of these features see Madianou (2005a).

9. The respective EU mean for television news is 68%, while for radio and newspapers it is 68% and 42% respectively. The figures reflect the period of the fieldwork but have remained unchanged (Eurobarometer, 2000).

10. In 1999 the Internet connection rate was 6% and although it has doubled in recent years (14% in    2003 according to the Eurobarometer survey) Greece continues to hold the lowest place in the EU together with Portugal (Eurobarometer reports 2000 and 2003).

11. Although most of the data concerns television news, inevitably some examples concerning other news media are included, as they are part of people's overall media resources.

12. The audiences' need to 'keep up' with reality is confirmed by two other studies on news (Gans 1979 and Jensen 1998, p. 58).

13. The other social uses of television are 'relational', involving television's capacity to facilitate communication or conflict (Lull, 1990, p. 35).

14. He refers to the private television channels.

15. This is evident in the specific features of the Greek political culture and the lack of a robust civil society (Demertzis, 1994; Diamantouros, 2000).

16. This is confirmed by a recent survey about viewers' satisfaction with television channels. The public channels had the highest percentage (NET, 72.1% and ET-1 69.5%) in terms of viewers' satisfaction followed by MEGA (67.1%) and ANTENNA (65.1%). Recall that the public channels' ratings are in constant decline (Taylor Nelson Sofres Metrisis, published in the daily *Eleutherotypia*, 29.5.2002).

17. This should not be taken to mean that the 'Cyprus problem' is not an issue that concerns Greece and its foreign policy, but rather that there is sometimes an observable discrepancy between the official discourse about Cyprus and the informal ones, which are often more ambivalent. Elsewhere, (2004a) I define the official discourse as the one that reflects government policy, while informal discourses are those circulating at an everyday level and do not gain public prominence. For a discussion on the Cyprus problem, also in the context of Greek - Turkish relations see among others Mavratsas (2001).

18. Recall, for example, the instances when they would phone in to voice their complaint.

## References

Bausinger, Hermann (1984) 'Media, technology and daily life'. *Media, Culture and Society,* vol.6 (4): 343-351.

Blumler, Jay (1991) *Television and the public interest: vulnerable values in Western European broadcasting*. London: Sage.

Canclini, Nestor Garcia (2001) *Consumers and Citizens: globalisation and multicultural conflicts*. Minneapolis: University of Minnesota Press.

Carey, James (1989) *Communication as Culture*. New York: Routledge.

Couldry, Nick (2003) *Media Rituals: A critical approach*. London: Routledge.

Demertzis, Nicos ed. (1994) *H Elliniki politiki koultoura simera*. Athens: Odysseas.

Diamantouros, Nikoforos (2000) *Politismikos dyismos kai politiki allagi stin Ellada tis metapoliteusis*. Athens: Alexandria.

Fraser, Nancy (1992) 'Rethinking the public sphere'. In Craig Calhoun, (ed.), *Habermas and the Public Sphere*. Cambridge. Mass.: MIT Press, pp. 109-142.

Gamson, William (1992) *Talking Politics*. Cambridge: Cambridge University Press.

Gans, Herbert (1979) *Deciding what's news*. New York: Vintage Books.

Gauntlett, David and Annette Hill (1999) *TV Living: television culture and everyday life*. London: Routledge.

Gitlin, Todd (1999) 'Public sphere or public sphericules'. In James Curran, and Tamar Liebes (eds.), *Media Ritual and Identity*. London: Routledge.

Gray, Anne (1992) *Video Playtime: the gendering of a leisure technology*. London: Routledge.

Gunter, Barry and Michael Svennevig (1987) *Behind and in front of the screen*. London: John Libbey.

Habermas, Jugern (1989 [1962]) *The Structural Transformation of the Public Sphere*. Cambridge: Polity Press.

Jensen, Klaus Bruhn (1988) 'News as Social Resource'. *European Journal of Communication*, vol. 3: 275-301.

Jensen, Klaus Bruhn (1998) 'Denmark'. In Klaus Bruhn Jensen, (ed.), *News of the World: World Cultures Look at Television News*. London: Routledge, pp. 39-60.

Lewis, Justin (1991) *The Ideological Octopus: An Exploration of Television and its Audience*. London: Routledge.

Liebes, Tamar (1997) *Reporting the Israeli-Arab Conflict: How Hegemony Works*. London: Routledge.

Livingstone, Sonia (2005) 'On the relation between audiences and publics'. In Sonia Livingstone, (ed.), *Audiences and Publics*. Bristol: Intellect Press.

Livingstone, Sonia and Peter Lunt (1994) Talk on Television. London: Routledge.

Lull, James (1990) *Inside Family Viewing: ethnographic research on television's audience*. London: Routledge.

Madianou, Mirca (forthcoming 2005a) *Mediating the Nation: news, audiences, identities*. London: UCL Press.

Madianou, Mirca (forthcoming 2005b) 'Contested communicative spaces: identities, boundaries and the role of the media'. *Journal of Ethnic and Migration Studies*, Vol.31 (3).

Mavratsas, Caesar (2001) 'Greek Cypriot identity and conflicting interpretations of the Cyprus Problem'. In Dimitris Keridis, and Dimitrios Triandafyllou (eds.) *Greek Turkish Relations in the era of Globalisation. Dulles*, VA: Brassey's. pp., 151-179.

Morley, David (1980) *The Nationwide Audience: structure and decoding. Television Monograph*. London: BFI.

Morley, David (1986) *Family Television*. London: Comedia.

Morley, David (1995) 'Television: not so much a visual medium, more a visible object'. In Jenks, Chris (ed.), *Visual Culture*. London: Routledge.

Norris, Pippa (2000) *A Virtuous Circle: political communications in the post-industrial democracies*. New York: Cambridge University Press.

Papathanassopoulos, Stylianos (1990) 'Broadcasting, politics and the state in Socialist Greece'. *Media, Culture and Society*, vol. 12: 387-397.

Papathanassopoulos, Stylianos (1999) 'The effects of media commercialisation on journalism and politics in Greece'. *The Communication Review*, vol. 3(4): 379-402.

Phillips, Anne (1995) *The Politics of Presence: the political representation of gender, ethnicity and race*. Oxford: Oxford University Press.

Philo, Greg (1990) *Seeing and Believing: the Influence of Television*. London: Routledge.

Putnam, Robert (2000) *Bowling Alone: the collapse and revival of American community*. New York: Simon and Schuster.

Robbins, Bruce (ed.) (1993) *The Phantom Public Sphere*. Minneapolis: University of Minnesota Press.

Schudson, Michael (1995) *The Power of News*. Cambridge, MA: Harvard University Press.

Schudson, Michael (2000) 'The sociology of news production revisited (again)'. In James Curran and Michael Gurevitch (eds.), *Mass Media and Society* (3$^{rd}$ ed.). London: Edward Arnold, pp. 175-200.

Silverstone, Roger (1994) *Television and Everyday Life*. London: Routledge.

Silverstone, Roger (in press) 'Mediation and communication'. In Calhoun, Craig, Chris Rojek and Bryan Turner (eds.) *International Handbook of Sociology*. London: Sage.

Warner, Michael (2002) *Publics and Counterpublics*. New York: Zone Books.

Ulrike Hanna Meinhof

# Chapter 5: Initiating a public: Malagasy music and live audiences in differentiated cultural contexts

Sonia Livingstone in her introduction to this volume raises some key conceptual questions, which frame the discussions in this volume in general and the concerns of this chapter in particular, namely, when is an audience (not) a public; when is a public (not) an audience? At the crudest level, the dividing line would place a public on the worthy, active, socially engaged, informed and self-reflexive side of the spectrum; while the audience would be relegated to the sphere of those who merely consume as passive spectators, or - if not entirely passive - at least without public commitment of any sort. In such a reading, publics seek to be informed, to reflect, and to act, reaching beyond the events through which they constitute themselves in the public sphere, while audiences enjoy what is on offer for the duration of an entertainment with no further consequences.

Within other branches of Cultural Studies, a more negative understanding of the 'public' underlines the coercive, normative and prescriptive nature of the role assigned to 'the public' in such dichotomies, reminiscent of the debates sparked off by the Frankfurt Schools' distinction between 'high' and 'low'/'mass' culture (for example, McCabe, 1986). Here a more positive understanding of what constitutes 'audiences' argues that all engagements - including those with the most mass produced forms of popular culture - are participatory and thus have public resonance (for example, Radway, 1984; Fiske, 1987). In that way, audiences, too, act in culturally significant ways, using their knowledge to adapt cultural forms and performances in meaningful, even potentially subversive and critical ways.

## Revisiting the author-text-reader triad

Such debates have a long history within cultural, media and communication studies, where they interlink with other discussions about the nature of the text itself and, more widely, about the triad of communication between author (as producer and performer), text, and reader/recipient, to use established semiotic vocabulary.[1] Here it is the relative privileging of one interpretative focus over the other that influences the appreciation or denial of the power of an audience to assert his or her own readings. An emphasis on production rarely integrates textual analysis and variant readings. A textual emphasis usually relegates the reader to that of an implied reader, who activates textual structures that impose their own authority through the semiotic codes themselves (language or any other visual/audiovisual form of culturally conditioned meaning making). Audience studies, on the other hand, tend to emphasise the multiplicity of meanings that are activated by readers. Attempts to analyse dynamic interactivity between production/author, the text, and the reader/audience - though often asserted as desirable in theory - tend to privilege one perspective over the other. (For these approaches, see Gripsrud, 1995; Fairclough, 1995; Buckingham, 1987).

Theorists in Media and Cultural Studies, in attempting to synthesize two dimensions of communication - the semiotic structures of the textual product and the activation of meaning at the point of reception - have for a long time postulated that all texts, while analysable as semiotic constructs, are 'open' and so allow multiple readings by differently situated 'readers' (see for example, Ang, 1986; Bennett, et al.1986; Graddol & Boyd-Barrett, 1994; McCabe 1986; Modleski, 1986). The process of reading texts - that is, the making of meaning at the point of reception rather than production - will depend on a large number of individual but also socially and culturally determined factors, including the different knowledge types which need or can be activated by the text and its reader (see also Meinhof & Smith, 2000). Textual structures do encode preferred readings, which are open to analysis, but these cannot guarantee they will be taken up. Hence, at best, there is a creative tension. This openness of interaction between text and reader allows analysts in Cultural Studies to 'rescue' seemingly shallow and despised popular culture texts - not necessarily by proving their subtlety or distinctiveness at the level of the text itself, but by examining the creative wealth of meanings engendered by readers of these texts. Such openness also allows us to interrogate the different interpretations of the same text by different readers without evaluating them as good or bad, correct or incorrect responses.

So far so good, but what if we investigate authors, texts and readers interdependently within their culturally situated contexts where each in turn construct texts from within the 'meaning potential' (Halliday, 1978) within their purview? If we do this, the cultural predispositions of authors and of readers - in particular their differentiated access to shared or private knowledge and skills, their emotional and/or intellectual commitment to particular value systems[2] - will render some texts and some readings more complex or more shallow, more complete or incomplete, more or less committed to action, more or less ethical, propagandist or distorted in intention and/or uptake than others. An emphasis on the potential for initiating and enabling certain meanings/actions rather than others at each stage of the author/performer - text - reader interchange thus reintroduces a critical and evaluative perspective into the analysis of communicative interaction. The understanding of how each of these can and do construct their meanings by different means - from authorial intentions, commentary or performance to textual product and recipients' uptake - thus provides a foil for critical assessment at every stage of interaction. It also shows the likelihood as well as the impossibility of certain preferred or less favoured meanings to be exchanged under particular contextual conditions. Significantly, where there is a need to appreciate the deeper context for an otherwise obscure or one-dimensional text, an element of agency and responsibility goes to the author/text producer/performer at the point of text-production or performance, as well as to the reader at the point of receptive 'text' recreation, without closing down any of the options for multiple encodings or readings.

In the absence of mutual knowledge between author/text and recipients, the sharing of presupposed information and knowledge becomes a central pre-condition for initiating 'an audience' into the reflexivity and understanding which defines a 'public' and its potential for engaging in considered action (Habermas, 1989/1962). Thus even if theoretical distinctions between the two are kept conceptually and normatively separate, 'audiences' and 'publics' can co-exist, and the boundaries between them blur in the same performative interactive space under particular conditions. The analysis of such interactions thus becomes less of a theoretical and more of an empirical question, approachable via fieldwork, text interpretation, interviews, and the associated ethnographic and discourse analytical/semiotic methods. Where these interactions take place in private spaces via radio, television, Internet, they can be difficult to trace empirically (but see Livingstone, Drotner and Mehl in this volume). An ethnography of live performances by comparison can offer easier access and valuable insights into the nature of such interactivity and the negotiation of meanings that are taking place between author/performers and audiences.

## Black 'roots' or 'world' music audiences and the public sphere

The following sections will try to elucidate some of these theoretical reflections by concentrating on one particular musical genre and its audiences. The genre focused on is that of 'roots' or world music, and the case study is of a musician from Madagascar performing in culturally differentiated settings in Europe. I will argue that 'world music' as it is being constructed via the music industry (CD covers, promotional schemes) and the media (radio and TV) in the western world[3] narrows the 'meaning potential' of some of the most powerful and creative works by African and other non-western artists (see also Barrett, 1996; Berger & Carroll, 2000; Clayton 2001; Irele, 2001). Western audiences are deprived of a whole layer of meaning that motivates these creations, and which is fully appreciated within the socio-cultural context from where such music originates. Performing artists on world music circuits tend to go along with the commercialisation of their music as exotic and 'other', allowing audiences to participate in the rhythmic and melodic quality of their creations, but making little attempts to transmit any fuller context. Yet, as this case study shows, western audiences of this music are entirely open to an initiation into the fuller meaning of such music, as and when they are provided with this opportunity. The detailed focus here is on two exemplary performances by a Malagasy artist in the spring of 2002, a period of grave political crisis in Madagascar. These were selected from a whole series of concerts by the same author/composer/performer and his group - a group I have observed in different cultural contexts in Europe and in Africa since 2001. The final section of this chapter will consider in detail how the artist used various strategies to initiate his audiences into the conditions in which they could become a public. However, before turning to this particular case study, we need to reflect on the conditions through which 'world music' is being constructed and received.

## Roots music and the media

Probably more than with any other musical genre, audiences of black African 'roots' or 'world' music in Europe are ethnically highly differentiated: from almost exclusivist diasporic to culturally mixed and/or purely white groups. This can be seen as and wherever such music is played or performed, be it on the radio or in live settings. In either of these contexts, the setting - mediated or live - is largely preconfigured. Audiences and artists and, in the case of radio or television, the moderators and their audiences, know what to expect from one another and construct their interactions accordingly.

Taken at one end of a sliding scale, we will find root music on community radio stations, stripped into slots that correspond to the national, ethnic and/or linguistic background of its 'diasporic' audiences.[4] For example, in Paris, home to a highly diverse population originating from all over the world, we find radio stations such as *FPP* (*Frequence Paris Plurielle*), which acts as an umbrella station for different independently produced diasporic productions. These include twice-weekly slots of the Malagasy *Radio Capricorne*, the weekly slot of *Espace Maghreb* as well as Maghreb *Pluriel, Visages du Kurdistan* (once per week), *Americas* (South American broadcasts four times a week) and so on. This situation is echoed in most capital cities in Europe with large (im-)migrant populations.[5] Often working from shoestring budgets with high or even 100% voluntary involvement by members of the sub-community, these broadcasts are largely by and for specific linguistically, ethnically and culturally defined groups with strong interactive links to the originating countries. Through these, 'purposeful networks' (Gillespie, 2002, p.169) are maintained at every possible level of the life of the sub-community, often complemented by websites which act as further platforms for information exchange about cultural, social and political events. Without any further commercial promotion, concerts and other artistic events by local and 'homeland' based artists thus easily attract audiences of hundreds, even thousands of people purely from within the sub-community itself and without any spread to the wider population of the city.

At the other end of the spectrum, 'world' music has grown from a niche market to one that enjoys considerable commercial success with a culturally diverse international audience. The label 'world music' itself tends to refer to those compositions that are largely produced by non-western musicians, usually originating from the developing world or diasporic settings, with lyrics written and performed in original non-western languages. 'Discovered' by western pop and rock musicians in the 70s and 80s,[6] music from African, Asian and South American 'roots' has gained unprecedented and increasingly high-status popularity. For

British readers there is a specialist monthly magazine (fRoots, with its influential editor Ian Anderson) in addition to a whole series of international web-sites. National and metropolitan radio, and to a lesser extent television, play a pivotal role as disseminators and promoters. In the UK, there are several radio programmes on *BBC Radio 3* (Andy Kershaw, Lucy Duran, and other more local stations such as Charley Gillet on *London FM*) dedicated to world music; since 2002 there has also been an annual world music awards scheme relayed on *BBC Radio 3* and on the digital television channel *BBC4*. Interestingly enough, world music tends to appeal to a relatively sophisticated niche market, often with 'left/liberal leaning' (Barnett, 1996, p. 241). Its fate on British radio and television is a case in point. One of the most important radio DJ's in this area in the UK, world music enthusiast Andy Kershaw, only as recently as April 2001 crossed a cultural shadow-line when his weekly show - transmitted for decades on the pop and rock music station radio BBC1 - was moved to the largely classical 'high-culture' station of BBC Radio 3.[7] Kershaw's transfer from a pop to a more 'high-brow' musical environment is further echoed by a plethora of other world music programmes also on *BBC Radio 3*. Foremost of these is the weekly programme *World Routes* presented by ethno-musicologist-cum-journalist Lucy Duran but there are also other eclectic evening music slots (such as *Night Waves; Junction*) as well. On the *BBC*, at least (and echoed in the classificatory systems of music shops) world music has been re-signified as music for a more discerning public than the young pop-music loving target group of Radio 1.

Given the relatively highbrow audience of *BBC Radio 3*, it is arguably somewhat surprising that relatively little is made of the socio-cultural background of the musicians and the lyrical content of their music. In most of these mediated contexts, the music is celebrated for its vitality and creativity - the rhythmic quality, the power of the voices and the blending of styles. Only occasionally is the cultural background of the singers discussed - Kershaw's special Haitian and Iranian programmes are the exception rather than the rule. Only Lucy Duran, a radio moderator and ethnomusicologist in her own right, regularly has guests in the studio with whom she discusses their social and cultural background, and occasionally refers to the content of their lyrics. But for most of the time, world music is set in a content-free space - an alternative and more sophisticated entertainment to the more predictable repetitiveness of pop and rock music, on a par with jazz, which made its entry into the realms of *BBC Radio 3* several years earlier.

World music audiences listen (or dance) to an often profoundly serious, socially and politically engaged, multi-encoded artistic form in a one-dimensional way, constrained as they are by the almost total incomprehensibility of languages such as Wolof, Hausa, Malagasy, Yoruba and Xhosa - to name but a few of the hundreds of native African languages of multi-lingual musicians that form the textual basis for their lyrics - to western listeners. Whether a song encodes a cry for freedom, or a call to arms and rebellion, an indictment of social and political problems, a celebration of love, nostalgia for a lost home, or hatred of an oppressive other, whether it is deeply religious or critical of fundamentalist fervour - western audiences remain largely innocent of content and potential agreements or contradictions with their own world views. Music is celebrated as universal non-verbal energy belonging to the realm of taste, embracing all people who share an appreciation for it without being disturbed by the implications of social or political meaning. The silence of the media on the content of the songs and the commercial practice of the music industry collude, with the result that it is still rare to find lyrics printed in the original language of the musicians and with a translation inside a CD booklet. Hence, neither CD buyers nor radio DJs receive much support from the recording labels. The existence of many sampler albums such as African Blues, African Guitar Legends, Arabesque, One World etc., further adds to this decontextual space. Barrett (1996, p. 239) argues that these covers play to a 'romanticised cultural aesthetic' of audiences 'not over-familiar with geographic spaces' with pictures and titles that promise 'luxury, global unity, authenticity, exotic difference, recreation and displacement' (see also Rasolofondraosolo and Meinhof, 2003, p. 130).

## Roots music and its live venues

Live music events and their audiences cover a similar spectrum. On one end of the scale, there are settings that are purely ethnically defined. So, for example, the Malagasy community centre in Paris, *Tana Orly* - significantly named after the capital of Madagascar Antananarivo, *Tana* for short, and located near the airport Paris Orly that Air Madagascar operates flights from - regularly features live concerts by Malagasy musicians flown in from Madagascar and/or French based Malagasy artists. Weekend concerts attract large, almost exclusively Malagasy audiences. On the other end of the scale, there are regular 'world music' concerts with ethnically mixed but usually predominantly white audiences. These often take place at venues chosen because of their reputations as hosts of world music or with a jazz focus, such as London's *Unity Chapel* or *The New Morning* venue in Paris, where internationally known African musicians such as Senegal's Youssou N'Dour and Baaba Maal or Mali's Salif Keita perform during international concert tours. In the UK these concerts are frequently recorded and shown late at night on national television, for instance, on *Channel 4*, *BBC2*, and more recently on the new *BBC 4* digital channel. Similarly, world music has found its regular slots in multi-art festivals, such as the annual Brighton Festival, and of course, with Womad - an annual open-air dedicated world music festival in Reading -again transmitted on *BBC Radio 3* and *BBC* television.

## The artists and their audiences

Having noted the quintessentially different character of world music performances and audiences that are ethnically/sub-community defined, there is also some continuum and overlap. It is true that, for the majority of African musicians in

Africa and in Europe, the world music scene remains a closed shop, usually controlled by western commercial interests and a tightly structured gate-keeping media. However, most world music artists, before having been 'discovered' by western record labels and promoters, originated from a more ethnically defined scene either in their countries of origin or in Europe. Once successful on the world music scene, the two audience groups often mingle at large concerts and festivals with different audience sub-groups claiming the musician as their own.[8] In other cases - especially where entry into the fame of world music is less established - artists retain links with their distinctly different audiences at distinctive pre-constituted venues. This latter phenomenon provides us with intriguing comparative data for our audience/public debate.

## Introducing the case study: Dama from Mahaleo

The remainder of this chapter is based on case-study research that focused on a well-known Malagasy musician, 'Dama' and his eponymous group 'Mahaleo', who, in spite of their chosen 'non-professional' status as musicians for 30-plus years and limited exposure on the international world music scene, have nevertheless performed in both settings. Since July 2001, and with the full agreement and collaboration of the artists concerned, I have conducted fieldwork in the form of participant observation, questionnaires, and interviews with audiences and artists during a series of solo and band performances by Dama and by Mahaleo. Performances took place in different cultural settings with ethnically, linguistically and culturally differentiated live audiences[9]. The aim was to investigate the similarities and differences in performance and audience reaction, and complement these by the musicians' own understanding of their practices of audience interactions. The selection of this particular group of Malagasy artists - apart from their personal accessibility to me as researcher - was based on a number of factors, but the most significant in the context of this chapter were:

The long-standing 'legendary' fame of Dama and Mahaleo amongst Malagasy people in Madagascar and abroad (Anderson 1999, p. 531), and their - albeit much more limited - presence on the world music scene.

- Their public role as professionals in non-musical careers in Madagascar, a feature known but rarely by their international audiences.

- Powerful lyrics with a pronounced socially committed content, often expressed indirectly through metaphor and metonymic characterisation, and to which non-Malagasy speakers have no access.

- The choice and sophisticated use of the Malagasy language that was revolutionary in 1972, but subsequently set off entire generations of followers. This is a layer of significance that, without any mediation, non-speakers of Malagasy cannot hope to appreciate.

Thus, there is a sharply pre-configured contrast between the two potential audience groups, the western 'world music' audience and the Malagasy audiences within and outside Madagascar. The music of Dama and Mahaleo is symbolic for a Malagasy identity, which allows people of Malagasy origin to celebrate, perform and retain cultural connections across transnational spaces. Through their music and lyrics, they have established themselves as deeply admired spokespersons for the concerns of the people and their social and political problems. Their significance was confirmed repeatedly in interviews conducted with members of their audiences at the various concerts, and with ad-hoc interviews with Malagasies in everyday settings. Malagasies all over the world not only know the musician(s) because of their huge repertoire of 300-plus songs, with a back catalogue of more than 30 years, but they also appreciate the artists for their social and political engagement in their everyday professional lives as doctors, politicians, civil servants and sociologists. Mahaleo's music, like that of so many other African artists, is inseparable from the public life and social concerns of the citizens of and from their respective countries. The lyrics of their songs - widely known by everyone and sung along in harmony during concert performances - reflect this engagement. The songs and their joint performance enable the confirmation of cultural identification, while at the same time articulating a critique of the many difficult social and political problems faced in their country (see also Rasolofondraosolo and Meinhof, 2003). None of this meaning potential of the music, which Malagasy audiences hear, see and engage with, is available to a western 'world music' audience.

## Audiences and publics

Given the theoretical assumptions underpinning this book, this chapter raises - and approaches empirically - the question of whether or not it is necessary or feasible to differentiate between, on the one hand, an informed engaged Malagasy 'public'; and, on the other hand, an exclusively taste and pleasure-oriented world music audience that, for lack of any fuller knowledge of the cultural context, is firmly removed from the public sphere in which these songs signify something more than simply musical vitality. African roots music plays a pivotal role in the cultural identity and social struggles of the people and the country from which it originates. As an artistic expression, its strength lies as much in its lyrics as in its musical form. The significance which African roots music has played in political struggles against apartheid in South Africa, in struggles for independence from colonial regimes (for example, in Zimbabwe and Mozambique) and new nation-building is well documented (see for example, Bender, 1985 and 1989; Connell & Gibson 2003, especially chapter 6). Mahaleo, too, started their career in 1972 as young student rebels during the General Strike, with songs against corruption and political abuse of power, and a more generalised commitment to the 'Malgachisation' of a French-dominated (post-) colonial cultural life. Occasionally banned from state controlled radio stations, they built their support during live concerts to tens of thousands, countering censorship by encouraging bootleg recordings, as well as with frequent concert tours to Malagasies abroad, mainly performing for the large diasporic communities in French cities such as Paris, Marseilles and Toulouse. Their 30th anniversary in 2002, during a career in which their support remained unwavering, coincided with a major political crisis, which in the first half of that year brought Madagascar to the edge of Civil War.[10] What interests us here is that, during the first half of 2002, many Malagasy musicians in Madagascar in Paris and other big European cities – though usually outside of any party politics – engaged fully in the political struggle for the unity of their country. Websites for *Radio Capricorne*, for example, and other support email links, rallied the Malagasy public in France and further abroad. They organised regular demonstrations in support of their newly elected, though not yet internationally-recognised President, Marc Ravalomanana; attacked the outgoing president Ratsiraka and his supporters for their campaign of blockade and sabotage against the *Hauts Plateaux* region and the capital city itself; and criticised the French for their unwillingness to recognise the new regime. During all of this, musicians played a major role: Malagasy artists based in France, such as Erick Manana, Lolo, Justin Valy amongst many others, joined forces with artists based in Madagascar on tour in France. The Malagasy diaspora in Paris was divided, with support also flowing to Ratsiraka. However, the energy of the majority of musicians was firmly placed within the new president's camp, and his promise of more democratic transparency, an end to corruption, improvement of conditions of life, and above all unity of Malagasy, be they from the coast or the highlands. Dama, whose full name is Zafimahaleo Rasolofondraosolo and whose audiences form the basis of this case study, was among those who performed at rallies, in Paris in January 2002 as well as in the capital city of Antananarivo during the spring of 2002. An independent MP from 1993 to 2003, Dama was pre-destined for this engagement. During demonstrations in Paris and in Antananarivo, he epitomised the role of the artist in the public sphere and continued his long-established role as an independent voice and a critical non-partisan artist-politician.

During the upheaval of May and June 2002, Mahaleo also performed live in Paris, first in the *Espace Chevreuill* (Nanterre) and then in *St Martin*, to almost 100% Malagasy audiences. In May, Dama also performed in the UK at the Brighton Festival of Arts to an almost exclusively white British audience, and again at a small private concert to a group of Malagasy and British listeners.

## Malagasy music in different 'home' contexts

A return to the division of audience and public would suggest that a world music event at the Brighton festival and a concert to Malagasy audiences by the same artist constructs very different levels of engagement. These are already preconfigured by the nature of the event, its venue, and its context, which create expectations between artist and audience/public that determine many of the interactions. However, there are surprising aspects to these representations that subvert such simple dichotomies. In an attempt to demonstrate this in detail, I will concentrate on two events: the concert in June 2002 at *St Martin* in Paris, where Mahaleo played to an audience of about 800 and who were almost exclusively of Malagasy origin, and the solo concert by Dama (with his percussionist Charle) at the Brighton Festival on May 23, 2002 to a mainly white audience of about 150.[11]

## Mahaleo for Malagasies

Given the preoccupation of many Malagasies at home and abroad during spring 2002 with the political future and unity of their country, and the immediate involvement of the musicians in some of the mass demonstrations, I had expected that the Mahaleo concerts during that period would have a strong political flavour. However, the interaction between audiences and the Mahaleo were more complex and their political implications much more indirect than I had anticipated. During concerts lasting between four and seven hours there was the usual selection of political and socially committed songs, but at no point did the interaction with the audiences transform into direct political opinion-making or appeals. A few references to the political crisis remained low-key, only serving to stress the need for unity. Instead, the artists created a communal spirit whereby they and the audiences together were co-performers and co-constructors of Malagasy identity, sharing concerns and celebrating their pleasures. Song selections included the joint performance of some of their most popular songs of the last 30 years: the arousing *'Morovoay'* where hundreds of people in the audience join from the first note with polyphonic singing and multi-rhythmic clapping; the love song *'Mimoza'* which always fetches one member from the audience on the stage to sing the female voice part of the duo; songs especially poignant in their referencing of key social and political problems (for example, *'Lendrema'*, *'Kobaka'*, and the newly written *'Malagasy Blues'*); as well as those appealing for unity (*'Nosy Milalao'*) and solidarity (*'Tsy Mirahaha'*). The call for unity and communality was furthermore implicitly reinforced by indirect metaphoric references in between the different songs, all performed in the Malagasy language. At the concert in *St Martin*, almost the entire night's talk-interludes by Dama and his brother - fellow singer and songwriter, Raoul - were couched in the form of an invitation to a shared meal. Prepared by the artists to feed 'the soul' of their invitees, Mahaleo were offering 'recipes for the day' consisting of many different dishes where everybody would find something to their taste (for example, sausages, rice and bread, sweet potatoes, even frog-legs), with enough food so that no one would need to remain hungry. The choice of the metaphor of eating together is particularly significant here in that it directly taps into a fundamental concept of Malagasy culture. This is the practice whereby all the people in a Malagasy village community, known as a *Fokonolona*, join in a shared meal, cooked together in large communal cooking pots, to which everyone contributes their share of rice or *Zebu* meat (Malagasy beef). The practice forms a central aspect of the Malagasy concept of *Fihavanana'*, or communal help and solidarity. In the social organisation of rural life, *Fihavanana* underpins all major social, legal, agricultural as well as family rituals and practices. Thus, the audience in *St Martin* had no problem in relating the metaphor of the meal and to its comprehensive appeal for unity and communality. Nor did they have any trouble in decoding the witty implications of the artist's allusion to the gradual closing down of the concert: 'Now we come to the dessert'. To this the audience responded in turn: 'No. No we don't yet want the dessert' and the artist countered: 'There are always people who want to eat dessert, others who want to take more main dishes, and others who still want to go back to starters. We'll need to find a compromise.' Mahaleo and their audiences, in drawing on and articulating through the music an extensive mutual knowledge, conviviality and communality, thus co-construct and confirm a mutual public sphere. From this context, further socio-political engagement and fund-raising schemes for developmental projects of individual group members emerged as easily as does the next promoter for another concert tour by the artists. Sharing in a musical performance and continuing with an engagement in local solutions for social and economic projects in Madagascar is part and parcel of the same public sphere which Mahaleo have successfully occupied during three decades, and across several generations of followers. From interviews I conducted with the artists and members of their audiences, which cannot be reproduced here, it became obvious that this is a shared agenda, intended and articulated by the artists themselves and by their public.

## Dama and the world music audience

By contrast, the situation at the Brighton Festival during the lunchtime concert by Dama and the drummer Charle could not have been more different. The lunch-time slots on Tuesdays and Thursdays were part of the Festival's innovations in 2002, intended to include more world music performances in its programme than had been the case in earlier years, when the music performed at the Festival had been largely dominated by classical music (concerts, operas, song recitals) and dance. Dama's concert had been advertised in the festival brochure through small flyers, and in a two-page article in *The Insight*, a Brighton newspaper. In the latter piece by Robin Pridy, Dama had been described as the 'Malagasy rebel' with a full account of his political and artistic career. However, only six out of the 60 people who returned their questionnaire to us had seen this article. As our questionnaire revealed, the predominantly local, white, British-born festival audience had been attracted by the festival brochure (67%) or had heard about it from friends (22%). The main reasons they gave for attendance (an open question) included: curiosity, experiment, novelty (32%), suitability of the time, which fitted in nicely with lunch-break (22%), love of world music in general (13%). Four respondents listed their personal connection with the country and their interest in Madagascar as their main reasons for attending. Ten respondents had heard of Dama and Mahaleo; 18 had listened to Malagasy music before. Amongst musical preferences, the majority listed classical music, jazz and world music, with *BBC Radio 3, 4,* and *2* as their main radio stations.[12] In short, the audience of the concert were a typical cross-section of the world music listeners targeted by *Radio 3*, with relatively demanding musical tastes and a limited knowledge of Malagasy music, but without any more detailed information or knowledge about Madagascar as a country or the musician's background in particular.

## Audience response

The rating of the concert revealed a triumph for the artists with a 100% success rate (80% ticked excellent, 20% very good). In the free comment section (which asked, 'what if anything did you particularly like/did not like about the event.') audiences listed the pleasure the music gave them, but many also stressed non-musical factors like, the inspiration, the warmth and the engagement of the musician; the involvement of audience and artists; the new understanding they had gleaned from the concert. Many stressed their willingness to be contacted again by the researchers and left email addresses or telephone numbers. A third of the audience stayed behind after the concert to talk to the artists, who reappeared in the auditorium shortly after the concert finished. Eight members of the audience specifically asked for more information and further connections, and were subsequently invited to a private concert with the express purpose of fund-raising for a developmental project in Madagascar at a private home. About 60 invited guests, including 40 Malagasies resident in the UK, attended this. I have listed these crude quantitative figures with some caution, and only as to complement and confirm my participant observations and analysis of the audience-artist interaction. On that basis I want to argue that, during the performance of about 70 minutes by Dama and Charle, a largely indeterminate festival-going lunch-time audience with no particular stake in anything to do with Malagasy social, political or cultural life was being initiated into the first steps towards becoming a public - eager to learn, to know more, deeply appreciative of the artist's own engagement, and in some cases willing to become financially involved. How could such an initiation be achieved in such a short space? In the last section of this chapter, I would like to analyse the different steps taken by the musician, which in my interpretation enabled this initiation.

## Strategies of involvement[13]

*Step 1: creating the first bond with the audience - greetings and friendship across cultural difference.*

Dama opened the concert with a greeting in Malagasy, which he explained and then used to make the audience respond (see in particular the passages marked in bold letters). He provided some cultural background, explained the different linguistic background (Malagasy and French), the largely unknown culture (where one knows about lemurs rather than the people) and the musicians' own reasons for coming to Brighton (wanting to learn, wanting to share their music, wanting to be representative for the people of Madagascar, wanting to bring friendship).

*Dama:* Manaona. In Malagasy language, Manaona means how are you.

Manaona? How are you?

*Audience reacts* (Good, fine/great etc)

*Dama:* Our mother language is Malagasy and in school, we learn the French language. However, to practice English we're here in England. And it's a very good pleasure for me and Charle to share you now music from Madagascar. Madagascar is well known by its lemurs but not really the people. That's why we are here. We are member of - two members of the people of Madagascar. And we begin with a song, the song of the orange. Orange is for me for us like a friendship a friendship and now we've brought to you an orange, and me and Charle we decide we say: mmh, how to give them that one orange. And ah - it's only one and there are many many people here, how to share it, and we say ok. we will sing to you a song, and the song is the song of the orange. And friendship is like this orange. The skin of the orange is not not really the true friendship, but the heart of the orange is really the friendship. And we give to you an orange without skin. Yes, the heart of the orange and the friendship from Madagascar.

Dama's explanation of the image of the unpeeled orange, *Voasary*, which was offered as a sign of friendship, uses 'author's license' since the lyrics of the song as written and performed by him are, in fact, a more sexy and tongue-in-cheek account of a young woman who is offered that orange by her lover after she knocked on his door three times. In the song, she is offered the peeled orange, whereas all the others before her had only been given the bitter peel. Malagasy audiences know this of course, but here the festival audience is being offered another image, which fits in better with the opening of a concert and metaphorically turns the gift of the concert into a gift of friendship to the audience. The listeners here are addressed as potential friends rather than distant audiences who sit back and enjoy.

*Step 2: Helping one another by sharing knowledge: turning the audience into helpers.*

We have two guitars, because this one is another tune, tune- tune, it's ok? - yes, and it is tuned like this little guitar, this is a *kabosy* - and it's a traditional instrument in Madagascar and we try to mix the traditional tuning with the guitar. And now that's why we have two guitar and normally we have another three guitar - the normal tuning ! and this is like *kabosy*, and this is another tuning - open tuning. And now we bring you in the countryside of Madagascar. And there are two powers in M - the traditional power in the rural country, and the administration power in the town. And 80% of the people are rural people in M. And we - our main activity is agriculture - artisanat - handicraft, and fish fish yes? Fishing, fishing ok thank you. And there our traditional - how to say it religion is we - our intermediaries - how to say it, yes, our ancestors - is our, and there are there is a life of ancestors - the old man and the old woman and after when they are dead they are - they begin the ancestor near the creator - yes - we say we don't say god we say creator - and this song is a song who which shows this two kind of power in Madagascar.

Dama, in this second extract that preceded the second song of the concert, *'Madirovalo'*, used a double strategy. On the one hand, he informed the audience about vital aspects of Malagasy culture, for instance, its predominantly rural culture, the significance of the ancestors for religious beliefs and wider cultural practices, including the use of a traditional instrument - the *Kabosy* (Malagasy lute) - and the open tuning of its strings. On the other hand, in a balancing of his role as the one who knows, informs and teaches the audience, he requested that they in turn support him in his struggle with finding the correct expressions in English, a request to which the audience complied with excited pleasure, calling out different English words from all sides of the auditorium. Dama thus employed his lack of fluency and grammatical accuracy in English to create mutuality between himself and his listeners.

The same double strategy of informer/help-seeker continued in the third break between songs:

> The most famous instrument in Madagascar, the *kabosy*. We haven't technology, television, or library and something like this to - *comment dit*? - *transmettre* - our *comment dit* - transmit our - *comment dit* - heritage - heritage, yes, cultural heritage, but we have old men and also the descendant, the descendant to the young people to *transmettre* - yes, to transmit - to make a transfer, yes.

> And the song is a song. In the village, musicians are playing roots music, violins, flutes, *valiha*, and in the middle of the village there is a very pretty young woman who is dancing. After in the middle of the song there is a very old woman who is coming with her *lamba*- what is this- *lamba*-

> Audience calls out suggestions

> eh yes shawl, and at the end of the song the old woman take the hand of the girl's hand, like this, and the sun is dying - is setting , thank you - now I make an exercise with my English - good, it's very good. The sun is setting - *comment dit* - the light of the sun traverse - yes?

*Audience calls out suggestions*

*Traverser* and it's the symbol of the traditional and the modern life in Madagascar. This is this song.


*Step 3: Sitting in the same boat, sharing the same problems. The audience and the artists - a community of concerned citizens.*

In the first three interludes, the audience ('You') was positioned on the other side of a cultural and linguistic space from the musicians ('We') and were appealed to as a group that is willing to be informed and to inform. In the next two lead-ins to song four (*'Kobaka'*, meaning 'Lies') and five (*'Tsy Mirahara'*, meaning, 'I don't care'), Dama appealed to the audience as members of the same political culture. In shared spaces like these politicians have to listen to the people and the public must vote and participate in public life. The responsibility of the politicians and the responsibility of the citizen are part-and-parcel of the same political agenda. Thus, Dama the politician and Dama the citizen stood on both sides of his song at the same time, with a simultaneous appeal to himself and to the people to whom he belongs. Both text interludes led to spontaneous applause from the audience before the songs.


*Dama:* Now a song for the politicians. Often the politicians are in their tower. And their towers are near the clouds. That's why they are far far from the people. And this song I write it and I write it for me, because even I am a member of Parliament without a party, I am an independent, yes? Sometimes we work more in the Parliament than in the countryside and that's why it's good for me to listen to this song to not to forget that I am not a member of Parliament without people

*Performs the song 'Kobaka'*

*Dama:*

When the politicians are too far from their people the people don't go to vote there are many many abstentions and everybody says *'tsy mirahara'* it don't matter. And this song is a song to - *comment dit interpeller?*

Audience calls out

Because when you don't go to vote its good for the politicians because even there are few people to vote the politician the politicians are always in their chairs and we must go to vote even we don't like the political games, yes? We must go to vote

After the opening guitar play of the song *'Tsy Mirahara'*, Dama engages the audience further by now teaching them to sing the repeat phrase *Tsy Mirahara* with him thus consolidating even more the audience's active engagement

*Step 4: Sharing the same pleasures: Teaching the audience how to sing in Malagasy.*

Perhaps its time to learn Malagasy language. You say *'tsy mirahara'*.

Audience responds

Again

*Audience responds*

Again

*Audience responds*

Again

*Audience responds*

Again

*Audience responds*

Good

Thank you.

Audience: Now what does it mean?

*Audience calls out various versions*: I don't care, I don't give a damn. It doesn't matter

Ah thank you. I don't care.

Plays opening tunes of song

Now you understand you can sing after me, right but not *tsy mirahara* but you open your voice and you open your heart and you open your eyes you open your ears and you open your body ok

With me after me.

*Audience performs the whole song with Dama*

The best choir in England you


*Step 5: Generalising the Malagasy political crisis (in the year 2002) to a problem that can be shared.*

Dama then moved on to the difficult political and social problems of Madagascar, not by referring to the concrete names of the politicians and the unresolved political crisis between the two presidential contenders, but by generalising the uncertainty of a people caught in a political dilemma. The song - ambiguously entitled 'Malagasy Blues' and especially written by Dama during the crisis of 2002 - is thus both specific for the crisis in Madagascar and has a more general appeal for people with an uncertain future. Similarly, the following song, (about the difficulty of a young man who leaves his village only to go under in the crowded capital city with no chance of ever returning), was introduced as a more generalisable social problem - that of the overcrowding of modern cities, and the difficulties faced by the poor, marginalised newcomer. The image of the insect attracted to the light that then burns its wings and dies, creates a further imagistic bond to the personal experiences of members of the audience.

*Dama:* Malagasy Blues. Now in Madagascar we are we have a very very terrible political problem in Madagascar now and the people wonder where they go their future is not clear now and we because first of all I am an artist and after a politician and we try to by our songs we try to give ways how to *comment dit*, to *sortir*?- to go out - the song is like this blues from Madagascar.


*Performs Malagasy Blues*


Many many people from the rural country go to the town and they are like the - *comment dit insectes* - the insects when the light is in front of them they go to the light and when they are in front of the light they touch the light and they are dead. Like this. The people from the rural country go to the light of the town - the capital of Madagascar is Antananarivo and like capitals all over the world many, many social problems and the song is the song of a rural human race. I don't say a man or a woman but the story of a rural people when they are in town they can't go back to their village because they are they have no money and the life is very difficult to leave yes

*Performs Fiainan' Antananarivo*

*Step 6: Subverting the divisiveness between North and South, rich and poor nations.*

In the next song, the concept of globalisation is evoked but only to undercut its economic and often divisive meaning between richer and the poorer countries. With the alternative 'globalisation of friendship', Dama appeals to shared understanding and the universality of emotions.

*Dama:* We think that now we live a globalisation yes economic globalisation and me and Charle we say why we try to promote another way another vision of the world and ok now economic is economic globalisation why not to promote friendship globalisation and this is this is a song of this friend ship of globalisation and of course we don't speak, we speak English and you don't speak Malagasy language and when we sing we sing in Malagasy language, there are many, many words that you don't understand but I am sure we are sure that you feel something isn't it and we think that even the words that we use you don't understand - our heart you understand what our heart feel and we understand also what your heart feel also, and hearts don't need interpreters that's why we think it's a very good idea a very good vision to put now - to to bid the friendshif the friendship - this is a song for this very very long term activity.

*Step 7: Celebrating togetherness and communality.*

Lastly, the appeal to friendship in the preceding songs was used as a signal for introducing himself and his percussionist Charle in their double role as sociologists and musicians, as well as to refer to the band Mahaleo itself and their 30th anniversary. For the final song, the guitar needed to be re-tuned for an open tuning similar to that, as explained earlier, for the *kabos,y* which Dama demonstrated on stage for the audience to hear and see. This set the stage for the final song, which is the most participatory of all, in that the audiences learned all the words for '*Roazy*' ('the rose' or 'mother nature'), that is, parts of her body, from the hair to the breast to the feet. By this stage, the somewhat restrained middle-aged lunchtime audience of the beginning sang in full voice and with great gusto.

*Dama:* Charle. He's a sociologist, a sociologist and he is my best friend over the world. Because our band is Mahaleo and this is an old band because this year we'll we'll celebrate our 30th anniversary. And he's my old friend with the band, in the Mahaleo band. And my name is Dama and I am an artist - *auteur compositeur*- author composer I write but I don't know how to read notes just by ears

And now the last song - ah ok (laughs) the last of the last.

Now I change (changes the guitar's tuning)

The story of the nature. Madagascar is like a paradise paradise island and nature is like a mother mother very big mother very very generous generous, yes it's ok? And they give so much to us human race but we don't give like she gives to us and that's why we we give to mother nature this song. And it's not a very difficult song because some words the key words that you need when you go to Madagascar we know them by this song. For example the name of mother nature is Roazy, and her hairs in Malagasy language means *Ny volony Ny volony (audience repeats)* and her eyes *Ny masony (audience repeats)* her ears *Ny sofony (audience repeats)* and this Roazy can give babies to the woman who can't have babies and she gives also milk to the babies when the babies are hungry. And this is the story of Roazy and we try to learn Malagasy language because it's the best way to learn language. Hands her hands *ny tanany (audience repeats)* and her what's the name of this breast *ny nonony (audience repeats)*, good and her tummy stomach, stomach yes? *ny kibony (audience repeats)* her feet *ny tongony (audience repeats)*, now

*Audience performs Roazy with Dama*

*Artists leave stage and reappear after loud shouts and clapping of hands for one encore*

It's a song that we sing the melody together it's very easy a soft song and in the song we say that sometimes we our life is like the waves of the sea sometimes down sometimes high sometimes down and sometimes, also, we feel so alone even there are many many people around us. And in this moment we really need a good friend not to to help you to like this to have your head more but not like this *(lets his head droop)* because if you do like this the weight of the problems can win but if you try to like this *(lifts his head)* you can win. Yes. This is the song. The melody is like this

*Herezo - opening phrase with 'lalala'*

With me

*Audience sings 'lalala'*

Very good, Very good, good, we feel good me and Charle because when you are used we are used that you listen to us but now it's a very, another situation that now we listen to you very good very good

*Performs song with audience - finish.*

## Conclusion

Earlier in this chapter I argued that commercial and media indifference to the often very rich linguistic, social, cultural and political context of a great deal of music, bracketed together under the label 'world music', deprives its western audiences of a significant layer of meaning that is readily accessible to listeners who share the same cultural background with their musicians. Yet audiences in both 'home' and 'world' music contexts can be encouraged to engage in a deeper involvement than that which is commercially available through the music industry, as long as the artists take seriously their role as cultural mediators. This is not to say that all African, or any other, musicians need to be engaged in this way. Music has every right to exist in different spheres of pleasure and entertainment without needing to play its part in the public sphere. I am simply drawing attention to cases where artists write lyrics and music, which they themselves perceive as socially and culturally significant in their original contexts. Here it is feasible to make this understanding available to the kinds of audiences for whom the genre appears to have particular appeal. This propensity in a 'world music' audience to engage in this way was one of the interesting results of a case study of contrastive settings for the same (Malagasy) performer and his music.

Lastly, it is necessary to highlight two key findings to emerge from this study. First, Malagasy audiences who already have a shared knowledge with a socially committed artist and the context of his music readily engage in a shared public sphere. Pleasure of listening and performing together (conviviality), sharing of purpose (communality), and the possibility of future action (social involvement beyond the confines of the concert) was part-and-parcel of the same interaction. Audience and artists from a shared social and cultural background engaged in identity performances that co-constructed and consolidated their public commitment and purposefulness as Malagasy citizens, however far away they live from their country of origin.

Second, world music audiences are usually ignorant of some of the most significant layers of meaning of the songs and artists they listen to. Yet, as was shown in the Brighton case study, such audiences readily take up the chance of further involvement and understanding as and when a committed and credible artist is offering it. There is the potential for such audiences to become initiated into the first set of conditions for entering a new public sphere through arousal by and pleasure in a music which still takes its public role seriously. Having, in many instances, grown up with and in the aftermath of socially committed music in the late 1960s and 1970s, which did put emphasis on musical as well as on textual meaning (Bob Dylan is just one of the most obvious examples), such audiences can be purposefully informed and engaged. If the results of the Brighton Festival study and other observations conducted in similar 'world music' settings with the same artist can be generalised, then it can be assumed that other artists in live concerts could also safely depart from their commercially constructed roles as purely ethnic, exotic performers, without risk of deterring any of their audiences. Such mutual understanding between audiences and artists might even eventually rebound on the world music industry's reluctance also to embrace the artists - where this is appropriate -in their roles as social commentators and actors in the public sphere.

## Notes

1. Text here is a semiotic construct referring to any cultural product, including that of music, so that 'authors' may be composers or writers; and 'readers' may be listeners or members of audiences.

2. That is, the entire contextualised nature of all meaning-making at the point of producing and responding to texts.

3. 'West' and 'western' is used here as a cultural rather than a geographic term denoting the post-industrial nations, especially Europe and the US, as against the developing world, here especially the African continent.

4. The term 'diasporic' is used here in its most neutral and widest sense, that is, to refer to groups of people living outside a country that they still consider to be their homeland and with which they maintain social connections. It does not pre-suppose lack of integration into their new homecountry. Nor does it automatically presuppose a sense of displacement or an emotional predisposition of nostalgia, longing or desire to return 'home', though these may well feature in the lives of particular individuals.

5. The EU project, Changing City Spaces: New Challenges to Cultural Policy in Europe, for which the present research acted in part as a pilot, researches these radio stations in seven capital cities in Europe: Berlin, London, Paris, Vienna, Rome, Ljubljana and Belgrade as part of a larger research project into cultural policy directed at cultural diversity in global cities. http://www.citynexus.com

6. Paul Simon, Peter Gabriel, or even further back George Harrison from the Beatles, are often quoted as its instigators; see for example BBC4's programme World Music.

7. Kershaw himself is somewhat self-conscious as well as tongue-in-cheek ironic about this transfer, referring frequently to his move as an entry into strange new territory, and pledging the same eclectic mix of music to the audiences that followed him across. In his first broadcast on Radio 3 on the 20th April 2001 he made continuous references to this new environment, and even two years later, he often refers to his musical selection as untypical and subversive of radio 3's mainstream offerings (Meinhof in preparation). Having recently been awarded an honorary doctorate from a British university, 'Dr Kershaw' has now added academic accolade to his extensive knowledge of the genre.

8. At an unusually small venue for the famous Senegalese singer Baaba Maal in Portsmouth in 2002, for example, groups of Senegalese students from Brighton pronounced to the researcher that this was 'their' man - since they were all from Senegal. A more mixed group of Africans claimed him

as African, while the predominantly white audiences appreciated him as 'theirs' in the word of shared musical taste.

9.  2001: Dama and percussionist Charle Grahamstown Festival of Arts, South Africe (July); Dama and other Malagasy musicians , Tana Orly, Paris (September);

    2002: Dama and percussionist Charle: Brighton Festival of Arts (May); Private concert, Seaford; (May) Mahaleo: Paris, Nanterre Espace Chevreuill (May); Mahaleo: Paris, St Martin (June); Dama solo, Holzhausen, Germany; (September) .

    2003: Dama and other Malagasy artists: New Morning (Feb); Dama solo: Centre for Black and Performing African Arts, Lagos Nigeria (April); Mahaleo: Espace Chevreuill, Paris (June), Mahaleo (without Dama) private concert, Paris (June); Dama solo, Rome (July).

10. The crisis was sparked by the presidential election in December 2001 that saw long-standing autocratic ruler Didier Ratsiraka lose to the former mayor of Antananarivo, Mark Ravalomanana. However, according to official counts, Ravalomanana received less than the required 50% of the total vote that would make a second round of voting necessary. This official count was disputed because of massive irregularities in the counting procedures, with supporters of Ravalomanana claiming above 50% of the vote and hence rejecting the need for a second round. To end the ensuing stalemate, Ravalomanana seized power in January 2002, with the support of millions and backed by a general strike that lasted for several months. Ratsiraka left for his home territory on the coast in Tamatave, supported by elite troupes of his Army while the remainder of the Army remained first neutral but later shifted allegiance to Ravalomanana, so inflaming some of the old divisions between the coastal people and the highlanders. Ratsiraka and his supporters systematically set out to isolate the highland regions with the capital city from the harbour towns, cutting supply lines from the coast, blowing up bridges and roads, and effectively sabotaging the infrastructure of Madagascar to such an extent that the centre ran out of petrol, food and medicines during several bitter months of dispute. However, Ravalomanana's support, which included a broad alliance of independent politicians and full support of all the churches, continued to hold up, A further election in May 2002 saw Ravalomanana's success confirmed above the 50% mark and, his recognition, first by the United States, then the European Union and crucially France. Ratsiraka fled the country into exile overseas and subsequent parliamentary elections in December 2002 gave Ravalomanana's newly founded party, *Tiako Madagascar* (I love Madagascar), a landslide victory. But it was at the expense of those independent candidates who had backed him during the crisis, but refused to join the new party. At present Ravalomanana's power is virtually unopposed.

11. All performances were observed, recorded on tape (by microphone from the hall as well as from the mixing deck so as to include audience reactions) and - where relevant - transcribed and translated into English. Apart from participant observation at the concerts and interviews with the artists, a questionnaire was added at the Brighton Festival Concert, to gauge a demographic profile and some quantitative audience reactions to the concert. We have since conducted a questionnaire survey at a Malagasy-organised concert at the New Morning venue in Paris in

February 2003, which confirmed informal observations of audience composition and response in the Malagasy-dominated settings.

12. Other demographic factors of interest: Age distribution biased towards middle age: 36-45 (33%) and 45-55 (22%), followed by the 17-25 (15%) and 26-35 year olds (12%). Annual income levels were moderate to average (possibly reflecting the 2:1 female preponderance and the below 25 age group student population), predominantly 10-20K (35%), and 21-35K (20), with some below 10K (18%) and a few above 36-50K (13%) and 51-70K (7%) respectively. Amongst the non-British audiences of altogether 15 respondents, almost everyone was born in another country in the world (for example, Singapore, Brazil, Hongkong, Capetown, Zimbabwe and two from Madagascar) Thanks goes to Leander Gloversmith for his help with administering and evaluating the questionnaires.

13. All the words spoken by Dama are transcribed verbatim, though pauses and fillers were not indicated. Audience reactions were indicated where it deemed relevant. The very frequent non-verbal responses by the audience, especially the requent laughter and signs of appreciation such as 'mmh' were not transcribed.

## References

Anderson, I. (1999) 'Madagascar" In S. Broughton, M. Ellingham and R. Trillo (eds.) *World Music*. Volume 1: Africa, Europe and the Middle East. The Rough Guides, 523-532.

Ang, I. (1986) *Watching Dallas*. New York: Methuen.

Barrett, J. (1996) 'World Music, Nation and Postcolonianism'. *Cultural Studies* 10 (2): 237-247.

Bender, W. (1985) *Sweet Mother: Afrikanische Musik*. München: Trickster.

Bender, W. (ed.) (1989). "Perspectives on African Music". *Bayreuth African Studies* Series (9). University of Bayreuth.

Bennett, T., C. Mercer, & Woollaccott (1986) *Popular Culture and Social Relations*. Philadelphia: Open University Press.

Berger H.M, & M.T, Carroll. (eds.) (2000) "Global Popular Music: The Politics and Aesthetics of Language Choice". Special issue of *Popular Music and Society* 24 (3).

Buckingham, D. (1987) *Public Secrets. Eastenders and its Audience*. London: BFI.

Clayton, M. ed. (2001) 'Music and Meaning" Special issue of *British Journal of Ethnomusicology* 10 (1).

Connell, J., C. Gibson (2003). *Sound Tracks*. Popular Music, Identity and Place. London: Routledge.

Fairclough, N. (1995) *Media Discourse*. London: Arnold.

Fiske, J. (1987) *Television Culture*. London: Methuen.

Gillespie, M. (2002) 'Dynamics of Diaspora: South Asian media and transnational cultural politics. In G. Stald & T. Tufte (eds) *Global Encounters. Media and Cultural Transformation*. Luton: University of Luton Press 189-196.

Gripsrud, J. (1995) *The Dynasty Years: Hollywood Television and Critical Media Studies*. London: Routledge.

Graddol, D. & Boyd-Barrett, O. (eds.) (1994) *Media Texts: Authors and Readers*. Clevedon: Multilingual Matters.

Halliday, M.A.K. (1978) *Language as a Social Semiotic*. London: Arnold.

Habermas, J. (1989[1962]). *Structural Transformation of the Public Sphere*. Cambridge: Polity Press.

Irele, A. ed.( 2001) "The Landscape of African Music." Special issue of *Research in African Literature* 32 (2).

McCabe, C. (1986) *High Culture, Low Culture. Analysing popular television and film*. Manchester University Press.

Meinhof, U.H. & Smith, J. (eds.) (2000) *Intertextuality and the Media: from Genre to Everyday Life*. Manchester University Press.

Modleski, T. (ed.) (1986) *Studies in Entertainment: Critical Approaches to Mass Culture*. Bloomington: Indiana University Press.

Radway, J. (1984) *Reading the Romance*. Chapel Hill and London: University of Carolina Press.

Rasolofondraosolo, Z, & Meinhof, U.H. (1993) 'Popular Malagasy music and the construction of cultural identities'. In S. Makoni & U.H. Meinhof (eds.) *Africa and Applied Linguistics*. AILA Review 16. Amsterdam & Philadelphia: John Benjamins Publishing Company: 127-148.

Roberta Pearson and Máire Messenger Davies

# Chapter 6: Class acts? Public and private values and the cultural habits of theatre-goers[1]

## Public and private values and the cultural habits of theatre-goers

In October 2003, Peter Hall, founder of the Royal Shakespeare Company and former director of the National Theatre, appeared on the BBC's *Breakfast with Frost,* discussing his current West End hit, a revival of Harold Pinter's *Betrayal,* and his career more generally. David Frost gently chided the director about his constant call for increased government subsidies to the theatre. Hall replied that while subsidies had originally been intended to reduce ticket prices and make theatre accessible to all, that had ceased to be the case. But, said Hall, the recently appointed new director of the National Theatre, Nicholas Hytner, had returned to the original intention of the subsidy by persuading commercial sponsors to underwrite the £10 per seat season during the past summer. Funding from private enterprise had replaced funding from the public purse. Does this imply that the theatregoers who availed themselves of cheaper theatre tickets by virtue of government subsidy constituted a public, while those who did so by virtue of commercial sponsorship were merely an audience? Or, are theatre-goers always a public because they gather in a public space? Jurgen Habermas believes that individuals at theatre performances, together with those attending rock concerts, party assemblies or church congresses, constitute *'occasional* or arranged' publics around 'particular presentations and events' (Habermas, 1996, p. 374). But Habermas' examples seem of a fundamentally different order. The 'publicness' of a party assembly, and even of a church congress, seems fairly straightforward, in that individuals have come together to debate issues most likely in a public space. But do individuals gathered in a public space such as a theatre or concert hall automatically become a public, even if merely seeking an evening's entertainment? This volume's essays primarily consider the public/audience rather than the public/private binary, although the latter is implicit in the former. A few of the essays touch on the public/private binary in terms of space while none do so in terms of funding. This essay addresses both senses of the public/private binary, first from a theoretical perspective and then from an empirical perspective, using data from a survey and focus groups conducted in September 2001 at the West Yorkshire Playhouse in Leeds.

In her introductory chapter in this volume, Sonia Livingstone argues that 'the common use of spatial metaphors to distinguish public and private only serves to exacerbate confusion. Space turns out to be ambiguous or shifting depending on its use'. Livingstone makes a persuasive case from an analytical perspective, but social elites have often judged entertainment media's potential for social good or harm precisely in terms of their publicness or privateness. In the nineteenth century the publicness of the theatre, particularly in the United States, a more robustly democratic institution than it is today, caused concern; theatre-goers were a cross-class clientele not bound by the rigid codes of etiquette that govern their twenty-first century counterparts. Audiences cheered, hooted, demanded replays of favourite bits, threw rotten fruit and, occasionally, the furniture. This unruly behaviour led to 'debates about live entertainments' in which audiences figured as 'dangerous crowds', not as publics (Butsch, 2003). Sometimes these potentially dangerous crowds posed a real danger, as in the Astor Place riots in New York City when an intensely patriotic mob rioted in protest against the patrician English actor Charles McCready. But innovations such as the proscenium arch and better stage lighting, of which permitted the lowering of the house lights gradually, tamed the theatre audience; the new medium of the cinema completing the transformation by luring away the working class patrons (Pearson, 2004). The thoroughly bourgeois respectability of the theatre partially accounts for the fact that since the early twentieth century neither policy makers nor academics have accorded its audiences much consideration. The cinema and its audiences have by contrast garnered a great deal of concern from both policy makers and academics. In the first decade of the twentieth century, the cinema, with its mingling of classes, races and genders in a dark, dangerous and unregulated space, became the nightmare vision of social elites, who sought to regulate both film venues and film content (Pearson and Uricchio, 1999). In the nineteenth and early twentieth centuries, 'public' was the bad term in the public/private space binary, with home entertainments seen as the middle-class remedy to the evils of the public sphere; thus Edison had initially conceived of his kinetoscope as a domestic medium, while home movie equipment rapidly became available to those who could afford it. The potential evil of the private became apparent with the new media of radio and television that addressed audiences as isolated individuals in their homes, away from the restraining social influence of public spaces. As Livingstone discusses in her chapter in this volume, the combination of children, bedrooms, computers and the Internet has intensified the discursive construction of the dangers of private space.

As social elites have judged the potential of the entertainment media for social good or harm in terms of their publicness or privateness, so audiences judge their worth, using what John Frow (1997, p. 77) refers to as 'different regimes of value':

> *Operations of distinction are at work in every cultural domain, and ... each involves the application of criteria of value, which are often incompatible with those operating in another domain. Heavy metal and bel canto opera, line-dancing and ballet are valued for different reasons, and their aesthetic dimension serves quite different purposes in each case.*

Although Frow does not say so, the publicness or privateness of a medium offers quite different pleasures. Audiences enjoy the performing arts (ballet, opera, the theatre, rock concerts, etc.) in part because of the liveness of both audiences and performers (see Auslander, 1999, on liveness). The presence of a live audience, a great deal of anecdotal evidence suggests, causes many actors to prefer the theatre to the cinema or television. The actors in a sense 'feed off' the audience, their performances energised and constantly mutating as a result. But the audience also 'feed off' each other, forming a transient community for the evening's entertainment. Kay Mellor, Leeds playwright and board member of the West Yorkshire Playhouse, as well as an accomplished television writer and actor, spoke of theatre audiences which 'laugh, learn to be affronted, intrigued, frightened, moved to tears, together with others' which 'heightens the experience' (Downing, 2001, p. 5). In this sense, perhaps the theatre draws on its roots in religious rituals, such as the Everyman plays performed in the medieval cathedrals and the Mystery plays performed in the medieval towns, in which theatre audiences might truly have been said to be a public learning the public lessons that held the culture together. Sharing the same space as the actors might not have thrilled a medieval audience, but can be a source of pleasure for a modern audience, accustomed to consuming the bulk of its entertainment in mediated form. The presence of the flesh-and-blood performers on stage, essentially in the same space as the viewer, adds to the special event quality of the theatre, the opera or the ballet. This liveness becomes yet more compelling with a performer already known to the audience in mediated form, which is why many of Britain's regional theatres have a 'star casting' policy, hoping to attract audiences with actors familiar from television or the cinema. We will say more about the 'effect' of star casting in persuading private television audiences to become public theatre audiences later.

Consumed in public like the performing arts, the cinema offers only half their liveness: the audience is live but the performers are mediated. Film viewers are at some level aware of shadowy figures in the surrounding darkness all laughing, or crying, or gasping or screaming in response to the same film, the audience, as in the theatre, forming a transient community that may intensify the experience. But the lower light levels, the photographed actors and realist filming conventions all make the public space of a cinema experientially more private than the public space of a theatre. As generations of film theorists have now speculated, watching a film is akin to a voyeuristic act, sitting unthreatened and unrecognised in the darkness watching a narrative unfold especially for you. With some exceptions (pubs, university halls of residence, prisons), television watching occurs primarily in the private space of the home; the medium's strong association with domesticity linked to the everyday (the regular, the repeated, the uneventful) in the work of such scholars as Roger Silverstone (1994) and Paddy Scannell (1996). This combination of domesticity and everydayness leads, some have speculated, to a different relationship between the audience and performer than that which occurs in the public media. Performers in the cinema and the theatre are distant and special, while television performers are, it is suggested, as close and familiar as one's family or friends. Psychologists Donald Horton and Richard Wohl dubbed this a para-social relationship, one that gives the illusion of face-to-face action despite being mediated (Horton and Wohl, 1956). In public spaces theatrical actors thrill viewers with their flesh-and-blood presence and cinematic actors titillate viewers with voyeuristic surveillance, while in private spaces television actors offer viewers a kind of friendship.

The public and private spaces of the performing arts, cinema and the television, offer audiences different pleasures, but in Britain, as in most of Europe, there is a strong tradition of public subsidy for all these media. Here we turn to the second sense of the public/private binary discussed in this chapter, that between public and private funding. In Britain, television receives the biggest public subsidy, since 'the BBC's licence fee is the single most significant single source of funding to the cultural sector' ('New Study', 2001). In the age of digitisation, cable satellite and audience fragmentation, the licence fee is subject to continued interrogation, but the BBC still constitutes the best case scenario for public funding being commensurate with public access: all those who pay to support the BBC can watch or listen to the BBC. This is not necessarily the case with other publicly subsided cultural forms, although constant lobbying from the cultural sector does sometimes result in increased subsidies. The National Campaign for the Arts announced in 2000 that 'the Government spending plans announced in July 2000 produced the largest ever increase in funding to the Arts Council. By 2003/4 the arts will have an extra £150 million a year in an increase of 60% in real terms' (National Campaign for the Arts). The government awarded this increased funding despite some evidence of declining audiences: 'it appears that adult attendances to the arts, built heritage and museums are declining. By 1998/99 ballet attendances were down 14% on what they had been in 1994/95; attendances at plays were down 8%' ('New Study', 2001). One would hope that increased public subsidies would correlate with increased attendance. Richard Eyre, distinguished theatre director, said in his report to the government on the Royal Opera House and the Royal Ballet:

> *Subsidy buys access to the arts, and access is the rationale for subsidy. It is the enduring belief in the civilising benefits that the arts bestow on a nation that has underpinned the development of the fertile cultural landscape we enjoy today, and which has allowed this country to thrive as a cultural force. The arts enrich all our lives, and it should be the birthright of all this country's citizens to be able to fulfil their creative potential as participants and spectators.*

Despite his idealistic rhetoric, Eyre was well aware that access to the arts was the birthright of the few rather than the many.

> *If it's in the nature of the performing arts that they can only be accessible to a few people at any one time, it's a tragedy that these people always seem to come from so limited a social and geographical spectrum.... The power to engender real access can, however, only be achieved in one way: by reducing ticket prices - at the very least for*

*first time audiences - and funding education so that the arts became a genuine 'choice', without carrying the baggage of class. In short, making the arts truly inclusive (Eyre, 1998).*

However, Eyre, like many commentators on culture, equates 'the arts' with viewership, with consumption, not with production or action. Yet participation in performance is accessible to any group of people willing to come together to mime, sing, dance or rehearse and act a scripted play, whether in a private (home) or public (village hall) venue. Amateur performance is rarely discussed as part of the 'performing arts' nexus, yet it is pertinent in any discussion of the boundaries between public and private, particularly with reference to state support for the performing arts (drama and music) in schools.

Cultural theorists accord with Eyre's sentiments, including his equation of performance with professionalism - not surprisingly since Eyre echoes, most probably unwittingly, Pierre Bourdieu's famous conclusions concerning class and cultural consumption. Working in this tradition and using Bourdieu's concept of restricted culture, Tony Bennett argues that 'the publicness of these institutions [libraries, art galleries, museums, concert halls and performing arts complexes] - their reliance on public funding and administration, their openness to everyone - places them, at least in theory, in the realm of unrestricted culture.' In practice, however, 'these institutions belong to the realm of restricted culture in the sense that their consumption - that is, the capacity to access them intellectually and culturally - depends on the acquisition of certain cultural skills, which, since these are selectively distributed via the education system, are socially rare' (Bennett, 1997, p. 91). The social rarity of competences to access publicly funded cultural institutions is not commensurate with the notion of the public good, at least in the utilitarian sense of the greatest good for the greatest number. Nor is it commensurate with the notion of a public composed of taxpayers, all of who support these cultural institutions while relatively few benefit from them in terms of direct participation. But not only taxpayers but also all citizens should benefit from publicly funded institutions, as they do from the National Health Service or state education, in which those paying different rates of tax nonetheless receive the same services. If citizens have an unrestricted right to health and education, should not the same hold true of culture? Might citizens have cultural rights as well as social rights; might they not be cultural citizens as well as social citizens?

Thinking about cultural citizenship first requires a definition of citizenship. Gerard Delanty says that 'in the most general terms, citizenship involves a constitutionally based relationship between the individual and the state' (Delanty, 1997, p. 285). Traditionally, theorists have conceived of this relationship with regard to rights within the democratic political arena, principally the universal suffrage. But within the western democracies during the last century or so the relationship between the individual and the state has expanded to encompass rights beyond the political. By the turn of the twentieth century, states had begun to regulate the relationship between individuals and economic institutions - the length of the workday, the minimum wage. The post-war emergence of the full-fledged welfare state expanded individual rights to include healthcare and shelter.[2] There is now some agreement that citizenship rights should embrace the cultural; that, as Eyre argues, all citizens should benefit from what David Chaney terms 'the appropriate cultural heritage' (Chaney, 2002, p. 168) and should be empowered by, as Bryan Turner puts it, 'the capacity to participate effectively, creatively and successfully within a national culture' (Turner, 2001, p. 12). But citizens' capacity for effective participation may depend on the capacity of the state to hand on and transfer to future generations the richness of a national cultural heritage' or 'a pattern of civilisational inheritance' which would involve 'museums and heritage strategies' (Turner, 2001, p. 12). Public policy is central to this conception of cultural citizenship. As David Chaney says: 'One way of understanding cultural citizenship, then, is as a complex of policy issues around both the provision of cultural facilities and the regulation of cultural industries' (Chaney, 2002, p. 168).

Presumably policy should ensure that all citizens have access to 'appropriate cultural heritage', 'national culture' or 'national cultural heritage'. Yet as Eyre, Bourdieu and Bennett assert, invisible barriers prevent access - at least to professional performances and exhibitions - to certain classes of people. John Frow speaks of the 'false openness of the apparently unrestricted public institutions of higher culture', which requires that, to 'enter them you have only to be interested in doing so, and this interest, along with the competences that tend to accompany it, just happens to be structured almost exactly according to the stratifications of social class' (Frow, 1997, p. 78). By virtue of ensuring the financial well being of institutions such as museums and theatres, either through direct funding or the encouragement of private funding, should not the state ensure the potential patronage of all citizens, rather than a culturally privileged subset? Or can the public funding of the arts be justified by conceiving of cultural citizenship as a passively enjoyed set of rights, honoured in the breach rather than in the observance, as is political citizenship? The democratic state bestows on all adult nationals certain political rights, which can for the most part be enjoyed passively; with certain exceptions, such as Australia, citizens can chose whether or not to vote. In many western democracies, increasingly larger numbers of people chose passivity over involvement yet still retain the right to be called citizens. The state through its cultural policies bestows on all citizens the right to participate in those traditional bastions of elite culture previously assumed the repository of a national or common heritage. If the barriers of social class cause people not to exercise their cultural rights, can the state nonetheless still justify supporting restricted culture for the few? Cultural citizenship, unlike political citizenship, requires participation; people must make decisions to consume certain cultural forms and must act upon those decisions. Political citizens can be part of a passive public; cultural citizens must be part of participatory audiences. Political citizenship can be formal but cultural citizenship must be substantive. If cultural citizenship consists partially of an individual's indirect relationship with the state through the patronage of publicly supported cultural institutions, then the state has the responsibility to ensure that participation is realised rather than merely potential. If access is differentially distributed by education or other demographic factors, the state is unequally distributing benefits for which all taxpayers have paid.

If cultural citizenship must be active, the existence of social barriers militating against participation then becomes as urgent a matter of public policy as does the large number of citizens opting out of exercising their political rights in the western democracies. Cultural relativists such as John Fiske or John Hartley might argue that commercial culture better meets the needs of the majority of the population than do the restricted cultural forms, which have been traditionally supported by the state. (The discourse of 'need' in these writers is an interesting shift away from the discourse of 'taste' and a return, in disguise, to the Arnoldian idea that culture has to be good for you, or at least make you feel better about yourself.) Bennett and Frow, together with their co-author Michael Emmison, respond to this challenge, asking whether we should be concerned that people chose not to visit art galleries or attend the theatre.

> *If the hierarchy of cultural values that places a special premium on the officially sanctioned culture of art galleries and museums no longer enjoys universal or even widespread acceptance; if those who do not participate in this realm do not experience this as a deprivation - why should these matters be of any general, let alone policy, concern?*

It is of concern, they say, because the ability to appreciate such restricted culture is strongly correlated with publicly funded education and with 'long-term and enduring distinctions of class'. Therefore, the state should invest in education that offsets 'the effects of different social backgrounds' in order to enhance the 'cultural life-chances of its citizens' (Bennett et al., 1999, p. 246). The absence of universal acceptance of the hierarchy of cultural values is reflected in debates about public funding, such as happened with the Royal Opera House. Perceived as elitist and inaccessible, the institution was awarded an increased subsidy only when its directors promised to build a wider audience, lower ticket prices and enhance the educational programme ('Extra Cash', 1998). Such debates result from what Nick Stevenson terms 'the attack on traditional divisions between high and low culture' which pose serious questions in terms of the common or national cultures that might be transmitted by public institutions. The diversification and fragmentation of public tastes and lifestyles have undermined a previously assumed 'cultural' consensus (Stevenson, 2001, p. 3). The cultural citizenship that we have discussed above might better be termed a common culturalist citizenship, now complicated by the collapsing of cultural hierarchies as well as by the recognition of multiculturalism. An appeal to a common culturalist notion of cultural citizenship as a justification for public funding will become more difficult for the erstwhile imperial powers of western Europe as the descendants of former colonial subjects form an increasing percentage of the population and demand recognition of their own heritage and lifestyles. Greater recognition of regional heritage in some western European nations such as Britain or Spain casts further doubt upon the notion of a unified national culture or heritage.

Consider, for example, the policy of 'saving art for the nation', that is, using public funds to ensure that certain artworks, seen as central to the Western tradition, remain in Britain rather than being sold to foreign buyers. Historian Tristram Hunt writing in *The Guardian* argued that it no longer makes sense to 'safeguard art "for the nation" in an age increasingly devoid of cultural homogeneity' Hunt said that a hundred years ago, when 'the fund to counter the export of art to America and sustain its civilising role in public galleries' was established, 'what ... constituted an idea of Britain was relatively simple... Across classes, regions and religions the British retained a cohesive idea of their nation as a beacon of civilisation'. By contrast:

> the past 30 years have seen a fragmentation of national and cultural cohesion. The old certainties of class, region and race, even of nationality, have become more complicated, with residents of the British Isles now possessing multiple, sometimes competing, identities. Growing numbers regard themselves as Welsh or Scottish rather than British; Londoner or Geordie rather than English; or Afro-Caribbean, south Asian or, even, European. (Hunt, 2003)

Hunt is here espousing what we would term a multi-culturalist citizenship, as opposed to the common-culturalist citizenship we have been discussing above. The majority of theorists using the term 'cultural citizenship' intend it in this sense, defining culture in its anthropological sense as a whole way of life and conceiving of cultural citizenship in terms of group identity; indeed, for some, the term becomes practically synonymous with identity politics (see, among others, Miller, 1998, and McGuigan, 1996.) In the multi-cultural theorisation of cultural citizenship, various groups within a particular society (people of colour, gays/lesbians, non-dominant language speakers) demand rights that recognise, legitimate and perpetuate their cultural distinctiveness. The state's encouragement of a multi-culturalist rather than a common-culturalist citizenship would clearly have implications for public funding policy. For example, some respondents to an audience survey included in a study of British multi-cultural broadcasting felt 'that the BBC has a greater duty than other channels and stations to cater for minorities, as minority communities pay their licence fee and should be able to benefit from the channels paid for from the fee' (Hargrave, 2002, p. 16). One of the purest media forms of multi-culturalist citizenship is the aptly named 'Radio Multi-kulti', which caters for the needs of many of Berlin's numerous immigrant and foreign-language speaking populations (www.multikulti.de).

This general and theoretical discussion of the spatial and funding public/private binaries can only be made operational in terms of particular empirical audiences.

How do particular audiences conceive of the different pleasures offered by media consumed in public and private spaces? Which audiences consume which specific kinds of public and commercial cultural forms? As we mentioned at the outset, our empirical data were gathered at the West Yorkshire Playhouse, a regional playhouse that originates its own productions. The funding mix of the Playhouse exemplifies the blurring of the private/public funding binary and attests to the tensions between common-culturalist and multi-culturalist citizenship that we have discussed above. The Playhouse raises more than 50% of its own funding from 'business in the form of sponsorship and from public bodies and charitable trusts in the form of fund-raising'. The rest of its income derives from 'central government in the form of Yorkshire Arts, and Leeds City Council and West Yorkshire Grants' (West Yorkshire Playhouse website). Yorkshire Arts is the only source of national funding for the Playhouse, the rest of the monies coming from regional sources. In England, national funding for the arts has a bias toward large institutions with a high public profile. In 1999, for example, the Arts Council of England gave £212.2 million to the ten Regional Arts Boards. 'Of this sum £69.9m (33%) was awarded to the following national companies: Birmingham Royal Ballet, English National Opera, Royal National Theatre, the Royal Opera House (including the Royal Ballet), Royal Shakespeare Company, and the South Bank Board' (National Campaign for the Arts). In 1998/99, England's fifty regional theatres, of which the West Yorkshire Playhouse is one, had to split £5.4 million from the Arts Council among them while the national companies received £22.85 million (National Campaign for the Arts).

In keeping with the perceived obligations of publicly funded institutions, the West Yorkshire Playhouse conducted a year long project funded by the Rowntree Foundation to encourage the residents of the nearby Leeds estate, Ebor Gardens, to take advantage of the publicly subsidised theatre on their doorstep. Data gathered during the project substantiates the views of Eyre, Bennett and Frow that invisible barriers exclude certain classes of patrons from certain forms of culture. Interviews with residents showed that many unfamiliar with the practice of theatre going felt insecure, unsure how to behave or how to interpret the experience. Said one resident: 'I think people always thought of the Playhouse as very off-limits, snobby, overpriced place. They used to walk past saying "That's not for me, you'd have to dress up"' (Downing, 2001, p. 20). Said another: 'You're never sure what it's going to be like, are you?' (Downing, 2001, p. 24). Some, rather than making a deliberate and conscious choice not to exercise their cultural citizenship rights by virtue of feeling excluded, had never even conceived of attending the theatre. As a community worker involved in the project said, the Playhouse 'might as well be a million miles away' (Downing, 2001, p. 20). The Playhouse staff had to overcome the misconceptions of those who had consciously rejected the Playhouse while convincing others that theatre going could be a pleasurable activity. The project had immediate and measurable success. Between December 1999 and July 2000, over 200 tickets were sold to Ebor Gardens community groups. Residents attended the theatre multiple times, often in family groups, and chose a wide range of plays

(Downing, 2001, p. 42). In sum, the project showed that 'the assumption held by residents that they would not be welcome in the theatre and the assumption held by the theatre that the residents would want something other than mainstream theatre experiences have both been undermined' (Downing, 2001, p. 8). Data from the 'In Our Neighbourhood' project also hints at the different modes of consumption of public and private entertainments. Before their involvement in the project, the only Leeds cultural institutions patronised by the majority of residents on the estate were the commercial cultures of the cinema or bingo (Downing, 2001, p. 23). Bingo players are aware of each other's presence but are intent upon the individual goal of winning; cinemagoers are intent upon the collective goal of consuming the narrative but are unaware of each other's presence. In the theatre, audience members collectively consume a narrative; the presence of others, as we have argued above, heightening the experience. Might the Ebor Garden residents introduced to the theatre have come to prefer that form of entertainment to the cinema or bingo? Or might they have sought different pleasures from the theatre than from the cinema or bingo? This brings us to our study with audiences at the West Yorkshire Playhouse.

## Empirical research with theatre audiences

Two senses of 'public' have been discussed so far in this essay: spatial and financial. Audience research such as ours interrogates both: it enters the public spaces of the theatre-goers and it investigates the factors that produce the desired commercial outcome of 'bums on seats'. Asking live audiences themselves about why they do or do not attend public performances, as a way of casting light upon these issues, is an approach that has not been much adopted in debates about access to high culture, partly because of difficulties of access - difficulties that we think should be overcome. As researchers and academic writers who may influence policy on these issues, we are part of the public domain ourselves - in both senses of the word public used here. We believe that directly engaging with the public is a way of addressing theoretical questions about culture, taste and class that cannot be substituted by speculation; in this we follow in the footsteps of Bourdieu and of Bennett and his colleagues in their Australian study (Bennett et al. 1999). As academic teachers and researchers, we are also publicly funded, which brings with it an accountability to civil society. Our research with live audiences and with some of those who provide entertainment for them proceeds from a conviction that research with cultural participants, whether producers or consumers, is needed to inform public policy as well as to test some of the hypotheses about public versus private taste presently circulating in academic discourses.

One of the most potent of these hypotheses is the proposed relationship between class and taste, and the linked relationship between education and cultural consumption. As Bennett et al point out:

*From Bourdieu's perspective, the forms of publicly funded culture developed over the late nineteenth and early-to-mid twentieth centuries - art galleries, museums, state-funded theatres, operas, music etc. - function as components of what he calls the field of restricted culture . . . to which access is restricted by the operation of a range of barriers. Bourdieu distinguishes this field from the field of large-scale cultural production (culture produced and distributed commercially by the mass media) in terms of their different relations to the education system.*

*(Bennett et al, 1999, p. 229-230)*

'Mass culture', so-called, is, in Bennett et al's formulation, 'more or less independent of the educational level of consumers', whereas museums, art galleries, theatres, and concert halls require special and 'rare' intellectual 'instruments' for deciphering the performances that are shown in them. They require, as Bennett et al put it, 'the acquisition of interpretative, intellectual and aesthetic skills, which far from being generally available, are selectively distributed via the education system' (Bennett et al, 1999, p. 230). The proposed links between levels of education and cultural consumption, as well as other demographic factors such as class, income, age and gender, were investigated in our research in West Yorkshire.

## Survey at the West Yorkshire Playhouse, September 2001

In 2001, Patrick Stewart, most famous as Captain Picard in the long running and successful television series *Star Trek: The Next Generation* and as Professor X in the blockbuster hit *X-Men* films, but also well-known for his theatrical work, including more than twenty years with the Royal Shakespeare Company, starred in the Playhouse's production of J.B. Priestley's *Johnson Over Jordan* - a difficult experimental play, not produced since 1939, which shows stages in the life of a middle-aged businessman as he lies on his deathbed. Stewart, known to the authors through their research for a book about *Star Trek*, arranged permission to distribute a questionnaire to audience members as he had also done for the audience of the Arthur Miller play, *The Ride Down Mount Morgan*, in New York, 2000. We also received permission to conduct several focus groups.

With regard to the public/ private binary, our primary interest at the West Yorkshire playhouse derived from our findings with theatre audiences in New York (Davies and Pearson, 2002). Can people who would not normally seek public entertainment in its elite form of Broadway theatre - people who, as Livingstone (in the Volume Introduction) puts it, 'engage with media purely for reasons of identity, pleasure, knowledge, lifestyle' - be persuaded to visit the theatre by the presence of a popular television actor? Television belongs to the so-called mediated private sphere, which also constitutes what Livingstone calls a 'third space'. Our primary hypothesis was that the presence of an actor familiar from this space might attract those who had never previously attended the theatre; Stewart might act as an inclusionary factor overcoming barriers of exclusion. We also hypothesised that those who came to the play primarily to see Stewart might have different consumption patterns than those who came for other reasons, particularly regular theatre-goers or J.B. Priestley readers accustomed to consuming 'restricted' culture (although, as readers of novels, such people can be characterised as private consumers of culture, not public ones). We also wished to test the anecdotal and impressionistic account of theatre audiences being composed primarily of the middle-aged, middle-class, white and well-educated.

In our survey, our operational definition of 'taste' was behavioural: we asked about what people did, not what they thought, felt or understood about it. The survey asked how often they went to the theatre, not how they responded to what they saw. The business of interpreting what people think, feel and understand about cultural products is, of course, important; it is what we engage in when we teach students about film, television, the arts, books and music, but it is an educational function, rather than a research function.[3] We also asked *why* people chose to attend the West Yorkshire play. The concern of Bourdieu and Bennett et al about the ways in which more or less educated people respond to and interpret cultural events presupposes that people are already there, or not there. But what do they think before they get there? Why do they *choose* to go, or not go?

We have argued elsewhere that Bourdieu and his followers do not adequately account for changes in taste (Davies and Pearson, 2002). We are interested in accounting for change both theoretically, in term of relating human and demographic factors to cultural behaviour, and pragmatically; it is of interest to both policy makers and cultural marketers to know what makes people seek out new experiences. It is also important for policy, especially the allocation of funding, to have information on stability, that is, what it is that persuades people to maintain their cultural behaviours. We have called the processes of cultural change, observed in our audience studies, 'crossover', and we have found that there are certain kinds of groups and individuals within audiences who are susceptible to 'crossing over'; we have labelled such people 'culturally permeable'. Such permeability may derive from a sense of being part of a 'public' as well as an audience; these could be people who see themselves as having a right to access forms of cultural experience, whether or not these are deemed appropriate for their age, class or interest group. Such culturally flexible people might themselves be said to constitute a bridge between the public and private - to be a component of Livingstone's 'third space'.

Bennett and Frow argue that the principal barrier to 'restricted' (that is, elite or difficult) cultural participation is lack of education. The relevant opposition is not so much between high and low culture as between extensive cultural practice and restricted cultural practice: those with the highest levels of education engage in the fullest range of cultural practices across the whole spectrum; those with the lowest educational levels are not so much the proponents of an oppositional or marginal culture as they are disengaged from cultural participation. As John Frow put it:

'Both in Bourdieu's work and in the Australian Cultural Consumption project, what 'high' cultural consumption tends to reflect is not class but education... it is not the case that the highest social classes have the highest levels of cultural taste' (Frow, 1997, p. 79). Similarly, Tony Bennett points out that going to the cinema, watching television, listening to the radio and sporting activities are fairly universal. Increasing levels of education have resulted in increasing levels of cultural participation for all activities. The rate of increase is greater in all of the examples of 'restricted' culture and, in some cases - orchestral concerts and opera - markedly so' (Bennett, 1997, p. 94-95). This suggests that, so long as everybody is exposed to different kinds of cultural forms educationally, then cultural access will be equally available to these people - an argument which should be treated with caution, especially in terms of educational policy. Simply exposing children to cultural forms and attempting to spread 'sweetness and light', by requiring all 14 year olds to learn Latin, or study Shakespeare, does not inevitably result in an adult population which flocks to read the classics or attend the National Theatre. Some 14 year olds, perhaps at a much later point in their lives, actually will do these things. We are interested in such people, who, rather than being narrowly indoctrinated by rigid and limited elite educational traditions as might have been the case in the past, are in fact the opposite. In an age of sophisticated and constant commercial and cultural pressure on young people to consume 'non-high' culture, those who choose to go to the theatre or listen to opera can rather be defined as transgressive. We suggest, paradoxically, that one of the triggers for these transgressive changes of direction in cultural behaviour, can be through exposure to popular cultural forms, such as television drama.

## Method and procedures of the study

The authors spent five days at the Playhouse during September 2001, collecting 961 completed questionnaires, distributed at five performances of *Johnson over Jordan* - two matinees and three evening performances. They also conducted three focus groups with 14 volunteer participants drawn from questionnaire respondents. These consisted of nine females and five males, divided into two groups of five and one of four. Below we discuss some of our findings in the context of the above discussions about public and private behaviour, and the relationships between taste, class, education and general media/cultural consumption.

We hypothesised that the presence of an actor familiar from commercial - and 'private' - culture, that is American commercial television (although, in the UK, possibly seen on the BBC) might attract those who had never previously attended the theatre. Obviously this particular actor, through being associated with a very popular 'cult' programme with a large number of organised and articulate fans, was even more likely to attract interest than other kinds of television actor. We therefore expected that many of the people attending the play might be fans of his programme - *Star Trek* - too. To test the first hypothesis - that they were there to see Patrick Stewart - we asked people their main reason for coming, and cross-tabulated this with their answers to the question: how often do you attend the West Yorkshire Playhouse? A wide range of reasons – not all listed – for going to the West Yorkshire Playhouse was given. We have tabulated the most frequently occurring here and looked at their relationship with frequency of attendance at the Playhouse (see Table 1).

The most striking statistic here was that 104 out of 205 first time visitors to the Playhouse – over 50% – said they came because of Patrick Stewart. Not surprisingly,

*Table 1: Frequency of attendance at the West Yorkshire Playhouse according to reason given for being at* Johnson Over Jordan

| Numbers attending West Yorkshire Playhouse | | | | | | |
|---|---|---|---|---|---|---|
| **Main reason for coming** | *Very often* | *Often* | *Some-times* | *Rarely* | *1st time visit* | *Total* |
| Patrick Stewart | 12 | 33 | 70 | 43 | 104 | 262 |
| J B Priestley | 16 | 52 | 43 | 10 | 14 | 135 |
| Both Stewart and Priestley | 5 | 19 | 24 | 8 | 12 | 68 |
| Friends and family | 2 | 10 | 26 | 5 | 33 | 76 |
| Curiosity | 5 | 11 | 13 | 6 | 1 | 36 |
| Opportunity | 3 | 5 | 6 | 7 | 10 | 31 |
| Subscription | 19 | 3 | | | | 22 |
| Publicity | 1 | 3 | 11 | 2 | 2 | 19 |
| *Total including all other reasons* | 95 | 182 | 276 | 109 | 205 | 867 |

the highest number of people who said they came 'very often' were subscribers, in other words, those who already had a financial investment in turning up frequently (19 people, 20% of the frequent attendees). But almost as many of the frequent attendees (16, nearly 17%) said they came for combined Stewart/Priestley reasons. We might also want to speculate that the 36 people, around 4% of the whole sample, who mentioned 'curiosity/general' as reasons for coming, were also drawn by the presence of the star, combined with the rarity of the Priestley vehicle. It is certainly clear from these responses that Patrick Stewart was a - indeed *the* - major factor in bringing first-time visitors to the West Yorkshire Playhouse.

But did Stewart also encourage people who did not go to the theatre generally to come to the play? Or were these people regular theatregoers who on this occasion just happened to be patronising the West Yorkshire Playhouse? One way of checking that the results tabulated in Table 1 were not just a 'West Yorkshire effect' was to look at the answers given to our question about theatre-going generally as a function of the reasons people gave for being in the theatre. Here the spread of responses was rather different (see Table 2).

Here we see that the Stewart fans claim to be fairly regular theatregoers, with the majority of them (221 out of 262 - 84%) going between two and twelve times a year. Eighty (30.5%) out of the 262 Stewart 'fans' go 6-12 times a year. However, 21 people (8%) of the Stewart group went less than once a year. These people are our 'permeable' group - clearly not regular theatre goers, but who on this occasion have been tempted into the West Yorkshire theatre by the presence of the TV star. Three said they never went to the theatre at all, so this was their first-ever theatre visit: it would have been illuminating to talk to these three people, but it was not possible to identify them from the anonymous questionnaire. What we think we are seeing with this group is the possible modification of people's cultural behaviour, indicating the influence of a 'private' media form, a commercial television programme and its star, entering into the public space of subsidised - and rather highbrow and difficult, in the case of *Johnson over Jordan* - theatre. A further revealing statistic from our data, in relation to the extent to which people were literally prepared to traverse spaces, both public and private, to see this play was the relationship between where they lived ('home base') and their reasons for coming. Among the 262 people who gave Patrick Stewart as their main reason for coming, 91 of them - 34% - came from other parts of the UK outside Yorkshire. Five of these came from outside the UK altogether. This compares with 25% of the whole sample (239 out of 918) that came from outside Yorkshire. In the comparable 'Priestley' group (134 people who'd given Priestley as their main reason for coming), only 19 per cent came from outside the Yorkshire area.[4]

Because the 'reasons' people gave for being in the theatre were so widely spread, comparisons between all groups based on their highly individualised 'reasons' would not have been meaningful. However, there was a substantial enough number of people in the Priestley group (134) to provide us with a comparable group for

*Table 2: Frequency of general theatre-going according to reasons given for attending* Johnson over Jordan *at West Yorkshire Playhouse*

| Numbers attending theatre | | | | | | |
|---|---|---|---|---|---|---|
| **Main reason for coming** | *6-12 times a year* | *2-5 times a year* | *once a year* | *less than once a year* | *never* | Total |
| Patrick Stewart | 80 | 141 | 17 | 21 | 3 | 262 |
| J B Priestley | 89 | 38 | 3 | 4 | 0 | 134 |
| Stewart and Priestley | 40 | 22 | 1 | 4 | 0 | 67 |
| Friends and family | 23 | 34 | 4 | 13 | 1 | 75 |
| Curiosity | 22 | 9 | 2 | 1 | 0 | 34 |
| Opportunity | 9 | 13 | 4 | 2 | 1 | 29 |
| Subscription | 22 | 0 | 0 | 0 | 0 | 22 |
| Publicity | 10 | 9 | 1 | 0 | 0 | 20 |
| *Total including all other reasons* | 423 | 340 | 42 | 48 | 6 | 859 |

looking in more detail at questions about 'the Stewart effect.' We carried out a number of comparisons between the 262 people who had said their main reason for coming to the play was Patrick Stewart, and those who mentioned Priestley as their main reason. Given our general questions about the relationship between class and cultural consumption, we did a breakdown of education and income between these two main 'fan' groups: the Priestley group and the Stewart group. We found that a higher proportion of Patrick Stewart fans (19.1%) than of J.B. Priestley fans (11.7 %) had ended their education by 18. There was also a higher proportion of postgraduates (42%) among the Priestley group than among the Stewart group (33.2%). These differences could suggest that the Stewart group might consist of more people who are not educationally 'capitalised' in the way that Bennett and Frow argue is necessary for full cultural participation. Further evidence for the Priestley group, but not the Stewart group, belonging to Bourdieu's 'restricted' consumption elite, came from answers to a question about what other events people had attended during the Priestley Festival. Other Priestley plays - *Eden End* and *Dangerous Corner* - were being performed and there was a programme of talks and discussions, screenings and an exhibition at Bradford Museum. Thirty people in the Priestley group claimed to have gone to these events, but only two in the Stewart group - these two had seen *Dangerous Corner*.

## Characteristics of first-time visitors to West Yorkshire Playhouse

Because there was such a clear Stewart effect on the first-time visitors to the West Yorkshire Playhouse, we took a closer look at the characteristics of these theatrical 'virgins'. Of the 216 first-timers who gave their age, the biggest group (55 people, 25.5%) was in the 26-35 age category; the next biggest (15.7%) were the 17-25 year olds, a very desirable category from the point of view of the theatre's marketing policy and also an interesting group in terms of cultural permeability and the influence, or otherwise, of education. Adding the eight young people under 16 (3.2% of first timers), nearly half (44.2%) of the first-time visitors were young; this compares with 25% of the whole sample in this age category. The most frequent theatre-goers in the whole sample were the middle-aged and elderly: 74% (75 people) of 56-65 year olds said they went to the theatre 6-12 times a year, and 65% of the 65-plus group (51 people) said the same. These constituted 21% of the sample. It might be seen as surprising that so many of those going out in public to the theatre, instead of staying safely at home, are elderly. Yet we found the same statistics with our New York sample (for our study in New York, see Davies and Pearson, 2003). This generation is used to going out for its cultural pleasures, whether to the cinema, or to the theatre, as well as being avid television viewers. Theatregoing may be a taste they acquired as they grew older, particularly with the development of an attractive new, publicly subsidised local theatre such as the West Yorkshire Playhouse, with its incentive of cheap matinees.

Generational patterns of consumption of culture, whether public or private, are clearly important and need more investigation. As 63-year old Estelle, a Leeds retiree in one of our focus groups' put it:

> I try now to give my granddaughter the chance that I didn't have, for children to come by taking them to the theatre. I've tried to take her to stuff that she could join in where kids are raving and banging balloons and all that. I think this will go into her head, and these to me are the theatregoers of tomorrow.

Estelle, as a wise grandmother, was not trying to prematurely 'educate' her little grand-daughter into more prestigious sources of cultural capital such as Shakespeare or Pinter; she saw the right way to introduce live performance to children as building on children's own tastes for carnival and comedy - an observation which suggests developmental reasons for cultural permeability or stability (see for instance, Davies et al, 2000, and Davies, 1989).

Income and education are indicators of class, so we looked at these in our first-time visitors. We found that the majority of first-timers were in the lower income groups: 23.5% earned less than £20,000 per annum, and around half of this group earned less than £10,000; 29% earned between £21 and £35,000. Around 8% of first-time visitors (24 people) had finished their education at 16; while 24 people (12.5%) completed it 18; a further 14 people (7.3%) were still students; and 16 (8.3%) had received Further Education. The rest - more than half - had higher, including postgraduate, education. Within the main sample, of the 602 people who had higher, including postgraduate, education, around 90% were regular or frequent theatre-goers - obvious evidence of a relationship between higher education and the sampling of 'restricted' forms of culture. This contrasts with the educational profile of our West Yorkshire first-timers, of whom only half had degrees.

## Private pleasures from public service broadcasting

We also asked what else our theatregoers liked to do with their leisure time – questions about TV viewing, cinema going and favourite TV programmes. Among the most revealing pieces of data - as we found with our New York theatre survey - was the answer to the question: 'what is your favourite TV programme'. 555 people answered, and rather surprisingly, even to us, the programme with the most votes - 35 - was *Star Trek*, followed by *Star Trek: The Next Generation*, with 27 votes. These constituted 11% of all programmes mentioned. The Top Ten is reproduced below:

| | | |
|---|---|---|
| 1. Star Trek | 35 votes | 6.3% |
| 2. Star Trek: TNG | 27 | 4.9 |
| 3. Fawlty Towers | 24 | 4.3 |
| 4. Frasier | 19 | 3.4 |
| 5. The Forsyte Saga (2002) | 15 | 2.7 |
| 6. The Simpsons | 15 | 2.7 |
| 7. Dad's Army | 14 | 2.5 |
| 8. Morecambe and Wise | 11 | 2.0 |
| 9. Friends | 10 | 1.8 |
| 10. Buffy the Vampire Slayer | 10 | 1.8 |

Following these, each with nine votes, were *Morse, Coronation Street, MASH,* and *Dr. Who. Star Trek: Voyager* got eight votes and *Star Trek: Deep Space Nine* got four. Even in the general sample, of whom around 600 people were *not* there because of Patrick Stewart, this table shows that *Star Trek* was the most popular television show by some margin, especially if *DS9* and *Voyager* are included. This is an audience that may be subconsciously, if we may quote Lord Hutton, influenced in its decision to go to see *Johnson over Jordan* by the cultural pervasiveness of this iconic television series.

Television taste cannot properly be assessed by looking at the numbers of votes cast (one of the reasons why programmes such as *The Nation's Favourite Book* are so spurious). As when we have asked this question in the past, people's answers were extremely diverse: 209 programmes were mentioned altogether, the majority of them having only one vote. Television, the great mass medium, generates very diverse and individualised choices - possible further evidence of the privatisation of cultural taste, but also evidence of a variety of cultural experiences being made available to a much more diverse range of the public than was ever possible before the medium's invention. Among the favourite programmes mentioned were *War and Peace; The Ascent of Man; 'Arts Programmes', The Brontes of Haworth; Shakespeare's Histories; The Blue Planet; Bob Dylan Live; Middlemarch; Civilisation; Persuasion; Heimat;* and *Alistair Cooke's America* - alongside a range of more lighthearted answers, ranging from *Bagpuss* through *Sergeant Bilko* to the Test Match and Football Italia. Defenders of public service broadcasting could advance such a range of genres as one justification for its continuance.

## Talking about theatre: the focus group discussions

Our final set of evidence on these questions of the relationship between the public and the private and how they are integrated in people's personal and psychological responses to cultural experiences comes from our focus groups. The Ebor Gardens residents, as we discussed above, became part of a theatre audience that learned to 'laugh, learn, to be affronted, intrigued, frightened, moved to tears, together with others' (Downing, 2001). Several of our focus group discussions echoed this.

One of our interviewees, Steven, a 41-year old postman-driver who was not a regular theatregoer, came to the play because he wanted to see Patrick Stewart. He said:

> *Every scene was fascinating; every scene was an eye-opener to me. I didn't get bored at all and didn't fall asleep or anything, although I was tired because I'd just come off nights. . . . I was actually dragged into coming to see it. I wasn't a sci-fi fan at all. . . I came along with Alison and was pleasantly surprised.*

Although Steven had come out of curiosity to see Stewart, his enthusiasm was for the actual experience of watching the play. In contrast to some other people who said they were sometimes bored, as a relatively inexperienced theatregoer, he was thrilled. His 'eyes were opened', not just to the play, but to the experience of being a member of a theatre audience.

For *Star Trek* fans like David, a data-base administrator, we thought that seeing their captain live in the theatre might be a somewhat alienating experience, making it difficult for them not to super-impose the image from the TV series onto the performance. Said David: 'No, I just separated him from that completely. I wasn't thinking of *Star Trek* at all.' David also made distinctions between different forms of liveness, including formulating a category of TV-viewing which, for him, had qualities of liveness: 'Next Generation Star Trek on television, it's got to be on the BBC otherwise I can't watch it. I can't watch it with interruptions and adverts and things.' Because of his desire to 'watch something all the way through' he objected to the intervals customary in theatrical performances because, for him, they broke into the 'liveness' of the experience –

> *the ambience, the feeling of what you're supposed to get from this play. I think if you've had a break then halfway through, you just lost it. . . . When watching television I just like to get the feeling of it and just be absorbed by the view, sound and just sit there and be absorbing it as a whole rather than the individual pieces.*

All of these comments stress the emotional intensity of experiencing performances, whether live or televised. Sam, from Oxford, said:

> *That is one of the exciting things about live performance - a different audience and a different performance can make an enormous difference to the way you perceive a play. Just the atmosphere can be completely different.*

Sally, a self-styled 'Trekkie fan' was an enthusiast for all forms of performance. Her account suggests that an aspect of the pleasures of sampling these diverse experiences is to integrate them into a sense of identity: of being 'an emotional person' and proud to be so. This is not an intellectual response, attributable to specialised education, although Sally was obviously very articulate:

> *What I like about sci-fi, particularly the Next Generation stuff, is the morality within it. Everyone is treated equally, everyone is given the same chance, no racism, sexism, nothing like that. The ideals of that world to me are fantastic, particularly with what happened this week [September 11th, 2001]. My passion is theatre. I love music. I've been to a concert in Manchester to hear them doing everything from Gershwin to Last Night of the Proms and again, it's the liveness, it's the reality of it that completely conflicts to the fact that I like sci-fi. But then the live aspects of actually just seeing something on stage, you empathise so much with those people. I went to see* Miss Saigon, *in London on my own, and I was crying my eyes out and I wanted to hold onto someone next to me, but I thought I don't know him. But you can get that in the cinema as well. . . seeing Saving Private Ryan, I was crying for the first twenty minutes.*

Our data, both quantitative and qualitative, suggest that for audiences, both public and private, commercial culture and public culture are not in fact divided. Our sample appears to be perfectly at home with both, although further analysis remains to be done on some of the inter-relationships between demographics, cultural behaviour and tastes, and also on the qualitative follow-up discussions. Obviously there are distinctions between what the different media can do for people, depending upon their private/public status. But our data reveal that members of the public, or members of different audiences, if we wish to characterise them in this way, are also capable of defining their own relationships with different media. Among them, there is no such thing as 'the theatre-going public' or 'the television-watching public'. There are simply different modes of engagement.

## Notes

1. The authors are grateful to Nick Mosdell, Research Associate at Cardiff School of Journalism, Media & Cultural Studies, who helped with the design and administration of the questionnaire and with the analysis of the data - an analysis which continues with his invaluable help. We also thank the staff of the West Yorkshire Playhouse, especially Kate Sanderson, for their help and we particularly want to thank Patrick Stewart for arranging access for us.

2. For a discussion of this 'expanded' citizenship, see Turner (1997).

3. We can say in passing that, as teachers, we believe we have much evidence for changes in taste and cultural behaviour in students as a result of the educational process. However, that is not our purpose here.

4. It is noteworthy that in both of these tables of 'reasons for going', 'publicity' plays very little part. The marketing manager, Kate Sanders, told us that the theatre's publicity had tended to target Priestley enthusiasts - but from these breakdowns this may not have been the most effective strategy.

## References

Auslander, Philip. (1999) *Liveness: performance in a mediatized culture*. London : Routledge.

Bennett, Tony. (1997) 'Consuming culture, measuring access and audience development', *Culture and Policy* 8:3.

Bennett, Tony, Michael Emmison and John Frow. (1999) *Accounting for Tastes: Australian Everyday Cultures*. Cambridge: Cambridge University Press.

Butsch, Richard. (2003) 'The Good, the Bad and the Well-Behaved: Images of Audiences'. Paper presented at the *American Cinema and Everyday Life Conference*, London.

Chaney, David. (2002) 'Cosmopolitan Art and Cultural Citizenship', *Theory, Culture & Society* 19 (1-2).

Davies, Hannah, David Buckingham and Peter Kelley. (2000) 'In the worst possible taste:

children, television and cultural value', *European Journal of Cultural Studies* 3:1 (Jan., 2000): 5-25.

Davies, Máire Messenger. (1989) *Television is good for your kids*. London: Hilary Shipman.

Davies, Máire Messenger and Pearson, Roberta E. (2002) 'Stardom and distinction: Patrick Stewart as an agent of cultural mobility - a study of film and theatre audiences in New York City' in Thomas Austin and Martin Barker (eds) *Contemporary Hollywood Stardom*, London: Arnold, 167-186.

Delanty, Gerard. (1997) 'Models of Citizenship: Defining European Identity and Citizenship', *Citizenship Studies* 1:3.

Downing, Dick. (2001) *In our Neighbourhood: a regional theatre and its local community*. York: The Joseph Rowntree Foundation.

'Extra Cash for the Royal Opera House', 17 December, 1998 http://news.bbc.co.uk/1/hi/entertainment/236990.stm.

Eyre, Richard. (1998) 'The Eyre Report', quoted in Peter Lathan, *Putting the House in Order*, 5 July. http://www.britishtheatreguide.info/articles/050798a.htm.

Frow, John. (1997) 'Class, education, culture', *Culture and Policy* 8:3.

Habermas, Jurgen. (1996) *Between Facts and Norms: Contributions to a Discourse Theory of Law and Democracy*. Cambridge: Polity.

Hargrave, Andrea Millwood, ed. (2002) *Multicultural Broadcasting: concept and Reality*, report commissioned by the BBC, Broadcasting Standards Commission, Independent Television Commission and Radio Authority, November.

Horton, Donald and Richard Wohl. (1956) 'Mass Communication and Para-social Interaction: Observations on intimacy at a distance', *Psychiatry* 19:3 found on http://members.tripod.com/~fandom101/para1.html.

Hunt, Tristram. (2003) 'Portraits of Us: As certainties of national and cultural identity fragment, does it still make sense to save art for the nation?' *The Guardian* (Oct. 14) http://education.guardian.co.uk/higher/comment/story/0,9828,1062619,00.html.

Miller, Toby. (1998) *Technologies of truth : cultural citizenship and the popular media*. Minneapolis: University of Minnesota Press.

McGuigan, Jim. (1996) *Culture and the public sphere*. New York : Routledge.

National Campaign for the Arts, Arts Factfile, http://www.artscampaign.org.uk/info.

'New study casts doubt on the value of state support for the arts'. (2001) British Theatre News, 29 July. http://www.britishtheatreguide.info/news/library/news/bl072901.htm.

Pearson, Roberta. (2004) 'The Menace of the Movies: Cinema Challenges Theater in the Transitional Period', in Charlie Keil and Shelly Stamp, eds., *American Cinema's Transitional Era*. Berkeley: University of California Press.

Pearson, Roberta and William Uricchio. (1999) 'The Formative and Impressionable Stage: Discursive Constructions of the Nickelodeon's Child Audience', in Melvyn Stokes and Richard Maltby, *American Movie Audiences: From the Turn of the Century to the Early Sound Era*. London: BFI.

Scannell, Paddy. (1996). *Radio, Television and Modern Life*. Oxford: Blackwell Publishers.

Silverstone, Roger. (1994) *Television and Everyday Life*. London: Routledge.

Stevenson, Nick, ed. (2001) *Culture and Citizenship*. London: Sage.

Stevenson, Nick. (2001) 'Introduction', in Stevenson.

Turner, Bryan S. (2001) 'Outline of a General Theory of Cultural Citizenship', in Stevenson.

Turner, Bryan S. (1997) 'Citizenship Studies: A General Theory', *Citizenship Studies* 1:1.

West Yorkshire Playhouse website, www.wyplayhouse.com.

Sonia Livingstone

# Chapter 7: In defence of privacy: mediating the public/private boundary at home[1]

## On the potentially dramatic consequences of new media

Claims about the transformative power of the new media encompass many dimensions of social life. One of the most widespread is that long-established and traditionally-significant boundaries between distinct spheres are being blurred or transcended (Lievrouw and Livingstone, 2002). These include the boundary between work and leisure (via home working, teleworking, flexi-working etc), between entertainment and education (as in the neologisms of edutainment and infotainment), between local and global (here we have glocalisation, the global village, etc), between producer and consumer (as products are co-constructed or socially shaped by consumers), between adult and child (as in the disappearance, or the death, of childhood), and between citizen and consumer (increasingly conflated as the citizen-consumer).

These are familiar boundaries that we have lived within and committed ourselves to, they institutionalise dominant values and they are regulated and reinforced at all levels from domestic practices to international law. Yet, they now seem to be, in these late - or even post-modern times, up for renegotiation. The increasing mediation of everyday life represents one among many social trends driving forward this discursive and material process of renegotiation.

The blurring of boundaries matters because what is at stake is a series of claims about power. Traditional distinctions, critical scholars argue, serve the interests of the cultural and political elite. Transforming or undermining these distinctions may, as those in cultural studies have advanced, open up new possibilities for the marginalised, the subaltern, the oppressed to regain some control over their lives. Alternatively, as many political economists would have it, such transformations are effectively exploited by powerful commercial interests, ruthlessly undermining any surviving spaces for the exercise of freedom by either the traditional elite or the masses. Whichever, if either, of these is the case, it is clear that any social change brings with it huge public uncertainty.

In relation to new media forms and contents this uncertainty provokes widespread anxiety, anxiety which precisely centres on this supposed undermining of familiar boundaries and hence of traditional hierarchies. Newspaper headlines regale us with claims that children are gaining access to what only adults are supposed to know, that commercial institutions are gaining control over education, culture and knowledge, that governments are extending their surveillance into our most private thoughts and practices, that global players are squeezing out local cultures and individual creativity, and so forth. On the other hand, although attracting less attention, the optimists also predict some grand futuristic consequences of the introduction of new media. The socially excluded may find new routes to participation. Knowledge is being democratised. Consumers get to create rather than passively receive content selected for them. Restrictive or discriminatory frameworks - of gender, race or disability - can be superseded. Local cultures can contribute to a global cosmopolitanism.

The boundary most pertinent to the present volume is that between public and private. Popular and academic discourse contains numerous claims regarding the role of the changing media environment in the privatisation of public space or, conversely, in the extension of the public realm into the domestic. This chapter examines the changing public/private boundary for children, young people and their families as new forms of media - most recently, the Internet - enter and become established within the home. The starting point is the intersection of three inflammatory terms in popular discourse - children, media, change - all of which reflect the perception that the conditions of childhood are changing and, moreover, that the media are changing the conditions of childhood. The endpoint of the argument will be to suggest that the exploration of one dimension of hypothesised change - the public/private boundary - has social, political and cultural implications beyond the particularity of children's media use.

## What's new? On mediated childhood

Sifting through popularly expressed hopes and anxieties to understand what is going on, what is really new, perhaps; we find two underlying claims. First, as already noted, there is the widespread claim that public and private spheres are becoming problematically blurred as a consequence of the impact of new media (cf. Habermas, 1969/89; Meyrowitz, 1985; Thompson, 1995). Second, a broadly celebratory discourse of active, media-savvy, sophisticated young people, supposedly pioneers in the new media-saturated late-modern or post-modern culture, exercising their cultural, civic and consumer rights to participate in society through globalised, mediatised youth culture (as discussed by Drotner, 2000; Seiter, 1999; Turkle, 1995).

Problematically, however, to endorse the first claim is to undermine the second. In other words, if young people are the agents of change, their activities serving to facilitate and mediate the transformative consequences of new media, then there is little to celebrate in young people's innovative activities if the consequence is the blurring of spheres best kept separate. On the other hand, if we deny that young people are the 'media-savvy' leaders of social change, we risk reinforcing exactly that long-established conception of young people that the celebratory approach was designed to counter, namely, the image of children as vulnerable, embarked on a process of development whose chances of success depend on protective sequestration during childhood and adolescence from the meanings and practices of adult society (Livingstone, 1998).

For example, in relation to the uses of the Internet, it is increasingly recognised that young people are often more expert than adults; indeed one wonders if they have ever before received such adult admiration for their skills and expertise (Livingstone and Bober, 2003). If the social consequences of new media are broadly welcomed for their creative or democratising potential, then the pioneering activities of children might be especially valued. But, if the new media environment is judged problematic, suddenly their expertise wins them an unexpected responsibility. They are then blamed for naively bringing pornography into the home, giving out parents' personal details to unknown others, giving up on the old-fashioned virtues of books or long-established standards of written language and communicative etiquette.

The strong feelings that these polarised positions arouse hint at a long history of cultural anxieties surrounding childhood in which society avows a positive view of children, yet systematically devalues, intrudes upon or excludes their needs and experiences (Qvortrup, 1995): they are disenfranchised within the public sphere, yet castigated for being apathetic or antisocial; they are subject to increasing surveillance, yet seen as deceitful or subversive; they lack the financial resources to be consumers, yet are criticised for their superficial consumerist values; and so forth.

The media are similarly associated with a history of public anxiety and ambivalence, often centring on their privatising effects on society. In tracing the long history of 'new' communication technologies, Flichy (1995; see also Butsch, 2000) argues that the social uses of the theatre, then the cinema, then radio, each underwent a transformation from a public occasion for 'collective listening to the juxtaposition of a series of individual listening experiences' in private (Flichy, 1995, p. 153). Today we are witnessing a similar transformation for television, the telephone and the computer – from collective to personal, from fixed to mobile, from focal to casual attention. For both media historians and for historians of childhood the boundary between public and private is particularly significant, serving to contextualise contemporary concerns about social change (Cunningham, 1995; Gadlin, 1978). I shall, therefore, make a short historical detour before addressing the question of whether and how children's engagement with new media contributes towards the renegotiation of the public/private boundary.

## Public and private dimensions of childhood

The historical changes to childhood over the past century or more rest significantly on a series of other shifts – including changes in the structures of employment, the education system, gender relations and the family, together with the rise of consumer culture, of a psychological or therapeutic culture and, of course, of youth culture (Hill and Tisdall, 1997). Overall, these changes position young people today in some ways as immature and in need of protection from potential harms, including from the media, but in other ways as in the vanguard, active pioneers in staking out new territories in youth culture. The outcome is a period of 'extended youth' in which young people are betwixt and between; caught in a series of cultural shifts, whose effects are at times contradictory rather than complementary.

Western industrial societies are delaying some of the traditional markers of adulthood, extending the years of education and pushing back the start of employment, of financial independence and hence of leaving the parental home. At the same time, at least by comparison with recent decades, it seems that society is bringing forward the age of sexual knowledge and experience, of lifestyle and identity choices, and of consumer spending power through the lucrative youth and, most recently, children's, market (Buckingham and Bragg, 2004; Kinder, 1999; Kline, 1993). To adult eyes, then, children are staying younger longer but getting older earlier. In some ways, they leave the privacy of the home and enter the public domain 'too early'; in other ways they delay entering the public domain 'too long', while bringing novel or disturbing elements of that public world into the privacy of the family. Hence, in the face of a changing media environment, we find longer roots for the 'vanguard' or 'pioneer' or 'youth as expert' themes characteristic of public discourse concerning the Internet, and for the moral concerns over impressionable children and anti-social youth, vulnerable to television influence, addicted to computer games and manipulated by advertisers.

The rapid pace of change in the media environment further exacerbates public anxieties - anxieties that, as noted earlier, not only mediate but also shape people's everyday responses to media. Gadlin (1978) argues that, to a degree that is historically distinctive, parents can no longer rely on their own childhood experiences to guide them in managing the spatial and temporal structures of their children's moral, domestic and family life - and this is particularly evident in relation to new media (from programming the video recorder, using SMS on the mobile phone, or searching or chatting on the Internet). Extending Gadlin's account of changing generational relations, Giddens (1993) proposes that we are witnessing 'a democratisation of the private sphere' (p.184), a historical transformation of intimacy in which children, along with other participants in a relationship, have gained the right to 'determine and regulate the conditions of their association' (p.185). Meanwhile parents have gained the duty to protect them from coercion, ensure their involvement in key decisions, be accountable to them and others, and to respect and expect respect. This conception of the 'pure relationship' contrasts strongly with the Victorian conception of the family based on hierarchy, authority and clearly demarcated roles.

The message from historians, then, is that contemporary families must negotiate a rapidly changing society without the traditional resources of hierarchical relations between the generations - with neither guidance based on strong parallels between the parents' childhood and that of their children, nor the moral right of parents to impose rules and sanctions without democratic consultation. Like their parents, so too are children posed with a series of challenges. Buchner et al (1995) argue that childhood increasingly includes the responsibility of constructing a 'leisure career' or 'biographical project', a responsibility that requires young people to anticipate future uncertainties and deal with risk and status insecurity in the context of a loss of traditional forms of family and community support.

Within this context of broader change - which includes the identification in the mid-twentieth century of adolescence (and youth) as a distinctive and problematic phase (Coleman, 1993) - that changes in the media environment should be located. In seeking to construct a biographical project, and in resolving the series of developmental tasks along the way - entering work, sexual maturity, political enfranchisement, financial independence, etc - communication plays a key role at all stages for young people, explaining why the various forms of media represent such significant resources or, at times, impediments. On a simple level, the media are available to fill the ever-growing leisure of extended youth. However, the media are far from neutral observers on the sidelines of change. Importantly, the media have remade themselves in recent decades - through youth television, pop music, globalised children's culture, the expanding magazine market, video games, etc - precisely so as to serve the needs, or to exploit, depending on one's political stance, the undoubtedly demanding task of 'growing up'. Identity development is thoroughly mediated, framed by the worlds of music, fashion, sport and lifestyle, and it is also increasingly problematic - witness the growth of stress, anorexia and depression among young people.

The media foster youth culture through both their contents and forms. Through their contents, they directly address the concerns, interests and experiences of young people. Through their forms, they provide the personalised, mobile, stylised, casualised media goods that today mark out the spaces and timetable of young people's lives. In so doing, and because of the multi-determined ways in which young people use them, the media contribute to a repositioning of young people in relation to the public and private spheres - casting them both as consumers and as citizens, in the present and for the future. One might argue that, to the extent that young people play a pioneering role in relation to the media, this is because society offers them few alternatives, positioning them so that the media offer a rare space for experimentation and expertise, providing a route - and hence also a focus of generational tensions - for the playing out of the consequences of wider social changes.

The combination of young people, positioned betwixt and between public and private spheres, and the media, with their unique power to penetrate private spaces and to construct publics (see Chapter 1, this volume), results in some ambiguous, exciting yet explosive renegotiations of what is public and what is private. Young people use the media precisely to push at, explore and transgress established norms of public and private. They relish the potential of the media to offer the flexible tools and the free spaces within which to construct their individuality and relationships. And they are at times naively blind to the power of the media to position them subtly but firmly, according to consumerist pleasures, external cultural prescriptions and powerful interests.

## Grounding theory in evidence

The analysis thus far has sought to understand how young people's media use in the twenty-first century is framed by broader changes in the relation between public and private spheres. But it has not yet moved beyond a polarised language of public and private, freedom and constraint, opportunity and danger. In the remainder of this chapter, I develop an analytic framework to distinguish three conceptions of the public/private boundary. These are illustrated with examples drawn from my recent exploration of children and young people's changing use of media in the context of home, school and youth culture. In 'Children and Their Changing Environment' (Livingstone and Bovill, 2001a), a project conducted across twelve European countries, a series of quantitative and qualitative comparisons sought to contextualise new media use in relation to older media, non-mediated leisure and the home. In 'Families and the Internet' (Livingstone and Bovill, 2001b), a series of ethnographic-style interviews and observations in thirty homes with children explored children's engagement with the Internet in its everyday context. And in my current research, 'UK Children Go Online' (Livingstone and Bober, 2003), these qualitative observations are examined systematically through a national survey of Internet use by children and young people.

In what follows, I stress that the analytic framework is not only derived from core theoretical distinctions and debates in social and political theory, but it also accords with the sense of everyday excitement, uncertainty and anxiety that, over and over again, emerges from interviews and observations with parents, teachers, children and young people as they attempt to make sense of new media in their daily lives.

## Unpacking the relation between public and private

So, what does the notion of the blurring of public and private spheres mean? In what respects is it occurring? Why does it matter? Underlying the often implicit, at times obfuscating, uses of the distinction between private and public, lie three key oppositions or sets of questions. These concern profit, participation and governance (see Table 1).

In keeping with the spirit of this volume, I have characterised these oppositions

Table 1: Opposing public and private

|  | In which 'public' means... | In which 'private' means... |
|---|---|---|
| **Profit: Questions of interest – who benefits?** | Disinterested, as 'in the public interest', 'for the public good', 'public sector'. Includes 'public service broadcasting' and 'public property'. | Commercial or commodified, acting in self-interest or for 'private gain', as in 'the private sector', 'private enterprise', 'private property'. |
| **Participation: Questions of social relations, common culture and in/exclusion** | Connected or engaged in a shared culture. As in 'public opinion', 'public participation', 'public space'. | Withdrawal or isolation, as in 'a private retreat'. Includes the possibility of idiosyncrasy or individualisation, as in 'private opinion' or 'personal choice'. |
| **Governance: Questions of visibility, rights, responsibilities and protection** | Accountability and visibility, 'making something public' or 'in the public eye', 'front stage'. | Privacy, secrecy, beyond surveillance, 'backstage', 'in private'. Includes 'the right to privacy' and the notion of 'invasions of privacy'. |

in Table 1 using phrases from ordinary language in order to acknowledge that they are firmly embedded - together with the theoretical and public discussions that employ them - in the particularities of the English language. Indeed distinctions, commonly confused in English, when loosely referred to as 'public' or 'private', may not be confused at all in other languages. Matters are further complicated by the widespread use of 'public' to refer to 'outside' and 'private' to refer to 'inside'. This conflates questions of governance with questions of participation: is the point about an activity being conducted 'outside' (or 'in public') that it is visible and so open to scrutiny, and/or that others can join in and share in the outcome?

The nature of media institutions particularly confuses. The press, for example, makes issues public in order to further private interests; public service broadcasters fulfil their remit by catering to minority tastes. Hanging out in the mall allows young people to congregate in public, but such provision is commercial. Joining a chat room allows a child to participate in public discussion from the privacy of their bedroom. Street corner culture seeks to subvert its public location by defying public norms. When claiming that the media alter the relation between public and private, we should be clear whether we mean by this to address questions of profit, of participation or of governance.

Beyond aiming for greater clarity, we should note the normative valorisation of all three oppositions. Generally, when we talk of the blurring of the public-private boundary, it seems that the primary concern is with the privatisation of the public domain, conceived negatively, while a reverse 'publicisation' of the private domain is relatively neglected. As argued in Chapter 1 of this volume, the fear is that citizens are undermined, downgraded to consumers through privatisation. Publics are undermined, downgraded to audiences. Common culture is undermined, downgraded to the pleasures of self-interested or alienated individuals. Moreover, this normative valorisation is strongly grounded in the effort to critique and rebuff the many and evident threats from the commercial or private sector to the public sphere, to democratic debate, to public service broadcasting, to common values. Most prominently theorised by Habermas in his theory of the public sphere (1969/89) and subsequently applied to the analysis of the mass media (Dahlgren and Sparks, 1991), 'the public' is now routinely construed positively while 'the private' represents threats, danger and loss.

While granting the importance of the defence of the public sphere, there must be space within the debate for a defence of privacy. Conceptually, the notion of the private has a series of positive meanings easily lost within the public sphere debate. The free market defence of the profit-motive is well known and, whatever one's politics, few in western society seek to overthrow capitalism. Rather than stressing the problem of withdrawal or isolation from community and political participation, the activities these terms characterise can be re-described as independence or even resistance. Although government accountability is socially valued, so too is the right of individuals to privacy and civil liberties, thereby curtailing excessive state surveillance.

Not only can these negative conceptions of the private be re-described more positively, but so too can the positive conceptions of the public be critiqued, especially as these are instantiated in particular cultural or social institutions. The public does not always act in a disinterested or public-spirited manner, for example, but instead can be motivated, prejudiced, righteous or irrational. Nor is participating in a common culture always admirable - the community can be coercive, homogenising, intolerant. Lastly, accountability pursued unwisely can undermine the very ideals it is meant to protect - witness the impact of 'audit culture' on public institutions (Power, 1999).

In addition to the conceptual revalorisation of privacy, in empirical terms it is evident from research with children that they are enthusiastic about 'the private' in all three senses. Young people like commerce - they enjoy advertising, they love merchandising, they want to see the latest blockbuster, to hear the new top-selling compact disc, to follow fashion trends. Furthermore, they want to be individual -

notwithstanding their adherence to peer group norms - , to construct a distinctive identity, to have their personal opinions taken seriously. And in seeking opportunities to engage in a privatised or individualised culture, or to lick their wounds when upset or constrained, they place a high value on their privacy. So, they keep a private diary, they hang out in their bedrooms, they seek numerous ways to evade the scrutiny of critical parents; likening the parental monitoring of their Internet use to being stalked or having their pockets searched (Livingstone and Bober, 2003); in short, they cry out - 'leave me alone'. While not intending here to offer a blanket endorsement of young people's enthusiasms, my point is to challenge any simple or straightforward mapping of public and private onto good and bad.

## Theorising the intersection of public and private

Returning to Habermas, it is significant that his primary concern was less with the privatisation of the public sphere than with the inter-penetration of spheres that 'should', in normative terms, remain distinct. In other words, his theory encompasses, in principle if not in emphasis, threats to the pure or ideal space of the private lifeworld of the family as well as the undermining of the public sphere by private or commercial interests. Importantly for the critical theory of Habermas, society is analytically divided not only into public and private spheres but also into the system world and the lifeworld.[2] In some respects akin to familiar sociological distinctions such as structure and agency, or institutions and habitus, or even macro and micro, the distinction between system and lifeworld illuminates the analysis of the public and private by subdividing each so as to produce four sectors or spheres of society. Crucially, it is the mutual intersection or inter-penetration of these spheres that is the focus of Habermas' critique. Moreover, it is the stress on process of intersecting or interpenetrating that can illuminate the social changes discussed in this chapter. In Table 2, I follow Fraser's account of Habermas (Fraser, 1990; Habermas, 1981/7).

The advantage of categorising sectors of society in this manner is two fold. First, one can analyse how a focal concept - media, audience, child - is materially positioned, and discursively mobilised, by each of these sectors. In Table 3, the model has been applied both to the media in general and, in italics, to the audience (including young Internet users) in particular. After all, in a media-saturated society, there is no aspect of society that is not both shaped by, and an influence on, the media.

The second advantage is that, instead of conceiving of a single intersection between public and private domains, this is replaced by a series of intersections - or inter-penetrations, or tensions - between each pair of quadrants. Of the several intersections possible, I will now consider in detail the three that concern the personal or intimate sphere - in ordinary language, the locus of privacy and its relations to the 'outside' world - in order to analyse young people's activities in relation to new media and social change (Table 4). I shall suggest in what follows

*Table 2: The spheres of society*

|  | **Public** | **Private** |
|---|---|---|
| **System** | The state | The economy |
| **Lifeworld** | The public sphere | The personal or intimate sphere |

that each of these three intersections centrally mobilises one of the key tensions underlying the public/private boundary.[3]

## Intersection of the personal sphere and the economy

Questions of interest or profit lie at the heart of the intersection of the personal sphere and the economy. Note, however, that in Habermasian terms this intersection is within the realm of the private, albeit between the system and the lifeworld. In other words, that which is described in the terms of common discourse as privatisation - meaning the private sector's commercialisation of or intrusion into children's leisure, identity and lifestyles - is not strictly speaking a blurring of public and private at all.

The crucial concern, then, is not that of the exploitation of the public by the private sector, but that of powerful business exploiting ordinary people. Many questions arise. Whose interests are served if children spend more time watching television, if they acquire more personalised media goods, if they engage with online contents and services? Are the interests of commercial providers necessarily in conflict with those of children and families? Can one preserve a public sector space within an otherwise commercial environment, and which alternative interests might this serve? Two complementary shifts support the increasing interpenetration (for this process is more unidirectional than mutual) of the personal sphere by commercial interests: the rise of individualisation and of commercialisation.

First, the social trend of increasing individualisation (popularly, if misleadingly, described in terms of privatisation or fragmentation of common - or public - interests; Livingstone, 2002), supports a diversification in taste, in leisure interests, in lifestyle preferences. These lifestyle tastes and preferences are, moreover, ever less determined by socio-economic factors or cross-generational inheritance. And they are greatly enjoyed, and enthusiastically entered into, by young people, keen to explore new and different identities, to play with alternative

| | **Public**<br>Audience as citizen | **Private**<br>Audience as consumer |
|---|---|---|
| **System**<br>Audience as object | The state:<br>Legal and regulatory frameworks for the media industry, including protection for 'fourth estate'<br>*Audience as object of media education and, through their vulnerabilities, of content guidelines and controls* | The economy:<br>Media industry, media markets, commercial logic of media, advertising and links to consumer markets<br>*Audience as commodity or market, characterised through ratings, market share and unmet needs* |
| **Lifeworld**<br>Audience as agent | The public sphere:<br>Media as forum for democratic debate, mediated community participation and public culture<br>*Audiences as active and engaged, informed, participatory and/or resistant* | The personal or intimate sphere:<br>Media providing the images, pleasures, habits and goods for identity, relationships and lifestyle<br>*Audiences as selective, interpretative, pleasure-seeking, creative in doing identity work* |

possibilities, to differentiate themselves from previous generations and from each other - creative but also fickle in this playful exploration. Children are enthusiastic adopters of consumer products associated with their favourite television programmes, sports teams, pop music groups - they want the wallpaper, the duvet cover, the collectable toys, the branded tee-shirt, the cuddly toys. On the Internet, their top search teams, their favourite websites, their preferred games, all pursue these themes.

That which, from a critical perspective, represents the driving force of private interests towards the multiplication of markets, the diversification of taste categories, the emphasis on markers of distinction and difference, represents for children and young people themselves the opportunity to experiment with and construct distinguishing and satisfying identities, the material focus for communication and, hence, relationships, and the resources for marking off boundaries from parents, family, 'others'. Moreover, insofar as young people do the unexpected in initiating new trends, which are only subsequently capitalised upon by the corporate sector - examples include 'grunge' fashion, rap music, text

*Table 4: Intersections between personal and other social spheres*

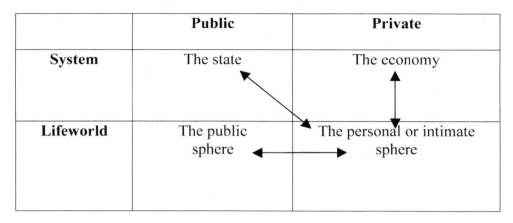

|  | **Public** | **Private** |
|---|---|---|
| **System** | The state | The economy |
| **Lifeworld** | The public sphere | The personal or intimate sphere |

messaging – their creativity in influencing both youth culture (within the lifeworld) and the economy (the system world) is significant.

However, the second shift surely is more influential. The lively and creative interests of young people are increasingly the target of a huge, commercialised, globalised leisure industry, devoted in its sophisticated targeting of youth as the new consumer opportunity; canny in its cross-promotion of non-media consumer goods within the media domain; ever more global in its reach; keen to evade or counter hitherto-dominant ethical norms that had regarded childhood as off-limits ('private'); and articulate in its reflexive adoption of child-centred discourses of children's rights, empowerment and identity as part of their branding and merchandising efforts (Kinder, 1999). So, the interests and anxieties of young people all become grist to the mill of mass consumerism. Individualisation is itself promoted by sophisticated marketing that simultaneously addresses ever more particular or esoteric niches while spreading ever more widely, ever more global in its reach. The outcome by no means necessarily serves the interests of young people.

A current example is the struggle to privatise online contents and services. Increasingly, online contents are branded and/or sponsored, organised according to normative preferred readings. Increasingly they contain difficult-to-avoid advertising. Behind the scenes, they collect personal data on the user's every click, search and download (Montgomery, 2001; Turow, 2001). The concept of the walled garden is symptomatic. Whether or not there are doors in the walls, commercial websites are typically designed to contain the user, to keep them on the site, enticing them with commercially themed contents, working rhetorically to make it unattractive or difficult to leave. The site for one football team contains no links to its rivals. The site for one television channel does not refer to any other. Each site offers a 'whole community', 'all' one could ever want to know, all the services one might want 'in one place'. These walled gardens implicitly, and firmly, counter the optimists' rhetoric of the Internet as a democratic and open space of links and connections, freedom and choice, not to mention anarchy and counter-culture (Burbules, 1998; Livingstone, 2002). Indeed, a casual comparison of public and private sector websites will generally substantiate this argument.

Moreover, although these contents and services are often enjoyed and desired by children, this does not necessarily justify the imposition of commercial interests on resources that could, to a far greater degree than occurs at present, serve children's interest. This argument can, in any case, be set aside for the time being because, thus far, children lack the critical literacy - awareness of online privacy rights, ability to detect sponsorship, recognition of commercial strategies and goals, etc - to judge fairly what these contents and services represent. Only once critical literacy is significantly greater can one consider the responsibility of users, especially children, in making their choices to engage with certain media or contents over others (Livingstone, 2004).

Most commentators, while recognising the role played by young media users - what Beck (1992) calls individualisation - would agree that the key driver of social change here is commercialisation, the activities of the economy or corporate sector being vastly more powerful than are the activities of users. As a result, many argue from a critical standpoint, that ever-younger children are drawn into a commercialised repackaging of peer, or youth, culture. Fandom becomes an increasingly dominant mode of engaging with popular (and even high) culture. Both peer culture and fandom become indistinguishable from consumer culture writ large - transacted and disseminated on a global stage. And the power of the private sector to impose its highly organised will on the private individual is such that few find it possible or desirable to stand outside consumer culture, though of course some, including some children, embrace alternative or anti-consumerist life choices. However, a critique and alternative may be developed as part of the larger public/private negotiation, in terms of the protection of public values, most significantly that of citizenship (for consumers are also citizens, for citizens require unbiased information and education), and in terms of rights (consumer rights, children's rights, civil liberties).

## Intersection of the personal sphere and the public sphere

The intersection of the personal sphere and the public sphere (see Table 2) blurs the public-private boundary within the domain of the lifeworld. Here, the central issue is that of social relations and common culture, in other words, participation. Since the lifeworld sustains society and carries the ideals of the culture, these questions are fraught, centring on how individual participation can contribute to the critical deliberations and community concerns of the public sphere. These anxieties regarding the vitality of the public sphere give rise to problems of regulation: since the public sphere cannot be created through coercion, what is to be done when individuals' desires draw them away from the community, being motivated by self interest rather than disinterestedness?

This concern over the blurring of spheres is somewhat misnamed, therefore, for popular and academic concern centres less on any growing intersection than on the growing separation between personal and public spheres. Early findings that children who spent a long time on the Internet became addicted, depressed, loners, exemplified such anxieties. But subsequent research tells the opposite story, for it now appears that - while the early studies, by necessity, examined early adopters who lacked friends online - today's youth have a critical mass of friends online (Subrahmanyam et al, 2001). The consequence is that online communication does not displace but rather supplements or even stimulates face-to-face communication, strengthening social networks (Livingstone and Bober, 2003), although whether this contains the seeds of future participation or of new social movements remains to be seen.

Clearly, young people have proved themselves the pioneers in both online and mobile phone communication, generating the customs and practices by which a peer group regulates its considerable volume of communication across diverse channels (see Drotner, this volume). As the empirical evidence repeatedly confirms, the driver of change in this public/private blurring is the activities of young people themselves, although the wider social conditions of childhood, including the many structures that serve to marginalise or exclude children, should not be forgotten.

However, such sociality has limits. Young people also express a strong desire to be alone, particularly when they find circumstances constraining. Here too the media are orchestrated to achieve this privacy. For instance, the media-rich bedroom, with its 'parents - keep out!' notice on the door (Bovill and Livingstone, 2001)[4]; the personalised media - walkman, discman, radio - that block out family intervention or interruption; the absorbed playing of computer games, writing online diaries (or 'blogging'), which are password protected, or the use of hidden files and other privacy tactics. Such activities are often interpreted by parents and other adults as hostile in intent: certainly they are symbolic means of inserting distance into relationships for, as noted earlier, the communal or domestic space, as with any public space, has a normative, coercive aspect which may override or marginalise particular individual interests. Recall Morley's (1986) image of the family living room in which the power inequalities of both gender and generation coincided to allow the father to dominate the media choices of other family members.

Conclusions regarding the mediation of the boundary between the public and personal spheres must therefore be qualified in terms of particular social relations and common culture. Participation in what, we should ask? For young people use media both to sustain and participate in peer culture, and to move away from and distance themselves from intergenerational or family culture. Recalling our earlier discussion of their uncomfortable positioning in an extended youth, betwixt and between independence and dependence, the public responsibilities of adults and the private protections of children, this is unsurprising. As Flichy (1995) argues, media allow family members to 'live together separately', so offering some resolution to the contradictions of modern family life. Taylor and Harper (2002) provide a telling illustration of young people using their mobile phones to text each other 'goodnight', supplementing, or perhaps replacing, the face-to-face 'goodnight' to their parents.

What are the implications of these observations? First, that participating in a common culture - sharing experiences, reaching decisions, negotiating values - depends ever less on the co-location of participants. Rather, the media serve to displace participation in time and space, permitting new forms of collectivity but perhaps also inhibiting old forms of deliberation, or introducing new grounds for exclusion. Second, parents are seeking the means, again using media, to counter the individualising effects of diverse and multiple media so as to sustain some degree of common culture within the home. Hence they may encourage eating together in front of the television, using sports or soaps to share some intimate time on the sofa, interacting together through a website, even instant messaging each other, or following up media themes to occasion family discussion, whether of an intimate or a political nature. Where once the structure of the home, and the media, demanded 'togetherness', today it must be more deliberately sought out.

Last, of course the challenge remains - how to encourage participation among young people not just in peer culture but also in the wider public sphere. Kimberlee (2002) suggests that, far from being apathetic or interested 'only' in alternative or identity politics, it is the extended youth, the altered trajectory in the transition from child to adult, which lies at the heart of the problem. As traditional structures of work, as well as traditional values and expectations, are lost, cues to participation and citizenship are no longer salient to young people. As Prout (2000: 304) points out, 'despite the recognition of children as persons in their own right, public policy and practice is marked by an intensification of control, regulation and surveillance around children', impeding rather than facilitating the ability of organisations to encourage children's participation. Hence, a number of commentators place the responsibility for the apparent distance between public and personal spheres less on the media (though there may be much that they could do to provide alternative cues to participation and citizenship), nor on children and young people, but rather on the structures of participation that seek to involve them.

## Intersection of the personal sphere and the state

At the intersection of the personal sphere and the state, crossing both the public/private boundary and the state/lifeworld boundary, questions of governance come to the fore. These oscillate between interventionist and *laissez faire* strategies, depending on the political climate. Also variable is whether the state seeks to regulate the relation between children and media by regulating the media or by regulating children, this latter by placing requirements on their parents or teachers.

In the UK, in response to the globalisation of media, among other factors, the current climate seeks to roll back interventionist regulation of the media, through state-imposed media content controls for example, replacing this with industry self-regulation, while shifting the responsibility for regulation from state to parents, teachers and children - itself a kind of privatisation of regulation. One key plank of the UK Office of Communication's regulatory framework is the promotion of media literacy - to ensure that users, especially but not only children, are equipped to make best use of the media and to avoid any associated dangers (Livingstone, 2004). Presumably, the successful promotion of media literacy will devolve responsibility to individuals, thereby legitimating 'lighter touch' regulation of the media industry.

However, the driver of social change here is public policy, itself driven in part by public opinion, so things move slowly, unlike processes driven by either or both of youth culture and commercial interests. Moreover, we are in a period of transition, with the media environment diversifying, globalising and commercialising ahead of both an updated regulatory framework and of public understanding of these changes. Consequently, we are witnessing a series of dilemmas where public and private values clash, and these in turn seem to exacerbate the oscillation between the inter-penetration of the personal sphere by the state and the withdrawal of the state from such intervention.

For example, the UK Government, in an attempt to encourage participation, recently promised every child an email address, but this promise was rapidly withdrawn when it was pointed out that listing children's emails on a school website might aid paedophiles more than politics. A similar dilemma arises when, on the one hand, the state aims to encourage children's online freedoms but, on the other hand, seeks to restrict them to certain approved activities other than those they might choose for themselves (often either private-intimate or private-commercial). Or when the education system hopes to facilitate the home-school link to encourage informal learning (a public good) without devoting teacher time to guiding parents in the use of the Internet (this being a domestic - that is, private - matter) and without acknowledging that the home-school policy further 'curricularises' leisure, turning parents into extensions of the (public) education system (Buckingham et al, 2001). Or when the state steps back from monitoring people's Internet use (an invasion of privacy) and instead encourages a market in online monitoring software with which parents can invade children's privacy themselves.[5]

The question of whose responsibility it is to regulate children's use of new media, (the state or parents, industry or users), and uncertainty over parenting roles and children's independence in the context of the 'pure relationship' (Giddens, 1993), is resulting in a tactical dance between parents and children. Parents attempt to control children's use of the Internet, children attempt to evade control: both resort to the rhetoric of trust - parents, in order to justify not regulating their children, children, in order to justify evading regulation. Both employ a range of subtle and not-so-subtle tactics, resulting in struggles over the decision to locate the computer in a public or private space, or to impose more or less draconian prohibitions on the use of interactive services, for example (Livingstone, in press). A simple example is that of the Sim Series software which supposedly promotes public values - teaching children 'about pollution, city planning, and the creation of healthy environments' (Calvert, 1999, p. 186); yet as any parent of a pre-teen knows, such software is gleefully played 'against the grain' - destroying the city, encouraging urban destruction, experimenting with the means of killing the inhabitants - in other words, precisely subverting such public values. On a more serious note, children who lack privacy offline may choose, or may even need, to seek it online for, as Navidi argues (2003), the threats to children's safety (physical, sexual and moral) within the so-called privacy of the home are, statistically, far greater than those external threats so often publicised through the press, making the Internet a potentially liberating resource. The point here is that, as Perri 6 (1998) argues, privacy is not so much about keeping secrets as about having control over who knows what about you - in other words, about choosing who you tell as well as choosing who you do not tell.

These questions and dilemmas of governance, protection and privacy have been analysed here from a broadly liberal perspective. That is, in terms of an oscillating closeness or distance between the state and the individual or the public and the private, and in terms of the dilemmas arising when rights conflict (the right of adults to access a non-censored Internet vs. the right of children to be protected from pornography, for example). But from a more critical perspective they can also be understood as the increasing incorporation of the private lifeworld by the state through the Foucauldian imperative to self-regulation. On this reading, policies such as the promotion of media literacy take on a more sinister aspect - demanding that individuals regulate themselves through becoming a good parent, a literate Internet user, a dutiful child, etc - in order to free commerce from content or trading restrictions or other obligations which may serve the public, rather than private, interests (Gordon, 1991). These injunctions towards self-governance represent a significant undermining of children's private lives (for children's and youth culture is, of its essence, playful, subversive, risky and hidden from adult eyes) and, potentially, an undermining of any benefits or freedoms to be gained from Internet access.

## Conclusion
This chapter has examined the experience of children and young people's uses of

new media to develop a wider argument about the renegotiation of the boundary between public and private. It proposed, first, that rather than simply claiming that public and private are becoming blurred, three distinct processes are occurring, these relating to three distinct, if interconnected, oppositions between public and private - one based on matters of interest and profit, one based on matters of participation and community, and one based on matters of governance and privacy. Second, and taking a lead from children's own positive evaluation of the private (rather than, or as well as, the public) poles of these oppositions, the chapter challenged adult-centred assumptions of the superiority of publicness. Children and, especially, teens co-opt the media in their own interests to create privacy for themselves, to explore their identity and self-development away from parents and other adults while, at the same time, forging a dynamic and sustaining peer network. In the third stage of the argument, Habermas' conception of society in terms of both a public/private dimension and a system/lifeworld dimension, was applied to media organisations and media users in order to contextualise the three oppositions - public interest/profit, participation/withdrawal and governance /privacy - identified at the outset.

The elaboration of this framework, exemplified through children's uses of new media, revealed the very different features, concerns and drivers of social change that characterise these three oppositions as they map onto the blurring or intersection of three domains: economy/personal sphere, public sphere/personal sphere and state/personal sphere. The claim that the traditional distinction between public and private is becoming blurred is thus unpacked into a series of distinct but intersecting questions of meaning, value, agency and responsibility. In short, 'public' and 'private' mean something different in different contexts, as part of distinct debates, and should not be confused or conflated.

Each of the arguments advanced here were stimulated by, and tested against, a child-centred research strategy (Corsaro, 1997), the point being to complement both an adult-centred and a media-centred approach. The advantage is that this allows the inclusion of voices too often marginalised in debates about children and media, bringing into focus a range of media uses not otherwise recognised (i.e. visible to adults, public) - the playful, secretive, evasive, tactical, subversive (i.e. the private). By contrast with a media-centred approach, a child-centred approach starts its story not from the perspective of changing media but from that of changing childhood, sidestepping the difficulties of technological determinism and of the media effects perspective. Grounding one's account first and foremost in children's lives rather than in technological innovation makes sense of empirical research with children and families, capturing the historically and culturally-contingent complexities with which new media are appropriated both into homes and more broadly into society. It is hoped that the present analysis provides a productive account of how the changing media environment alters the opportunities and dangers for social, economic and political engagement that face young people and their families.

## Notes

1. Many thanks to the colleagues with whom these ideas have been discussed: Magdalena Bober, Moira Bovill, Nick Couldry, Daniel Dayan, Kirsten Drotner, Peter Lunt, Mirca Madianou, Dominique Mehl, Ulrike Meinhof, Dominique Pasquier, Roberta Pearson and Andrea Press. Earlier versions of this chapter were presented to the *European Communication Congress,* Munich, 2003, and to the *Information, Communication and Culture Conference,* Oxford 2003. A shortened version of this chapter has appeared in *Journal of Media Practice* 6:1.

2. Outhwaite (1996, p. 369) defines 'Lifeworld' in Habermas' usage as extending Husserl's usage so as to encompass 'relatively informal ways of life, contrasted with market and administrative systems, as well as to a cognitive "horizon of meaning"'.

3. This framework can encompass further sources of public/private intersection. For example, the question of broadcasting regulation versus liberalising the market lies at the intersection between state and economy. The economy and public sphere are linked in, for example, the question of commercial funding for public participation initiatives (as in the debate regarding the liberating or corrupting influence of the talk show). Lastly, the tension within the public domain between system and lifeworld is evident in attempts to use publicly-owned media services to enhance citizenship participation (as in e-democracy initiatives).

4. As I have argued elsewhere (Livingstone, 2002), staying at home is framed, to a significant degree, by the meaning of 'going out'. Especially for parents of younger children and of girls, going out is risky while staying home is safe. A privatised, media-rich bedroom culture is also supported by the apparently progressive exclusion of children and young people from public places in society (as funds for youth clubs are withdrawn, as hanging about on street corners is discouraged, public leisure facilities are beyond the financial resources of many).

5. The invasive rhetoric of the software market is clearly evident in product names - e.g. *Cybersnoop,* and in product claims - *Cybersitter,* says the promotional materials, 'works by secretly monitoring all computer activity' so as to 'see exactly what your children have been viewing online [and] monitor chat room sessions, instant messaging, email' (www.cybersitter.com). This is not to say that the external threats to children's privacy are not real: consider the dilemma over equipping the mobile phone with GIS capability - on the one hand, this frees the child by permitting parents to monitor children's location, but on the other, it places the child at risk, for ill-intentioned adults may also monitor children's movements.

## References

6, Perri (1998). *The Future of Privacy. Volume 1: Private life and public policy*. London: Demos.

Beck, U. (1992). *Risk society: Towards a new modernity*. London: Sage.

Bovill, M., and Livingstone, S. (2001). 'Bedroom Culture and the Privatization of Media Use'. In S. Livingstone, and Bovill, M. (Ed.), *Children and Their Changing Media Environment: A European Comparative Study* (179-200). Mahwah NJ: Lawrence Erlbaum Associates.

Buchner, P., Bois-Reymond, M. d., & Kruger, H.-H. (1995). 'Growing Up in Three European Regions'. In L. Chisholm (Ed.), *Growing Up in Europe: Contemporary Horizons in Childhood and Youth Studies* (pp. 43-59). Berlin: de Gruyter.

Buckingham, D., Scanlon, M., and Sefton-Green, J. (2001). 'Selling the Digital Dream: Marketing Educational Technology to Teachers and Parents'. In A. Loveless, and Ellis, V. (Ed.), *Subject to Change: Literacy and Digital Technology* (pp. 20-40). London: Routledge.

Buckingham, D., and Bragg, S. (2004). *Young People, Sex and the Media: The facts of life?* Houndmills and New York: Palgrave Macmillan.

Burbules, N. C. (1998). 'Rhetorics on the Web: Hyperreading and Critical Literacy.' In I. Snyder (Ed.), *Page to Screen: Taking Literacy Into the Electronic Era* (pp. 102-122). New York: Routledge.

Butsch, R. (2000). *The Making of American Audiences: From Stage to Television 1750-1990.* Cambridge: Cambridge University Press.

Calvert, S. (1999). *Children's Journeys Through the Information Age.* Boston: McGraw-Hill College.

Coleman, J. C. (1993). *Understanding Adolescence Today: A Review. Children and Society*, 7(2), 137-147.

Corsaro, W. A. (1997). *The Sociology of Childhood. Thousand Oaks*, California: Pine Forge Press.

Cunningham, H. (1995). *Children and Childhood in Western Society Since 1500.* London: Logman.

Dahlgren, P., & Sparks, C. (Eds.). (1991). *Communication and citizenship.* London: Routledge.

Drotner, K. (2000). 'Difference and Diversity: Trends in Young Danes Media Use.' *Media, Culture & Society, 22(2),* 149-166.

Flichy, P. (1995). *Dynamics of modern communication: the shaping and impact of new communication technologies.* London: Sage.

Fraser, N. (1990). 'Rethinking the public sphere: a contribution to the critique of actually existing democracy.' *Social Text*, 25/26, 56-80.

Gadlin, H. (1978). 'Child Discipline and the Pursuit of Self: An Historical Interpretation.' In H.

W. Reese & L. P. Lipsitt (Eds.), *Advances in Child Development and Behavior* (Vol. 12, pp. 231-261). New York: Academic Press.

Giddens, A. (1993). *The Transformation of Intimacy: Sexuality, Love and Eroticism in Modern Societies*. Cambridge: Polity Press.

Gordon, C. (1991). 'Governmental rationality: An introduction.' In G. Burchell, Gordon, C., and Miller, P. (Ed.), *The Foucault Effect: Studies in Governmentality* (pp. 1-51). Chicago: University of Chicago Press.

Habermas, J. (1969/89). *The structural transformation of the public sphere: an inquiry into a category of Bourgeois society*. Cambridge: MI. Press.

Habermas, J. (1981/7). *The theory of communicative action, Vol 2. Lifeworld and system: a critique of functionalist reason*. Cambridge: Polity.

Hill, M., and Tisdall, K. (1997). *Children and Society*. London and New York: Longman.

Kimberlee, R. H. (2002). 'Why Don't British Young People Vote at General Elections?' *Journal of Youth Studies, 5*(1), 85-98.

Kinder, M. (Ed.). (1999). *Kids' Media Culture*. Durham: Duke University Press.

Kline, S. (1993). *Out of the Garden: Toys and Children's Culture in the Age of TV Marketing*. London and New York: Verso.

Lievrouw, L., & Livingstone, S. (Eds.). (2002). *Handbook of new media: Social shaping and social consequences*. London: Sage.

Livingstone, S. (1998). 'Mediated childhoods: A comparative approach to young people's changing media environment in Europe'. *European Journal of Communication, 13*(4), 435-456.

Livingstone, S. (2002). *Young People and New Media*. London: Sage.

Livingstone, S. (2004). Media literacy and the challenge of new information and communication technologies. *Communication Review*, 7: 3-14.

Livingstone, S. (in press). 'Children's privacy online: Experimenting with boundaries within and beyond the family.' R. Kraut (Ed.), *Information technology at home*. Oxford: Oxford University Press.

Livingstone, S., and Bober, M. (2003). *UK children go online: Listening to young people's experiences*. London: LSE Report, launched 16 October 2003. Available at www.children-go-online.net.

Livingstone, S., and Bovill, M. (Ed.). (2001a). *Children and their changing media environment: A European comparative study*. Mahwah: Lawrence Erlbaum Associates.

Livingstone, S., and Bovill, M. (2001b). *Families and the Internet: An observational study of children and young people's Internet use*. Public report. London School of Economics and Political Science.
http://www.lse.ac.uk/collections/media@lse/whosWho/soniaLivingstonePublications3.htm

Meyrowitz, J. (1985). *No sense of place: The impact of electronic media on social behavior*. New York: Oxford University Press.

Montgomery, K. (2001). 'The New On-Line Children's Consumer Culture.' In D. Singer & J. Singer (Eds.), *Handbook of Children and the Media* (pp. 635-650). London: Sage.

Morley, D. (1986). *Family television: cultural power and domestic leisure*. London: Comedia.

Navidi, U. (2003). *Presentation at the Experts' Meeting, Children, Mobile Phones and the Internet*, Mitsubishi Research Institute, Tokyo, 6-7 March 2003. See also http://www.childline.org.uk/ (last checked 31/1/2003).

Outhwaite, W. (Ed.). (1996). *The Habermas Reader*. Oxford: Polity.

Power, M. (1999). *The Audit Society: Rituals of verification*. Oxford: Oxford University Press.

Prout, A. (2000). *Children's participation: control and self-realisation in British late modernity*. *Children & Society, 14*(4), 304-315.

Qvortrup, J. (1995). 'Childhood and modern society: a paradoxical relationship'. In J. Brannen & M. O'Brien (Eds.), *Childhood and parenthood* (pp. 189-198). London: Institute of Education, University of London.

Seiter, E. (1999). *Television and New Media Audiences*. New York: Oxford university Press.

Subrahmanyam, K., Greenfield, P., Kraut, R., & Gross, E. (2001). The impact of computer use on children's and adolescents' development. *Journal of Applied Developmental Psychology, 22*(1), 7-30.

Taylor, A. S., & Harper, R. (2002). 'Age-old Practices in the 'New World': A study of gift-giving between teenage mobile phone users'. Paper presented at the SIGCHI Conference on Human Factors in Computing Systems: Changing our world, changing ourselves table of contents, Minneapolis, MN, USA.

Thompson, J. B. (1995). *The media and modernity: a social theory of the media*. Cambridge: Polity.

Turkle, S. (1995). *Life on the Screen: Identity in the Age of the Internet.* New York: Simon & Schuster.

Turow, J. (2001). 'Family boundaries, commercialism, and the Internet: a framework for research.' *Journal of Applied Developmental Psychology*, 22(1), 73-86.

Kirsten Drotner

# Chapter 8: Media on the move: personalised media and the transformation of publicness[1]

The gameboy, the discman, the mobile phone, the PDA, the MP3 player - since the 1980s portable, personalised and interactive media have signalled a transformation in relations between people and media. This has been from stability to mobility, from a situation in which the use of media devices was restricted to a location and to a time, to a situation in which media objects may accompany individual users across shifting settings and times of the day.[2] Mobile media potentially link individual users to any other point of digital communication, everywhere, at any time, through various forms of interactive media practices. This transformation equally signals a reorientation of peoples' appropriation of mediated time and space as they develop more personalised interactive forms of communication such as sms (short messaging services), mms (multimedia messaging service that combine text, audio, still and live images), chat and gameworld interaction. The latest generation of mobiles possesses both communication and computing capabilities (email, Internet access, GPS), a combination which is dramatically changing media culture in countries such as Japan and Hong Kong.

Thus, the increased individualisation and mobility of contemporary media culture invites conceptual reconsideration of the time, spaces and social relations within which media practices develop and become institutionalised. And the technological fusion of computing and mediated communication invites similar reconsideration of the interactive forms and communicative functions that mobile devices help facilitate, hamper and contest. Since these concepts have been developed within media studies in relation to mass media and their respective institutions, it is rewarding to take these forms as our conceptual points of departure. Crucial elements here are the relations between public and private spaces, the formation of audiences and publics, and the ways in which both of these sets of relations are implicated in various forms of mediated textual practices.

How do people lay claim to public and private spaces when using mobile media technologies? Do the nearly ubiquitous presence of mobiles in many countries help weaken chronological time or, conversely, reinforce it? Do the portable and personalised media serve to challenge notions of media audiences, as these are traditionally constituted through the uses of newspapers and film, radio and television? Can we speak of mobile publics? What communicative forms and functions are enhanced through interactive, mobile media, and how do these relate to prevalent genres within the traditional mass media? These are the main questions that I will attempt to answer in this chapter.

My empirical focus is on mobile phones, which on a global scale are the most widely used of the mobile media. They are also useful objects of study if we want to consider the complexities of contemporary media culture, which is increasingly characterised by technological convergence, individualised interactivity and mobility. Mobiles are at once stand-alone technologies and part of an interlaced media ensemble: phone numbers used for downloading ring-tones and logos are found in magazines; pictures from mobiles are put on the Internet; sms is applied by TV broadcasters in their invocation of audiences. Mms icons draw on brands and star images known from other media. The combination of communication and computing in the most advanced devices lead people in the industry to seek for new names such as wireless devices, handsets and handhelds to cover the diversity of services and functions. I shall retain the term mobile phones since it is the common term used in most countries and signals a key function of use.

Like most other portable and interactive media technologies, mobile phones in general and sms in particular were first widely taken up by young people and older children in post-industrialised societies where mobile phones are both a symptom of and solution to the demands made on spatial flexibility, temporal coordination and personal identity performance. Since these groups are pivotal to the socio-cultural transformations of the relations between audiences and media mentioned above, they constitute the focus of my empirical examples.

Moreover, my focus is on European contexts of appropriation and use. While mobiles are adopted in all post-industrialised societies, there are still marked differences in the technologies applied, the institutional frameworks of distribution and the socio-cultural contexts of use. In technological terms, Japan leads the way with its wide dissemination of 3G mobile handsets that allow email communication and access to the Internet with a range of websites, as well as integration of text, sound and image, in addition to ordinary call functions.[3] Europe is dominated by the so-called 2.5G system that allows the data connection to be 'always on' and has swifter data transmission than the 2G system that is the norm in North America. In terms of take-up, Europe leads the way with 73 mobile phone subscribers per 100 inhabitants in 2001; followed by Japan (59 per 100) and the USA (46 per 100). With 278 million mobile subscribers in the EU by 2001 (an 18% increase since 2000), they outnumber landlines by 72 million (Lumio & Sinigaglia, 2003, p. 4). Notably in Europe, the tremendous popularity of short text-messaging has given unsuspected revenues to content providers and operators - in 2001, for example, two billion messages were sent in Denmark, with a population of 5.2 million, against 2.4 billion messages sent in the USA, which has a population of 280 million (Cancel, 2003). Furthermore, ring-tones and logos account for 39% of the total value of the European mobile market (Impe, 2003). For obvious reasons, the telecommunications industry is intensely preoccupied with developing convergent, mobile media.

## Public discourses

While mobile phones and other portable media technologies have received little systematic scholarly attention in comparison with the personal computer and the Internet, mobiles have not been short of public and commercial attention. Since their inception, mobile phones have been visible to the public eye and ear. When still-pricy devices in the 1980s and early 1990s, they were flaunted by well-off, young adult males as status symbols and discursively humoured by public wit. For example, in Swedish a mobile phone was a *yuppie nalle* (yuppie teddy), in German it became a *handy* and in Danish a *mobilos* (signalling low-status Spanish). From early on, mobile phone conversations on private matters conducted in (semi-) public spaces, such as trains, restaurants and shops, were objects of public discussion and at times self-admonished regulation (Ling, 1997). The often self-conscious positioning by the early adopters as trendsetters only added to the intensity of the debate.

The wide adoption of mobile phones through the 1990s, not least by the younger generation, and the concomitant domestication of the technology has been accompanied by new public discourses. Foremost among these is a discourse of risk, which comes in several forms. One is the perceived health risk of the devices, with cancer as a prime suspect, a suspicion that is being reinforced with the erection of new 3G masts in many European countries. In addition, the health discourse has intermittently focused on the physical damage to thumbs caused by excessive short-text messaging.

Another risk discourse focuses on the material aspects of theft and exorbitant phone bills. Downloading and sending icons and pictures can be quite costly and the expense is not stated up front. Organisations and societies representing consumers and children have voiced concern about industry responsibilities in terms of underage users, responsibilities that are particularly difficult to deal with, as content providers differ from operators. In Japan, the risk of sexual abuse has been very prominent for some years (Kioka 2003, Takeyama 2003), and this discourse is entering Europe along with the introduction of 3G handsets. Less tangible, but equally pervasive in the risk discourses, is the alleged danger text-messaging poses to the print literacy of the young ''thumb tribes'. With its 160 characters, it invites unorthodox forms of spelling that are clearly at odds with the proficiencies taught at school and hence judged deficient by educational standards.

While public discourses lay claim to negative effects of mobile phones, the commercial discourse through the 1990s has been concerned with promoting more optimistic views. When the technology was still a novelty, its safety aspects were stressed: if you need help, a mobile at hand means it is only a call away. Parents could keep track of the whereabouts of their teenage children at night and monitor daily coordination of family life. Today, when the technology has become a taken-for-granted tool in many parts of the world, the discourse of connectivity and creativity, flexibility and fun has pre-eminence, as is seen on operators' and content providers' homepages. For instance, ''bringing dreams to life' (DoCoMo), ''Mobile moments - mobile lives' (Ericsson), ''Motorola - intelligence everywhere' (Motorola), ''Nokia - connecting people' (Nokia).

A primarily negative public discourse versus a primarily positive commercial discourse mirrors a predominant pattern when new media technologies are introduced (Jensen, 1990; Drotner, 1999). The new gadgets become simple seismographs of complex socio-cultural problematics and they offer welcome projection screens for scenarios of the future. Since the younger generation is among the early adopters, these dichotomies play into established discourses on childhood; discourses that since the 18th century have been characterised by an opposition between protection and autonomy (Gillis, 1974; James et al. 1998; Qvortrup 2000). The more personalised and portable media technologies such as the mobile phone serve to radicalise these well-known positions, since the phones are associated with individual ownership and personal priority of use, and since their handiness make them inconspicuous yet effective means of social coordination and interaction beyond the confines of the home and the control of adults.

## The discursive hinterland

Still, the public and commercial discourses on mobile phones are not only about the material objects of communication. Crucially, they centre on the substance and form of communication itself and the contexts of its use. Private conversations in what is considered public spaces like streets, shopping malls and markets; public performances (such as voting for a candidate in *Big Brother*) conducted in the privacy of the home; collective short text-messaging as part of community campaigns - these are all examples of ways in which the mediated interactions through mobile phones serve to question received notions of what is considered public and private space, what it takes to be part of an audience versus part of a public, what is considered intimate talk and public speech.

These notions are rooted in the idealist Enlightenment tradition that Jürgen Habermas takes as his historical point of departure and in the normative ideal in his influential theorisings on mediated communication in modernity (Habermas 1962/1989). According to this ideal, the public sphere is a partly mediated sphere of rational communication and social regulation. Here, publics form and are sustained through their communicative practices that aim at reaching consensual action and intervention. Matters from the private sphere of home and work can be debated as long as the debate is kept on a general level. These private matters concern domestic issues of the home, which Habermas terms the intimate sphere, and they concern economic issues of production such as labour disputes, safety conditions and investments.

In many Western societies, this ideal has had what may be termed a "reality effect" in modernity. It has constituted the basis of communicative practices, institutional locations and legal regulations, just as its respective spheres have operated as formative bases of audiences and publics.[4] As is evident, the concept of public denotes a physical or virtual location (public place or space), an aspect of society (the public sphere) and a group of people (the public) that knowingly perform particular social functions with particular social aims. These variations of the concept are often conflated in popular as well as scholarly discourses with decisive contradictions as a result (see Livingstone's introduction to the present volume). Defined as a group of people, a public is perceived as a narrower term than an audience, since it only operates within or in relation to the public sphere, conducts itself through abstract debate, and aims at reaching collective and consensual social action. Audiences are constituted through their mediated meaning-making processes, that can be individual as well as collective, and that can take place in the privacy of the home or on the job, as well as in public spaces. Both the concept of audience and public are premised on the notion of spatial separations of social life, separations that in a symbolic, and often very literal, sense are tied to specific locations. The public sphere, thus, only exists as a meeting ground because public and private domains of life are segregated.

The Habermasian concept of the public sphere would suggest that popular discourses on the introduction of mobile phones centrally concern the challenges mobile communication poses to received notions of what constitutes 'proper' communicative issues in different areas of society, just as the discussions lay claim to shifting boundaries between audiences and publics. When the central communicative devices through which publics are constituted and maintained can no longer be relegated to particular physical or imagined settings, when communicators themselves are on the move, then the received notions of media and mediators are played out in new ways and our analytical concepts are called into question.

In seeking to understand these reconfigurations, we may draw on the definition of the public sphere put forward by German sociologist Niklas Luhmann (1995; see also Baecker 1996). According to this definition, the public sphere is a continuous social process, mainly performed through the media, whose central function is to offer a reflexive perspective on the system. Hence, it signals a reduction in the complexity of modern society for its members, a signal that serves to ease individual conduct and social continuity. Luhmann, unlike Habermas, has no normative ideal of reaching consensus or facilitating joint social action. Rather, his systems theory harbours a sceptical positivism whose main objective is a continuation of the system, irrespective of its character.

One need not buy into Luhmann's positivist epistemology in order to appreciate some of his insights. That the media serve to reduce social complexity by simplifying, coordinating and framing entertainment and information is well known from audience studies, rituals and genre theory. Watching the daily soap episode or reading the newspaper serves as temporal demarcations in the flow of daily life and as symbolic reminders for audiences of their social belonging (for example, Silverstone & Hirsch, 1992; Couldry. 2003). Likewise, genres may be seen as recognisable matrices of interpretation, as results of tacit contracts between producers and audiences to get something understandable yet interesting (Neal, 1980).

In the case of mobile phones, we may further contextualise their social ramifications by drawing on recent theories on modernity and on individualisation. Contemporary societies have variously been defined as, for example, information societies, learning societies, knowledge societies and network societies (Masuda, 1980; Husén, 1986, Stehr, 1994, Castells, 1996/1998). Irrespective of scientific traditions, these definitions focus on the constitutive role played by media and information and communication technologies (ICTs) in all areas of modernity. The complexity and differentiation of most societies and their increasing interconnectedness necessitate flexible coordination of actions - and hence continuous communication. A majority of this social communication is mediated, as we know.

The enormous increase in the use of mobile technologies is premised upon such social formations, just as these technologies serve to further the growth of social complexity. Mobile phone communication allows, and demands, people to be always available; it facilitates ad-hoc communication and co-ordination as part of the flow of daily activities; and it allows for readjustments to and comments on social action. All this seems to reduce the complexity of social organisation. But at the same time, mobile communication serves to widen people's range of possible contacts, and do so at all times and in all places, a process that in itself tends to increase rather than reduce complexity (Rasmussen, 2000).

In modernity, the handling of complexity is increasingly an individual affair. Individualisation may be defined as a socio-cultural process whereby social interdependence is played out as individual transactions, a paradox that is often lost in popular discussions on the ''me generation' and similar normative discourses (Beck & Beck-Gernsheim, 2002). What Anthony Giddens calls 'the reflexive monitoring of daily life' (Giddens, 1991) is one of the main results of individualisation in modernity, and much of this monitoring is mediated. The flexibility, portability and communicative ease of mobile phones make them prime means of handling this individualised monitoring in modernity. Late childhood and youth in many ways condense the claims made to indvidualisation, since identity work is at the fore in all areas of life - school, family, peers and also, for a good many, work. Hence, it is no wonder that the younger generation constitutes the early adopters of mobile communication in most parts of the world.

## Permeable spaces

The portability of the mobile phone is its crucial feature. This means the spatial reconfigurations of mediated communication are at the core of its social functions. Landlines connect places with places, and so when people call a fixed phone, they call a particular place - other people (or devices like answering machines) in that place may stand in for the recipient of the call (Geser, 2002). Mobile phones make direct connections between individuals or, in the advanced versions, between individuals and satellites or Internet nodes (and then on to one or many recipients). They can go almost anywhere their users go; they traverse spatial boundaries and so they serve to diminish the concreteness of place in favour of the concreteness of the communicators. This, of course, is why a standard remark of a mobile conversation is about location: 'Where are you?' or 'I am now on the bus'. Unlike landline calls, mobile communication does not assume place; it has to be confirmed, legitimated, and explained - which again requires more text, talk or visual demonstration.

The portability of mobiles serves to make spatial boundaries more permeable and to increase the importance put on the communicative connectivity over communicative context. Mobile communication foregrounds a conception of space, less as physically bounded entities or locales, and more as socially shifting processes defined by communicative practices and their relevance. To be part of a mobile network of callers or text-messagers is highlighted more by users than their actual or virtual location. A television viewer or a radio listener may be conscious of the existence of other viewers or listeners; indeed, this potential self-consciousness is arguably constitutive to the definition of an audience in the sense of an interpretive community predicated on its spatial distribution (Fish, 1979).

Conversely, mobile audiencing is much more focused upon connectivity itself than upon its spatial context. Particularly with the younger generation, mobile interaction will often be a social affair including several people at either end and so there will be interplay between the physical and the virtual audience. A clear example of this interplay is children riding on a school bus and making mobile conversations between the front- and back-seat kids. From an adult point of view such conversation is at best a waste of money but, as is evident for any witness to such an incident, for the participants it is precisely this playful connectivity between place and space, between physically and virtually located audiencing, that makes calling relevant and fun - passing the handset around, listening to sniggering on the phone, looking towards the other end of the bus. This interplay is seen most clearly in terms of conversation, while the potentially more collective nature of sms tends to foreground the spatiality of audiencing: sending multi-messages, knowing that your message may be passed on to a range of people unknown to you.

Mobile, mediated practices constitute communicative spaces that cross the domains of public, semi-public and private locales and their respective normative barriers. In public spaces, the normative clashes resulting from these crossings are less regulated than is the case in semi-public spaces such as restaurants and classrooms (Ling, 1997, 2000; Licoppe & Heurtin, 2002). Overhearing a private conversation in a public space may cause personal curiosity or irritation, but rarely collective reaction. In semi-public spaces such reaction can be, and often is, institutionally guaranteed. In private places such as the home or the job, mobiles supplement landlines, with fewer challenges of spatial boundaries as a result. Here, clashes are primarily caused by the individualised nature of mobile communication, with mobile calls being reserved for personal calls that, moreover, signal ''ultra privacy' to other members of the private household who may want to monitor the degrees of privacy (Drotner, 2001).

## Flexible time

Mobile communication can be synchronous (conversation), asynchronous (sms, mms, email, voicemail) and both (web chat, Internet) - and it can be round-the-clock. These temporal possibilities are more diverse than those found in landline telephony and in mass communication - the latter offering time shifts via the VCR, repetitions of items such as commercials, and simultaneity via live-broadcasts. However, broadcast audiences cannot influence the sequential arrangements of production, and they largely accommodate themselves to media schedules. As audience studies have demonstrated, the routinised flows of radio, television and the press serve to orchestrate audiences' temporal experiences of everyday life rather than the other way round, and they continue to do so to a great extent, despite the means of time-shifting by the VCR (for example, Scannell, 1988; Larsen, 2000). Media use makes abstract, chronological time tangible and anchored in relation to daily routines, and this mediated notion of time is reinforced through textual formats obeying sequential structuring - the weekly gameshow, the daily newspaper, the hourly radio news.

Mobiles facilitate *ad hoc* mediated communication, which is also reciprocal. Social arrangements can be coordinated, modified and changed literally as people go along. Mobile communication, too, operates as an anchoring of chronological time, but not as fixed points of demarcation. It is a provisional handling of time that aligns mobile communication with a sense of temporal ease and fun rather than the fixities and duties of sequential time management - one may always make a new call, send another icon along. Still, this 'ad-hocratism' (Rheingold, 2002) makes time something to be always aware of - as an expanded momentariness during a call, a reflection on past messages sent, short-term planning of whom to reach next. These potential contradictions make the temporal aspects of communication more noticeable for mobile users than tends to be the case with broadcast audiences. In that respect, mobile and Internet interactions are similar, the main difference being that mobile communication combines temporal flexibility and fluidity with a set of permeable spatial qualities.

## Affirmation of social roles

The most noticeable aspect of mobile phones, and certainly the one drawing most immediate attention, is its impact on social interaction, not least in public and semi-public spaces. In both formal and informal settings, mobile communication adds an extra dimension to interpersonal communicative practices: place-based activities and conversations are interspersed by space-based mobile communication, and this creates an often intricate monitoring of roles, both for speakers and listeners, particularly in the case of mobile conversation (sms is silent and tends to be more unobtrusive).

When mobile talk is undertaken amongst anonymous others, the speaker negotiates a private, virtual role and a public, physically located role, while most listeners find various ways of displaying what Erving Goffman calls ''civil inattention' (Goffman, 1963, p. 85). Unlike calls to particular places via landlines, mobile callers cannot anticipate the situated role of the recipient, and hence virtual role-regulation is often part of the opening of conversation, adding to the role-monitoring between social roles. These processes are particularly evident when there is a marked gap between roles undertaken in the social and virtual spheres – one may think of mobiles ringing during a classical concert or a conference, situations that often cause embarrassment, both on the part of recipients and listeners (Ling, 2001). Naturally, these are also among the situations when mobile users put their device on hold, thus balancing their wish to be online with the demands made by the conventions of social etiquette. Still, explicit, interpersonal regulation is rare in anonymous and non-institutional frameworks, although general rules of conduct may be imposed in institutional settings such as airports and cinemas.

When mobile talk is undertaken among acquaintances, there tends to be a narrower gap between social and virtual roles, more normative consensus on what roles are acceptable and a clearer regulation of normative transgressions (Ling, 2001). This is seen with the mobile phone uses of the younger generation, with which in-group norms abound – down to the style of phone covers and sms acronyms – and which are mostly self-regulated. Since their uses are also of a more collective nature, they add to the complexities of role monitoring: the roles of speaker and listener are often interlaced when phones (and conversational control) change hands and remarks from bystanders become part of the conversation.

With George Herbert Mead, (1934) it may be argued that these complexities orchestrate an oscillation between the psychological positions of 'I', 'me' and 'you' that is, an oscillation between an internal and an external perspective on communication that opens a space for self-reflexion. From a sociological perspective, we may say that mobile phone uses serve to complicate what Erving Goffman calls the 'face work' necessary in modern social life. Unlike landline conversations, mobiles do not mediate between a known 'backstage' (the location of speakers) and 'frontstage' (the virtual space of conversation) (Goffman, 1971). Rather, they require negotiations of various front-stage performances (Ling, 1997) - roles cannot be assumed, they have to be affirmed. Hence, these negotiations tend to highlight the existence, even the necessity, of roles and facework. Not least with young people, the concepts of Mead and Goffman help illustrate how mobile phone uses both afford and affirm a reflexive self-monitoring that offsets the playful and performative aspects which the uses also incur.

Moreover, these processes take place in social settings characterised by self-regulation rather than institutional regulation of norms. Obviously, this opens the possibility for shifting the power relations of communication from explicit, institutional levels to more fluid, interpersonal levels. Institutions 'will lose much determinative influence of what is 'really going on' on the level of social communication and interaction' (Geser, 2002, p. 32). While this shift may not cause the demise of a publisher or broadcaster, it does serve to complicate the ramifications of audiencing.

## Adaptable audiencing

In terms of social relations, the concept of the audience encompasses the relations between producers and receivers mediated through various textual modes. Thus, mediated interpretive practices are at the core of what constitutes an audience. But these practices are differently contextualised both in institutional and interpersonal terms, and they give rise to different forms of interaction between producers and receivers.

Broadcast producers address their audiences as anonymous entities - broadcasting is, indeed, about the potential reach of anyone but no one in particular (Scannell, 2000). Broadcasters are institutionally located and audiences are positioned as part of physically bounded and stable communities, even when these communities are imagined or interpretive. The intensified audience interactions with broadcasters through email, sms or phone calls serve to highlight the reciprocity of communication between producers and audiences, whose engagement is called upon. However, these forms of interaction are still directed to institutional locations, defining the issues of interaction, and gatekeeping who gets a call through, an email cited, an icon displayed during a show.

Mobile communication is a stand-alone activity but also institutionally framed by content providers and operators, a fact that any parent paying the phone bills of teenagers will confirm. But the institutional framework is virtually invisible during use; speaking or texting seems institutionally unmediated and hence interaction is all. Mobiles are personalised in many ways. Interaction is transient, it is always to be interrupted or continued, and it cannot 'fall back' on institutional continuities of production. It has to be individually confirmed, continued or rejected; and its substance and form can be personally shaped and modified. Unlike broadcast audiences, mobile users are performers investing their energies in more transient media practices whose communicative rules they seem in a position to influence. Does this make them a non-audience?

It certainly makes them a different type of audience than broadcast audiences. If we retain the basic definition given above, that is, that mediated interpretive practices are at the core of what constitutes an audience, then mobile communicators *are* audiences: conversation as well as texting, image production and reception involve contextualised interpretations of sign systems. But broadcast and mobile audiences are positioned very differently in terms of spatio-temporal and institutional relations as we have seen. Spatial permeability, temporal flexibility and institutional invisibility all serve to foreground the procedural nature of signification, so 'audiencing' may be an apt term to denote what is going on in mobile communication. As we shall see below, the interactive nature of mobile communication serves to strengthen a sense of dynamic in these processes.[5] Still, since audiencing centrally concerns interpretive procedures, these processes must be differentiated in relation to the sign systems involved.

Mobile conversations, being personalised, synchronous dialogues, highlight the performative aspects of audiencing.[6] Moreover, in communicative terms, if not necessarily in social terms, they display the horizontal positioning of the speakers, unlike the more hierarchical positioning of broadcast audiences *vis-à-vis* the producer. Such audiences may explore para-social interactions (Horton & Wohl, 1956) in the privacy of their homes with public newscasters and gameshow hosts positioned within clear, institutional frameworks, and they often know that they are part of an audience.[7] Mobile communicators extend seemingly de-institutionalised discourses of intimacy with close friends or partners into public spaces. This horizontal positioning serves to strengthen communication between equals irrespective of location (peers, family, friends); and so we see that mobile calls will often deepen established bonds, at times to the exclusion of strangers.

According to the Italian ICT researcher Leopoldina Fortunati,

> the possibility of a nomadic intimacy is achieved, but at the same time there is the refusal to discover and directly experience everything that the social space can offer.

> (Fortunati, quoted in Geser, 2002)

Fortunati does not expand on the very fact that communication about intimacy may change when conducted in public and hence she fails to address what happens to audiencing when issues, which have been relegated to the private sphere of broadcast audiences, are taken into public. What 'nomadic intimacy' signals is the contested nature of the boundaries between public and private places, between social and virtual spaces, and between shared and private forms of communication.

As a communicative practice, nomadic intimacy is simultaneously a textual and social process. It may encompass discourses on private matters, and it will often encompass the deportment of the speakers, who may close off their body language or retreat from co-located social interaction, demonstrating 'the importance of maintaining a buffer around them'. This makes several researchers conclude that the extension of private space into public space becomes an encroachment upon that space. The callers 'colonize a part of the public sphere [sic] and reduce it slightly by their unwillingness to participate' (Ling, 2001, p. 16, 23). Still, such conclusions underestimate the socio-cultural varieties of mobile audiencing.

For the conflictual practices in negotiating public and private space are minimised when conversation is a more collective affair, as is often the case with children and young people who routinely interlace social and virtual interactions. As we noted, mobile communication both enables and enforces self-reflexive monitoring of various front-stage performances and this monitoring is intensified with users' oscillation between social and virtual practices. Here, intimate discourses are generated within collective and self-reflexive communicative processes that afford a self-consciousness of audiencing, a possibility of sharing and arguing about private issues, which may attain aspects of public performances, and publicness, as will be discussed below.

Sms and mms allow asynchronous communication with multiple recipients, and these practices facilitate swift communication from one to many to a degree that is impossible with mobile p2p conversation. Such features equally make these sign systems more similar to broadcast audiencing. Each recipient of a text message will know the phone number of the sender, but cannot trace other potential recipients. In social terms, these structures strengthen loose ties within and between networks, that is ties that lie dormant until it becomes relevant to make contact (Grannovetter, 1973). Unlike connections made to place-based audiences, as in broadcasting, or links made to de-localised individuals, as in mobile conversation, texting may link shifting networks of people as long as these have a mobile at hand.

*Thus a new, more fluid culture of social interaction can emerge which is less based on ex-ante agreements, but more on current and ad hoc coordination which allows people to adopt to unpredictable short-term change in circumstances, opportunities, or subjective preferences and moods.*

*(Geser, 2002, p. 16)*

Through its network links, sms eases the rapid formation and extension of groups. The ways in which these formations operate in relation to notions of audiences and publics are largely a result of differences in the aims of communication and in people's positioning relative to those aims.

## Portable publics

The proliferation and domestication of mobile communication through the 1990s has been instrumental in changing the conditions of group formation on interpersonal as well as on macro-levels. Gate crashing is now very much a result of potential partygoers having their handsets switched on and being able to locate and follow where the action is. In the sprawling urban centres, young people co-ordinate their daily, and particularly, nightly activities and interests through their mobiles. The devices not only accompany the male street cultures that young men, particularly working class, have traditionally shaped and shown, they also act as transformative agents of these cultures by affording a new sense of publicness: the users are at once in public and a (potential) public, they claim public settings while forming communicative networks on issues and interests that they may relate to other potential publics. While these networks are transient, they are nevertheless dialogic and self-defined, thus opening spaces of performative and playful reflection and deliberation.

Particularly for young women, this new sense of dual publicness seems of significance. Whether warranted or not, many female informants stress that their mobile increases their sense of security in public places, and hence the mobiles serve as enabling tools for young women to not only claim the night, but to claim public places as spaces of personal affinity and autonomy. But does this make them a public, even a potential one, as indicated above? The answer crucially depends on our position in addressing the contested discourses regarding publics, as well as when and where they may be located. As is evident from the above, mobile communication, by cutting across familiar oppositions, facilitates new sets of questions, asking also *how* publics may be formed and transformed.

To the extent that mobile communication advances a sense of belonging to public settings, a sense of being able to 'do' public communicative performances, on private matters, it also serves as an important lever of what social scientists define as civil society (for example, Lister, 1997, Janoski, 1998). The Swedish media researcher Peter Dahlgren, drawing on that tradition, has developed the conceptual dimension of civil society, a development that is particularly helpful in seeking to define the new constellations between audiences and publics brought about by contemporary media culture (Dahlgren, 1995, 2003). From his conceptual perspective, Dahlgren focuses on what he terms 'civic cultures', that is:

> ... *how people develop into citizens, how they come to see themselves as members and potential participants in societal development (...) The media, both the traditional*

*mass media and the newer interactive media, constitute the dominant site of modern public spheres, and thus via their form, content and specific media logics, contribute directly and routinely to the character of civic cultures.*

*(Dahlgren, 2003, p. 3)*

While Dahlgren does not ignore the empirical dimension of civic cultures, his conceptual dimension of civic cultures holds an innovative promise in seeking to define key elements in contemporary audience-public constellations. This conceptual take allows us to begin to ask how publics and audiences are resourced. What are the socio-cultural conditions by which social agency is achieved, practiced and opposed? In which ways do media (old and new) operate in relation to those processes? Answers do not focus upon the location of civic cultures as spatial categories - for example, in relation to the familiar distinction of Habermas between private and public spheres. Rather the answers focus on locating civic cultures as communicative practices that people shape across different settings and textual repertoires.

From such a perspective, it seems obvious that mobile communication may enhance a sense of affinity to public settings, of being entitled to speak and be heard, even if it is still too early to conclude what this mundane empowerment implies for social engagement and action in the longer term. It is also evident that, from the point of view of a civic cultures perspective, the practices of nomadic intimacy that mobile communication advances into public space are ways in which, not least, young people widen the scope of what may be defined as 'worthy' of public discourse and thereby add a new dimension to the 1970s feminist slogan that, 'the personal is political'.

On a grander scale, mobile phones, in addition to dynamically updated websites, have already had an immediate political impact. These new media have eased the rapid mobilisation of large-scale protests such as the anti-globalisation demonstrations at the WTO conference in Seattle in 1999, the World Bank meeting in Prague in 2000 and the successful overthrow of Philippine president Estrada in 2001. Their assumed political implications have caught the public and professional interest to a greater degree than is the case with the everyday uses (Geser, 2001; Rheingold, 2002; Pertierra et al. 2002). How may we understand such protests in relation to concepts of media audiences and publics?

Clearly, the mobilisations are different from audiences (and from audiencing) in their collective, physical manifestations and in their shared aims and actions. In some sense, they are more like crowds or mobs in that they seem amorphous from the outside and are adaptable to changing circumstances.[8] Still, unlike crowds in the traditional sense, rapid, mediated communication is instrumental to the formation of these protests, a factor that opens communicative spaces within the networks and between networks and the public spheres formed by broadcast media such as television.

For example, Pertierra et al. (2002) demonstrate that during the uprising in the Philippines, a host of text messages were initiated by organised, political activists and acted as catalysts to - rather than instigators of - political opposition which had already formed, not least through radio and television (a six-hour daily TV coverage of impeachment preceded the massive demonstrations in Manila). And so, while Rheingold's radical conclusions about spontaneous, political activism brought about by mobile media resonate better with the positive, commercial discourse on mobiles than with mundane empirical facts, research does validate the central importance played by mobiles and the Internet in the media ensemble:

> *These technologies allowed their users to momentarily suspend their class, educational and ideological differences, and establish virtual communities - of texters, web-surfers, etc. - that were united by their antipathy to the then acting President. These technologies thus facilitated communication and cooperation between groups normally located at opposing ends of the ideological divide.*

> *(Pertierra et al., 2002, p. 120)*

As the Philippine example demonstrates, mobile communication may buy into other forms of systematic deliberation, and the immediate activating force of the mobiles lies in their 'capacity to expedite the arrangement of rallies' (Pertierra et al., 2002, p. 121). Operating collectively through mediated communication and sharing a common aim of action, such protests do, indeed, resemble the traditional Habermasian notion of a public. Moreover, the existence of and contestation between several publics may arguably nurture members' reflexive communicative competencies and add to the effectiveness of their actions. Still, mobile protests also differ from received notions of a public in that the communicative spaces opened by these groups oscillate between individual and collective forms of communication; they enable brevity of information, not nuanced argumentation; issue-based action not systematic deliberation - be it in the idealist form of reaching consensus or in the positivist form of reducing complexity through the voicing of difference and disagreement. Hence, sustained political arguments in the familiar sense cannot be voiced or heard by the mobile publics, nor is communicative permanence secured, making it hard for institutional insights of mediation to be systematised and explored as learning processes for the future.

Mobile, civic cultures, as well as networked demonstrations, challenge our received notions of what constitutes audiences and publics, perhaps also what publicness is. As such, mobile and interactive media highlight the need for conceptual transformations in view of these trends. First, and most important, they enforce and allow us to frame our analytical questions differently. With Dahlgren, we may ask how publics are formed, not just who they are or where and when they are visible. That is an increased professional interest in the socio-cultural conditions of communicative agency. Second, we need to contextualise the mobile and interactive media uses within the entire media ensemble. From such a perspective, it seems evident that mobile media do not undermine or abandon the formation of audiences and publics as we know them; but they do serve to make these processes more complex. We can no longer assume that audiences are based on spatially segregated communities, nor that all publics are temporally stable fora of systematic and sustained argumentation. In tandem with the increasing importance played by mediated communication for social regulation, the formation of 'grand' publics diminish, or are accompanied by the formation of what we call 'portable' publics, whose composition is more flexible than traditional publics since they may change from issue to issue. Third, we need to study the relations between audiences and publics. The transient nature of the portable publics also makes them more permeable with 'nomadic' audiences. Since most people in networked societies variously occupy both positions, the important division is perhaps not so much between audiences and publics, but between online and offline groups. This development, in turn, adds to the social pressure put on traditional public spheres, since their existence cannot be taken for granted but has to be legitimated in action.

Individualisation in modernity both enhances and enforces continuous monitoring of social roles in all spheres of life. From that perspective, mobile audiences arguably ease the processes of monitoring by adding an extra interpretive dimension, highlighting, and often negotiating, the duality of social and virtual interactions. The monitoring going on in the portable publics, on a daily basis, between individual and collective interactions may afford public engagements and affinities that can spur public communication at large, while in itself seeming less geared towards sustained public deliberation and debate.

## Interactive expressiveness

So far, our analysis of mobiles has focused on their spatial, temporal and social aspects, what may be termed a user-centred perspective on mediated communication. But what do people talk about? Which types of print, visual and mixed messages circulate? These questions concern the meaning-making substance and form of mobile communication, and they focus on the media perspective on communication. Naturally, this perspective is crucial to a socio-cultural understanding of media - if mediated meaning-making was irrelevant to people why would they use media in the first place? So, a joint user and media perspective, social and textual, facilitates more nuanced studies (Drotner, 2000).

While this joint perspective is a demanding task in any media study, it is even more daunting in analyses of interactive media such as the web, email, gameboys and mobile phones. With these technologies, the text, always an elusive and contested entity, is apparent only at the moments of interaction, and in many cases it may be modified and deleted. Legally-protected rights of privacy make it even harder for the ambitious researcher to access textual transactions on mobile phones.[9]

Let us therefore start with a functional typology of mobile communication following Roman Jakobson's classic scheme (Jakobson, 1960/1985). At one extreme is the short message conveying the caller's wish for the recipient to perform some sort of action. Such messages serve a conative function. At the other extreme, there are messages whose substance is relatively unimportant but which operate as signs of connectivity. These messages serve a phatic function and are very common in mobile communication, particularly with young people and women (Drotner, 2001, Geser, 2002). Many mobile owners leave their phones on not so much for being available for calls but to have the satisfaction of hearing little beep tones when receiving a text message, often without bothering to read it. A similar phatic function is seen with another popular texting format, namely, the goodnight messages sent to partners and close friends.

The phatic function of connectivity demonstrates perhaps the greatest discrepancy between the evaluations made by users and non-users, and by adults and kids. Adults and non-users tend to judge mobile communication in terms of its effectiveness, economy and substance - all of which call for brevity and immediate relevance. Conversely, users evaluate mobile communication in terms of its affect, performativity and form. For example, in a qualitative study on children's media uses, a parent expressed near incomprehension of his daughter, aged nine, who would sms her best friend next door every morning, ten minutes before meeting her to go to school (Drotner, 2001). In a similar vein, repeated calls and text messages are deemed pointless by non-users on grounds of triviality, while users find satisfaction in these messages as affective tokens of social bonding. Thus, the phatic function serves to push the communicative focus of mobile interaction from substance to process, from *what* is being communicated to *that* communication takes place at all. The dispersion of audiences and publics across a variety of sites and sources of expression may add to this shift of focus in that commonality has to be continuously articulated and affirmed.

Mobile interaction not only serves different communicative functions. As we have already seen, it equally takes several forms. *Sms, mms* and calls on to email and web chats in the 3G systems. While all of these forms are interactive in nature, they nevertheless display increasing degrees of communicative complexity - and responsibility on the part of users. For example, the asynchronous, inexpensive and conventional character of sending an icon or a text message makes it less demanding as a communicative act for the sender as well as for the recipient.

Due to the limitation of characters, the sender may resort to standard formulations in texting and feel less pressure on individualised impression management than when placing a regular call. Especially for boys and young men the communicative standardisation, and hence emotional distance, implied in short text messages ease contact with the opposite sex - even to the point of candidness: 'ice can be broken, intentions declared and invitations offered, all without the risk of embarrassment' (Plant, 2000, p. 19). Thus, boys and young men will send text messages and icons with sexualised content to girls they fancy - as emotional test balloons let out from a distance: 'Hi, sweetie! So wonderfl to b with u 2day. So GOOD we talked yesterday!!! Just want to say ILU. Happy training! xxx T' (Rasmussen, 2002, p. 19).

Receiving and responding to standard icons, text messages and calls demands knowledge of communicative variations in order to correctly decode the various forms and act appropriately. As we saw, mobile communication foregrounds self-regulation of social roles to a greater degree than mass-mediated forms, and hence it involves more personalised fine-tuning of communicative competencies and textual repertoires. One must know when to decline a response, answer an sms with an sms, or upgrade the intensity of communication and make a call. Thus, mobile phones not only demand extensive monitoring of social roles, as already noted, but since these social roles are largely constituted and played out through communicative processes, the social monitorings are simultaneously textual monitorings.

If radio and particularly television have rightly been seen as windows to the world opened from within the living room (Meyrowitz, 1985), and if the recent trends of reality formats on television and the Internet may be seen as mediations between social and virtual intimacies (Mehl, 1996, Dovey, 2000), then the extensive take up of mobile phones in many ways signals an extension of the living room into the world. Or more precisely, they signal a range of intimate, mediated interactions across social and virtual spaces and they do so around the clock. This transformation of public space into a 'common living room' (Kopomaa, 2000) is routinely deplored as an intrusion of the trivial and mundane into the loftier, more abstract realms of publicness, both in its spatial and social sense. Alternatively, the transformation is hailed as a victory of innovation and individual activism undermining old-fashioned institutions and hierarchical structures. These dichotomous discourses tend to underestimate the complexities involved in practicing the social and textual 'mobilization' of mediated communication. These practices involve tentative transformations of our understandings of both audiences and publics, as we have seen.

## Media and media studies on the move?
So far, the Internet has claimed much more intensive scholarly interest than mobile phones in exploring the possible transformations of audiences and publics, and few attempts have been made to relate the two sets of transformations. Scholars from audience studies primarily focus on everyday uses of the Internet including gaming, chatting and texting (for example, Sefton-Green, 1998; Svenningson, 2001; Wellman & Haythornthwaite, 2002); ICT researchers study e-learning and computer users' acquisition of digital competencies - mostly within formal settings

of teaching (O'Malley, 1995; Garrison & Anderson, 2003). In addition, scholars of political communication focus on the ways in which democracy and citizenship may, or may not, be resourced by net communication (Schiller, 1999; Granjon, 2001; Jenkins & Thornburn, 2003).

There are good reasons to argue for a transgression of these professional boundaries. First, most people occupy positions as both audiences and publics at various times and in various sites and settings, and researchers may easily overstate the importance played by one or the other by focusing on either and so miss the interlacing of both. Second, as Peter Dahlgren (2003) argues, we need to understand why people join, evade or are excluded from participating in public forms of communication, and the answers lie, not in the public sphere itself, but in civic cultures enabling or disabling social affinities, and in the fissures generated by media that transgress or challenge established boundaries between the two. Hence, we need to study the relations between audiences and publics from a more holistic perspective. Third, and perhaps most important, Internet and mobile technologies converge in the 3G handsets. The Internet operates on a global scale, and on both civic and commercial grounds, even if the latter seem to encroach upon the former. Thus, users may appropriate Internet communication both as citizens and consumers, and intricate mixtures of the two (as on political consumer sites). Mobile devices operate on strictly commercial grounds, and to most people they do not have global reach. Thus, users may appropriate mobile communication mostly as consumers, even if the portable nature of mobile phones, as we have seen, may facilitate an affinity to public space and to speaking in public (and as a public), not least for groups that have been marginal to these fora in the past.

The convergence of mobile and Internet communication is likely to throw into relief some well-known problematics as well as some new possibilities. The telecommunications industry is determined to reap the commercial gains in advancing mobile services, despite dot-com setbacks and real divisions between content providers and operators. The 3G technology is being introduced in Australia and Europe and it is already widely adopted in Japan. In the push for more commercial services - mms and web services offering gambling, games and girls - more big players are likely to use gatekeeping formats and forms of communication. Conversely, it is precisely these multi-functional formats that hold the greatest, creative potentials for users - they can become performers in multimedia interactions and advance their multimodal competencies.

Hence, we face a scenario, familiar to earlier media developments, in which some of the important stakes are the power over the rights to access and use; the universality of information and entertainment; and the legal status of intellectual property rights. While mobile technologies do not change the stakes in this scenario of the immediate future, at least they add yet another medium through which audiences and performers, publics and producers, may lay claim to these stakes. Perhaps their greatest potential lies in the ways in which they widen the subjective conditions for democratic engagement. This is not so much in facilitating visible, political demonstrations as in the more taken-for-granted practicing of publicness, in extending our imagination of what it takes to perform audiencing, of which issues can be shared through mediation, to partake in shifting the boundaries between public and private domains, between the modes of talk and the means of action.

## Notes

1. I would like to thank the following colleagues for stimulating discussions and timely critique: Peter Dahlgren, Daniel Dayan, Ditte Laursen, Sonia Livingstone, Mirca Madianou, Dominique Mehl, Ulrike Meinhof, and Roberta Pearson. A shortened version of this chapter has appeared in *Journal of Media Practice* Vol 6:1.

2. The camera and transistor radio are important mobile media, too, and share central aspects with contemporary mobile media: like many interactive media, the camera puts the user in a position as producer of visual images and serves as lever of people's visual awareness; like most portable media of today, the transistor radio is first appropriated by younger people and operates as an integral element in youth culture. Both are personalised media with a rapid take-up upon introduction.

3. Japan's largest operator is NTT DoCoMo (DoCoMo means anywhere) that in 2001 held 60 per cent of the national market and which in 1999 launched the so-called i-mode that allows email communication, access to Internet with highly popular dating sites, which are mobile chat rooms. The operator KDDI has introduced a camera unit, a GPS navigation system and a moving image transmission system, while J-Phone has been successful with Sha-mail through which users may send and receive still and moving images along with text mails. In 2001, KDDI and J-Phone each held 18 per cent of the Japanese market (Nikkei Research 2003).

4, The reality effect of the public sphere ideal includes, not only the obedience to its ramifications but, equally important, the challenges to and violations of the ideal, e.g. through minute and concrete accounts in the public sphere of sex and violence, and through the publication of celebrities' and politicians' private affairs. This dualism is evident throughout modern media history, as in the so-called penny dreadfuls of the 1840s in Britain, in the popular press early in the early 20th century and in today's webcam mockeries.

5. That mobile communication seems to highlight the processual, fluid nature of audiencing more than is the case with broadcast audiencing should not be conflated with degrees of interpretive activity. Both broadcast and mobile audiences are involved in sense-making processes of involvement, comment and possibly critique.

6. Similar performative aspects are evident in the use of 3G technologies on dating sites, when pictures are taken, or sound bites recorded and sent. Conversely, the GPS facilities are less conspicuous than sms, emailing or going on the Internet, since they operate without any actions

on the part of the user. This invisibility seems, indeed, part of the problem with children's use of such devices - they don't know they are being tracked (Takeyama 2003).

7. Fan cultures and ritualised live broadcasts are clear examples of reflexive audiences (e.g. Katz & Dayan 1992, Stacey 1994, Baym 2000). But, in more mundane terms, reflexive audiencing is found in people's watching of the national news, in net gaming and in special radio channels for e.g. teenage listeners.

8. Howard Rheingold's book *Smart Mobs* (Rheingold 2002) is a clever pun on the relations between social formations and mobile technologies.

9. Most "textual" analyses of mobile communication rest on users' accounts or logs or on archival material provided by individuals and institutions such as is the case with the text message archive at the Finnish Information Society Research Centre. Examples of more textual approaches to mobile phone culture, focusing on single entities, are found in e.g. Androutsopoulos & Schmidt 2002, Kasesniemi & Rautiainen 2002, while Laursen (forthcoming) studies sms and conversation sequences.

## References

Androutsopoulos, Jannis & Gurly Schmidt (2002) 'Sms-Kommunikation: Etnografische Gattungsanalyse am Beispiel einer Kleingruppe', *Zeitschrift für angewandte Linguistik* 36: 49-80.

Baecker, Dirk (1996) 'Oszillierende Öffentlichkeit', in Rudolf Maresch (ed.) *Medien und Öffentlichkeit: Positionierungen, Symptome, Simulationsbrüche.* Munich: Boer Verlag.

Baym, N. K. (2000) *Tune In, Log On: Soaps, Fandom, and Online Community.* Thousand Oaks, CA: Sage.

Beck, Ulrich & Elisabeth Beck-Gernsheim (2002) *Individualization.* London: Sage.

Cancel, Claus (2003) 'Mobilvaner' [Mobile Habits], *Politiken* 5.6.: 19.

Castells, M. (1996/1998) *The Rise of the Network Society.* Malden, MA: Blackwell.

Couldry, Nick (2003) *Media Rituals: A Critical Approach.* London: Routledge.

Dahlgren, Peter (1995) *Television and the Public Sphere: Citizenship, Democracy and the Media.* London: Sage.

Dahlgren, Peter (2003) 'Net-Activism and the Emergence of Global Civic Cultures'. Paper presented at The 16th Nordic Conference for Media and Communication Research, Kristiansand, Norway, August.

Dovey, John (2000) *Freakshow: First Person Media and Factual Television.* London: Pluto Press.

Drotner, K. (1999) 'Dangerous Media? Panic Discourses and Dilemmas of Modernity', *Paedagogica Historica* 35, 3: 593-619.

Drotner, K. (2000) 'Difference and Diversity: Trends in Young Danes' Media Cultures', *Media, Culture and Society* 22, 2: 149-66.

Drotner, Kirsten (2001) *Medier for fremtiden: børn, unge og det nye medielandskab.* Copenhagen: Høst & søn.

Fish, Stanley (1979) *Is There a Text in This Class: the Authority of Interpretive Communities.* Harvard, MA: Harvard University Press.

Garrison, D. R. & Terry Anderson (2003) *E-learning In the 21st Century: A Framework for Research and Practice.* London: Routledge-Falmer.

Geser, Hans (2001) *On the Functions and Consequences of the Internet for Social Movements and Voluntary Associations.* University of Zürich. www.socio.ch/movpar/t_hgeser3a.htm (consulted 9.6.2003).

Geser, Hans (2002) *Towards A Sociology of the Mobile Phone.* University of Zürich. www.socio.ch/mobile/t_geser1.htm (consulted 9.6.2003).

Giddens, Anthony (1991) *Modernity and Self-Identity.* Cambridge: Polity Press.

Gillis, John R. (1974) *Youth and History: Tradition and Change in European Age Relations, 1700-Present.* New York: Academic Press.

Goffman, Erving (1963) *Behavior in Public Places: Note on the Social Organization of Gatherings.* New York: Free Press.

Goffman, Erving (1971) *Relations in Public: Micro Studies of the Public Order.* New York: Basic Books.

Granjon, Fabien (2001) *L'Internet militant: mouvement social et usage des réseaux télématiques.* Rennes: Éditions Apogée.

Grannovetter, Mark (1973) 'The Strength of Weak Ties', *American Journal of Sociology* 78, 6: 1360-80.

Habermas, Jürgen (1962/1989) *The Structural Transformation of the Public Sphere.* Cambridge, MA: MIT Press. Orig. 1962.

Horton, D. & R. Wohl (1956) 'Mass Communication and Para-social Interaction: Observations on Intimacy at a Distance', *Psychiatry* 19, 3: 215-29.

Husén, T. (1986) *The Learning Society Revisited.* Oxford: Pergamon Press.

Impe, Marc van (2003) 'The Market for Ringtones and Logos will be Non-existent in 2005', *Nordic Wireless Watch* 13.12. www.nordicwirelesswatch.com/wireless/story.html?story_id=2565 (consulted 8.6.2003).

Jakobson, Roman (1960/1985) 'Closing Statement: Linguistics and Poetics,' pp. 147-75 in Robert E. Innis (ed.) *Semiotics: An Introductory Anthology* Bloomington: Indiana University Press. Orig. 1960.

James, Allison et al. (1998) *Theorizing Childhood.* Cambridge: Polity Press.

Janoski, Thomas (1998) *Citizenship and Civil Society.* Cambridge: Cambridge University Press.

Jenkins, Henry & David Thornburn (eds) (2003) *Democracy and the New Media.* Cambridge, MA: MIT Press.

Jensen, Joli (1990) *Redeeming Modernity: Contradictions in Media Criticism.* Newbury Park, CA: Sage.

Kasesniemi, Eija-Liisa & Pirjo Rautiainen (2002) 'Mobile Culture of Children and Teenagers in Finland', pp. 170-92 in James E. Katz & Mark Aakhus (eds) *Perpetual Contact: Mobile Communication, Private Talk, Public Performance* Cambridge: Cambridge University Press.

Katz, Elihu & Daniel Dayan (1994) *Media Events: The Live Broadcasting of History.* Cambridge: Harvard University Press.

Kioka, Yasumasa (2003) 'Dating Sites and the Japanese Experience'. www.childnet-int.org/downloads/tokyo%20conference%20proceedings.pdf (consulted 9.6.2003)

Kopomaa, Timo (2000) *Speaking Mobile: The City in Your Pocket.* Helsinki: Gaudeamus. Outline on: www.hut.fi/Yksikot/YTK/julkaisu/mobile.html (consulted 9.6.2003).

Larsen, Bent S. (2000) *Medier til hverdag, en undersøgelse af mediebrug og hverdagsliv.* [Everyday Media: A Study on Media Uses and Everyday Life] Ph.d. dissertation. Faculty of the Humanities: University of Copenhagen.

Laursen, Ditte (forthcoming) 'Please Reply! The Replying Norm in Adolescent SMS Communication'. In Richard Harper et al. (eds) *The Inside Text: Social Perspectives on SMS in the Mobile Age* Dordrecht: Kluwer Academic Publishers.

Licoppe, Christian & Jean-Philippe Heurtin (2002) 'France: Preserving the Image', pp. 94-109 in James E. Katz & Mark Aakhus (eds) *Perpetual Contact: Mobile Communication, Private Talk, Public Performance* Cambridge: Cambridge University Press.

Ling, Richard Seyler (1997) "'One Can Talk about Common Manners': The Use of Mobile Telephones in Inappropriate Situations". In Leslie Haddon (ed.) *Themes in Mobile Telephony. Final Report of the Cost 248 Home and Work Group* Farsta: Telia.

Ling, Richard Seyler (2000) *Norwegian Teens, Mobile Telephony and SMS Use in School.. FoU Report 7* Oslo: Telenor Research and Development.

Ling, Richard Seyler (2001) *The Social Juxtaposition of Mobile Telephone Conversations and Public Spaces.* Oslo: Telenor Research and Development. www.telenor.no/fou/publisering/rapporter/R_45_2001.pdf.

Lister, Ruth (1997) *Citizenship: Feminist Perspectives.* London: Macmillan.

Luhmann, Niklas (1995) *Die Realität der Massenmedien.* Opladen: Westdeutscher Verlag.

Lumio, Martti & Lucia C. Sinigaglia (2003) *Telecommunications in Europe* Brussels: Eurostat. www.europa.eu.int/comm/eurostat/Public/datashop/print-product/EN?catalogue= Eurostat&product =KS-NP-03-012-__-N-EN&mode=download (consulted 8.6.2003).

Masuda, Y. (1980) *The Information Society.* Tokyo: Institute for the Information Society.

Mead, George H. (1934) *Mind, Self, and Society.* Chicago, IL: University of Chicago Press.

Mehl, Dominique (1996) *La Télévision de l'intimité.* Paris: Seuil.

Meyrowitz. Joshua (1985) *No Sense of Place: The Impact of Electronic Media on Social Behavior.* New York: Oxford University Press.

Neal, Stephen (1980) *Genre.* London: British Film Institute.

Nikkei Research (2003) "Japanese Monthly Market Update", June. www. Nikkei-r.co.jp/English/mag/magazine0206.htm (consulted 8.6.2003).

O'Malley, Claire (ed.) (1995) *Computer Supported Collaborative Learning.* Berlin: Springer.

Pertierra, Raul et al. (2002) *Txt-ing: Cellphones and Philippine Modernity.* Manila: De La Salle University Press.

Plant, Sadie (2000) *On the Mobile: the Effects of Mobile Telephones on Social and Individual Life.* www.motorola.com/mot/documents/0,,297,00.doc (consulted 10.6.2003).

Qvortrup, Jens (2000) "Macroanalysis of Childhood", pp. 77-97 in Pia H.Christensen & Allison James (eds) *Research With Children: Perspectives and Practices* London, New York: Falmer Press.

Rasmussen, Ditte (2002) "Sms: mere end en sprogtrend" [Sms: more than a linguistic trend], *Vandfanget* 7, 2: 18-20.

Rasmussen, Terje (2000) *Social Theory and Communication Technology.* Aldershot: Ashgate.

Rheingold, Howard (2002) *Smart Mobs: The New Social Revolution.* Cambridge, MA: Perseus Publishing.

Scannell, Paddy (1988) *"Radio Times*: The Temporal Arrangements of Broadcasting in the Modern World", in P. Drummond & R. Paterson (eds) *Television and Its Audiences* London: British Film Institute.

Scannell, Paddy (2000) 'For-anyone-as-someone Structures', *Media, Culture & Society* 22, 1: 5-24.

Schiller, Dan (1999) *Digital Capitalism.* Cambridge, MA: Cambridge University Press.

Sefton-Green, Julian (ed.) (1998) *Digital Diversions: Youth Culture in the Age of Multimedia.* London: UCL Press.

Silverstone, Roger & Eric Hirsch (1992) *Consuming Technologies: Media and Information in Domestic Spaces.* London: Taylor & Francis.

Stacey, Jackie (1994) *Star Gazing: Hollywood Cinema and Female Spectatorship.* London: Routledge.

Stehr, Nico (1994) *Knowledge Societies.* London: Sage.

Svenningson, Malin (2001) *Creating a Sense of Community: Experiences From a Swedish Web Chat.* Ph.d. dissertation. Linköping University, Sweden.

Takeyama, Masanao (2003) 'Children and Mobile Technology: the Japanese Experience'. www.childnet-int.org/ downloads/tokyo%20conference%20proceedings.pdf (consulted 9.6.2003).

Wellman, Barry & Caroline Haythornthwaite (eds) (2002) *The Internet in Everyday Life.* Oxford: Blackwell.

Ulrike Hanna Meinhof

# Appendix: Audiences and publics: comparing semantic fields across different languages

*'When I use a word', Humpty Dumpty said in a rather scornful tone, 'it means just what I choose it to mean - neither more nor less'.*

*'When I make a word do a lot of work like that... I always pay it extra'.*

*(Lewis Carroll, Alice in the Looking Glass, 1872, here reprinted 1973; p 274-5)*

## Introduction

With this appendix we attempt to sketch out the semantic fields of 'audiences' and 'publics' as these words are put to work in selected European languages, focusing on the mother-tongue languages of the contributors to this volume and the target languages of their research. The decision to include this appendix arose from discussions among the contributors when it emerged that key words and concepts often have different meanings in the linguistic and epistemological context of our various academic traditions. It also aims to redress, where possible, the undue dominance within media studies of English-language concepts. When adopted uncritically, a simple translation of concepts from the English may hinder and obscure rather than help to clarify both theoretical exposition and the analysis of empirical phenomena in other linguistic, cultural and intellectual contexts. As Kirsten Drotner observes:

> *comparing the semantic fields of 'audience' and 'public' in English and in most lan-*
> *guages on the European continent, one is struck by the absence of the term 'audience'*
> *as a commonly used phrase in continental languages. This lack includes German, the*
> *mother tongue of Jürgen Habermas whose* Strukturwandel der Öffentlichkeit *has*
> *been instrumental in much debate in media studies over the last 20 years and an,*
> *often critical, instrument in the development of audience studies. It seems paradoxi-*
> *cal that the international scientific community has struggled to unravel the complex*
> *relations between audiences and publics and come to terms with their political impli-*
> *cations without realising the fact that English is the only major scientific language in*
> *which the term 'audience' figures as a common category.*

These terminological differences, and the potential problems arising from adopting terms with different connotations, prompted the writing of the dictionary entries in this appendix. The concepts selected for our appendix are investigated in relation to the different linguistic and conceptual traditions of our respective countries. Our aim is to draw a map of overlapping conceptual fields relating to 'audiences' and 'publics', as these frame our debates in this volume. At the very least, we hope to clarify what may cause considerable confusion when terms are translated or adopted into different languages without any attempt to uncover the different implications and evaluative connotations of certain concepts. As will become apparent below, the differences are especially marked between English/French and the other European languages.

Like all words, the meanings of 'audience' and 'public' have not remained fixed during their long histories. The 'open class' of words in the lexicon of any language is the least stable of all and is constantly evolving. Words are borrowed from other languages, they expand, contract or split, they move up or down the evaluative ladder, they form derivatives and compounds, they are part of constantly evolving sub-fields of synonyms, antonyms and hyponyms. They acquire metaphoric or technical meanings separate from the literal, every-day or 'folk-linguistic' usage and so on. Words in semantic fields are like particles, in that any movement or realignment of one area often affects another. These re-significations may no longer be visible on the surface of a language at any particular moment in its evolution. Hence tracing the origins allows us not only to uncover some of the archaeology of our lexicon but also to reflect on some interconnections and evaluative connotations which may otherwise remain obscure.

The most important contribution of these appended lexical entries from a range of European languages - Danish, German, Greek, English, French and Slovenian - is simply to make English and non-English native speakers and readers of our chapters (here written in the English language) aware of the fact that, within our respective mother tongues, we cannot assume equivalence of meaning. *Mouse or Rat* is the title of a recent study by Umberto Eco (2003), with the telling subtitle *Translation as Negotiation*. The latter process is precisely what we are hoping to engage our readers with - a more consciously negotiated platform for our discussions about people and processes in the mediated world of cultural dialogue. Whether a mouse is or is not a rat (in Latin, the same word, 'mus', refers to either) may well be another 'Alice in Wonderland' question. Our dictionary gives us the opportunity to define either one of these in the context of their native linguistic and cultural habitat. Like all dictionary entries, these invite browsing rather than consecutive reading. Rather than summarising the similarities and differences between our languages in one interconnecting piece, we have kept the specific entries separate even where similar points emerge. There are, however, some very notable overlaps and gaps, which we summarise below.

## Comparative comments

Etymologically, because of their roots in Latin, the two key terms 'audience' and 'public' have more or less obvious cognates in all our languages, with the exception of Greek, and Slovenian, in the case of audience, but their semantics differ widely (see below). The root of the word 'public' (English), 'public'/'publique' (French), 'Publikum' (Danish and German), 'publika' (Slovenian) is in all cases the Latin word 'publicus'; the root of the word 'audience' (English), 'audience'/ 'auditeur' (French), 'Audienz' (German), 'audiens' (Danish), is Latin 'audientia'/ 'audire'.

Only the English seems to have a more or less binary division between 'public' and 'audience', with partially marked positive or negative connotations respectively, although all languages have words to capture the entire semantic field (for example, German 'Öffentlichkeit' vs. 'Masse'), often with positive or negative connotations. Furthermore, only the English and the French seem to use the word 'public' ('public'/'publique') as a generic word which encompasses the meaning of 'audience', together with a normative connotation which links it to the common good. The other languages do not have a normative distinction based on the root of the word 'public' but employ different words for the normative connotation. Hence, 'audience' in German is 'Publikum', in Danish it is 'publikum', in Greek it is 'akrostirio' or 'teletheates', in Slovenian it is 'občinstvo', 'publika', 'poslušalstvo', 'gledalstvo', or 'bralstvo'. The normative public or public sphere in German is Öffentlichkeit', in Danish it is 'offentlighed', in Greek it is 'koino' or 'dymosia', and in Slovenian it is 'javnost'.

Apart from general terms for 'audience', all our languages have related terms, which differentiate the channel of communication according to whether it is auditory, visual/ audiovisual, or visual only. See, for example, English, 'listener'; German, 'Zuhörer'; Danish, 'tilhører'; English, 'viewer'; German, 'Zuschauer'; French 'spectateur', 'téléspectateur'; and English, 'reader'; German, 'Leser'; French, 'lecteur', etc. Also, most languages can further expand the terminology within the lexical field, according to academic, official and everyday usage (for example, academic German 'RezipientIN').

However, in some specialised fields the French term 'auditeur' carries connotations of a 'circumscribed activity'. This specialised meaning also exists in German and in English (to audit a course) but only in a university setting: here the term 'Hörer', though not 'Zuhörer', is used for someone who has enrolled to listen to some lectures without undergoing a degree course. In Danish, 'auditør' is a specialised term denoting a public official who deals with, for example, military offences. A specialised meaning of 'audience' in the sense of a formal hearing with someone of superior status also exists in English, French, German and Danish.

## Dictionary entries

Entries are listed in the following order: English (Sonia Livingstone), German (Ulrike H. Meinhof), Danish (Kirsten Drotner), Greek (Mirca Madianou), Slovenian (Sabina Mihelj), and French (Daniel Dayan). The categories in our dictionary entries do not all follow identical patterns but are intended to cover the most relevant information about the semantic fields of 'audience' and 'public' in our respective languages. They comprise all or most of the following categories: current established dictionary meaning, etymology, typical usage, connotations and associations, derivatives and relatives. Each entry includes a commentary on the most relevant aspects in each language, including the use of specialised academic terminology.

## English (Sonia Livingstone)

### *'Audience'*

#### Current established dictionary meaning
Noun: (1a) the act or state of hearing. (1b) a formal hearing or interview (with the Pope, the King). (1c) an opportunity of being heard (being given an audience with). (2a) a group of listeners or spectators. (2b) a reading, viewing, or listening public. (2c) a group of ardent admirers or devotees (e.g. see Longman's Dictionary of the English Language, Merriam-Webster online dictionary).

#### Origin of term/history
Middle English (Fourteenth century), from Middle French, from Latin, *audientia,* from *audient-, audiens,* present participle of *audire* ( to hear).

#### Typical usage
Collective term for people attending a public communication, whether hearing or viewing, whether co-located or dispersed, e.g. an audience for television, a concert, the theatre or a political meeting.

#### Connotations and associations
The collectivity here is commonly, though not necessarily, understood by association with the masses (that is, as an aggregate of like-minded, possibly irrational or emotional individuals) and as passive in role (receivers rather than participators in or producers of the communication). Hence 'audience', especially by comparison with 'public', is often taken as a disparaging, even a negative term.

#### Derivatives
John Fiske (1992) transforms the noun into a verb, 'audiencing', to convey the active role of participating as an audience in communication; increasingly used in cultural and communication theory in the plural only, 'audiences', to convey the heterogeneity and diversity within 'the audience'.

### Relatives

Viewers (of television), listeners (of radio, music); less often used in relation to print media or interactive media (where consumer - q.v., or user, are being applied, albeit uneasily).

## 'Public'

### Current established dictionary meaning

As an adjective: (1a) Exposed to general view; open. (1b) Well-known, prominent ('a public figure'). (1c) Perceptible, material. (2a) of, relating to, or affecting all the people or the whole area of a nation or state ('public law'). (2b) of or relating to a government.

As a noun: (1)the people as a whole; populace. (2) a group or section of people having common interests or characteristics (' the reading public', a film star's public). In public ('in public view').

### Origin of term/history

Middle English *publique* (Fourteenth century), from Middle French, from Latin *publicus;* akin to Latin *populus* meaning, the people. Possibly influenced by *pubes* - grown-up, adult (see Longman's Dictionary of the English Language).

### Typical usage

Used so widely, and as part of so many noun phrases, as to combine and confuse the distinct but overlapping meanings above - visible, prominent, perceptible, governmental, national, universal, popular, social, humanitarian, accessible, open. Most often used to refer to the population of a nation, although occasionally of the globe, insofar as they may be assumed to have a set of common concerns, interests, understanding and needs.

### Connotations and associations

A collectivity that is assumed to be homogeneous, singular in its actions and claims. The recent academic attempt to pluralise 'publics', to convey heterogeneity, is not widely used beyond the academy, and introduces confusion regarding the claims, scope and interrelations of these 'publics'.

### Derivatives

Many. In addition to those noted above, there are: public domain, public convenience, public house, public enemy, public health, public relations, public school, etc. Also - publishing, publicity.

## Relatives

See list of terms under 'typical usage'. Many relatives or synonyms take adjective and noun forms (popular/the population; national/the nation).

## Comment

The dictionary meaning for 'audience' (c.f. Longman and Merriam-Webster dictionaries) combines both ends of the communication chain - hearing and being heard, though the more common use is to stress the role of the hearer or receiver rather than the speaker or producer of communication. This definition includes the 'rational' dimension of hearing - as a public, and the emotional dimension - as an ardent fan. It also encompasses both the act (e.g. paying attention to a communication) and the collectivity of individuals who commit the act. However, the common usage often conveys a negative meaning when applied to mass-mediated communication (though not for live events). Reception studies, on the other hand, represents an approach to audiences that seeks to emphasise the agency involved in receiving or decoding a communication text, together with the symbolic and social links between receivers and producers. Particularly useful as a collective noun that spans media - can be used to include readers, viewers and listeners of radio, press, books, television and the cinema.

Significantly, for a changing and converging communications environment, it does not happily encompass interactive or online media - computers, telephone, games machines, Internet. Hence the term 'user' or 'consumer' of media is gaining currency. However, it is significant that until recently the consumer has been used far more in an official discourse of markets, economics, business and government policy than as part of ordinary language. In ordinary language, people shop, buy, want, need, use, but they do not 'consume' or think of themselves as consumers. Note also that it is mobilised neutrally by official discourses (consumers are spending more) or theorised within economics (consumer confidence measures) or, more negatively and critically, in sociology (through the theory of mass society - mass consumption). More recently, the term has gained some positive connotations, through the advent of consumer rights as part of a broader growth in rights discourse. Very recently, 'the consumer' has become a term in official discourse connoting being a beneficiary of government policy, so gaining the connotation of citizenship (as in 'citizen-consumer)'. Yet 'consumer', like 'user', lacks the collectivity of an audience and, together with 'public', all three terms lack the clear reference to communication - the encoding and decoding of a symbolic message - thereby rendering 'audience' of continued utility.

As regards the dictionary definition of 'public', it is worth noting that the link to political theory, democracy and citizenship is one made by academics, but is only indirectly present in the dictionary definitions. Notably, there is little or nothing in the dictionary definition which implies agency - active participation, deliberation or mobilisation, even though, in academic discourse, 'public' is normatively marked as positive (rational, active, collective, embodying both rights and responsibilities, and strongly linked to citizenship). Further, although the dictionary definition is descriptive/neutral rather than clearly positive in its connotations (think of publicity, public house), in ordinary language the public is often contrasted positively with the private (as in public service, public interest, public welfare); what the public wants has rhetorical force, though it may not be respected (cf. public opinion). Note that there are many more adjectival uses than noun uses, though it may be that the noun is used more frequently.

## German (Ulrike Meinhof)

Translations of (and the German conceptualisation of) 'audience', as well as of 'public', overlap insofar as they refer to a collective of people who are recipients of cultural artefacts or participants in cultural events. Hence it is impossible to make a clear distinction between them to capture the different connotations of the English terms. Terms differ, however, depending on specialist or general usage. The most usual translations of both 'audience' and 'public' are:

• for specialist usage in German media theory: *RezipientIN* (m/f).

• for general usage: *Publikum* (neuter) or, if specified according to medium of reception: for listening, the singular or plural *Zuhörer, with collective Zuhörerschaft; for viewing, sg or pl Zuschauer*; for reading, sg or pl. *Leser* with collective *Leserschaft* (f), *Leserkreis* (m).

## *'Audience'*

### Dictionary translations

Langenscheidt English/ German (1977): (1). *Anhören, Gehör* (for example, a hearing); (2) *Audienz:* a formal reception or hearing with a high status official (from the Latin *Audientia*, meaning hearing or attention from audire; hence, *hören* (to hear, to listen); (3) *Zuhörerschaft, Publikum, Anwesende, Besucher;* (4) *Leserkreis.*

Collins English/German (1994): (1) *Publikum* (Theater, TV) *Zuschauer, Zuhörer, Zuhörerschaft*; (2) *Audienz* (formal interview).

Oxford Duden English/German (1997): (1) *Publikum* (listeners, spectators); (2) *Audienz*; (3. *Publikum* (readers), *Leserkreis* (readership).

## 'Public'

### Dictionary translations

Langenscheidt English/German (1977): (1) *Öffentlichkeit*; (2) *Öffentlichkeit, die Leute, das Publikum, Kreise, Welt.*

Collins English/German (1994): (1) *Öffentlichkeit*; (2) See also: *theaterinteressierte Öffentlichkeit*) Oxford Duden English/German (1997): (1) *Öffentlichkeit, Allgemeinheit*; (2) *Publikum, Leserschaft.*

### Current established dictionary meaning(s) of translated term and its synonyms

Publikum (n)(noun) (see also: *Zuschauer/ Zuhörerschaft*) refers to:(1) Collective term for listeners (*Zuhörer*) or viewers (*Zuschauer*) of an event or a genre/setting/media (perceived as a unit). (2) Collective term for a group of people who are interested in art, science etc. (3) Collective term for visitors to a place, a pub, a restaurant etc.

### Origin of translated term and historical development

*Das Publikum* has the same origin as the English word *public*: Latin: *publicus, meaning öffentlich* (see entry under 'public'); (Theater) *Publikum. Publicum vulgus*, meaning das gemeine *Volk* or general public. As a noun it is only used in the sense of 'audience'. As an adjective and verb derivative, *'publik', 'publizieren'* etc are loan words and (high register) synonyms for German *'öffentlich* 'and *'veröffentlichen'* (i.e. the English making public or 'publish'). The term *'Publikum'* only came into use with the advent of professional actors and is probably derived from French or English. Before then, in all early drama there was no separation between performers and audiences, since performers emerged from within the audience and acted as their representatives. Even in medieval drama in the market place, the *'Publikum'* still emerged from amongst the performers (*Darsteller*) and had to be given space to be heard (Von Wilpert, 1969, p.607-8).

### Typical usage

Theatre/ live performances/ media (film/ tv/ cinema/ newspaper). Derived from the theatre, but now applicable to all mediated settings as well (often as a compound - *Fernsehpublikum* for TV, *Theaterpublikum* for theatre, *Kinopublikum* for cinema).

### Connotations and associations

*'Publikum'* stresses a collective but this is seen in neutral terms. It can have positive or negative connotations by the addition of evaluative adjectives: *'kritisches/ interessiertes Publikum"*, *'unkritisches/ desinteressiertes P"'* (critical/ uncritical;

interested, uninterested audience/ public. In these combinations *kritisches Publikum*, for example, would translate into English as 'critical public/ audience').

## Derivatives
Related idioms and derivatives only exist for the other meaning of 'public', as in 'public sphere', which translates as *öffentlich'*, *Öffentlichkeit*: *'publizieren'* (to publish), *publik machen* (to make public). (*Publik* is restricted to educated usage).

## Relatives/ synonyms
*Zuhörer,* 'listener' can be singular or collective. *Zuhörerschaft* (literally: *'hören'* and the particle *'zu'* from the preposition 'to' implies active listening as against *'hören'* which means to hear. *Nutzer/ user* (used in both German and English version, especially for new media).

*Verbraucher/ Konsument* (mainly used for consumption of material goods; not normally applied to media).

## Comment
As shown by the dictionary translation of both words, 'audience' and 'public' can be translated as *'Publikum'* insofar as the terms refer to participants, listeners, viewers, be it media (TV, film, radio, print media) or live public events (theatre, concerts, speeches). There is no equivalent to the negative connotations of English 'audience' (see Sonia Livingstone's entry) in the German concepts of *Publikum, Zuhörer, Zuschauer* etc. They straddle the meaning of both audience and public. There is no German term that could capture the distinction between the public and the audience in the corresponding English collective terms for participants in a live or media event. (A more negatively loaded term is *'Masse'*, as in *Massenmedien,* 'mass media' *Massenunterhaltung,* 'mass entertainment' etc.).

The English word 'the public' or 'public' in the sense of pertaining to the public sphere translates as *"Öffentlichkeit"*, commonly understood as able to be heard or seen by everyone, taking place in front of an audience as in *öffentliche Veranstaltung* - public assembly, meeting, event; *das öffentliche Wohl* - the public good. It has a different etymological basis from *Publikum* (see also the Danish entry, which is directly related). *Öffentlichkeit* has a long discursive history in academic theory stemming from the Enlightenment, and has continued with discussions of and about the Frankfurt School's critique of the mass media. In this context it has a strong normative character. In theoretical works translated from German theory English translations of 'public'/ 'public sphere' originate from German *öffentlich/ Öffentlichkeit* (for example, Jürgen Habermas, 1962 *Strukturwandel der Öffentlichkeit. Berlin: Neuwied* has been published in English as *Structural Transformations of the Public Sphere*). Both *Masse* and *Öffentlichkeit/ öffentlich* are similar to the positive/ negative connotations of the English terms 'mass' and 'public'/ 'public'/ 'public sphere'.

In specialist usage in media theory, *'Rezipient'* is used. Metzler Lexikon Medientheorie, Medienwissenschaft (2002) has an entry on *publizieren,* 'to publish', but refers *Publikum* to *'Rezipient'* which is linked to *Rezeption.* The origin of *Rezipient* is the Latin *recipere,* meaning to receive; but in literary/media theory it is a direct loan of 'reception' from Anglo-American theories. *Rezeption* in German-speaking contexts is regularly applied within literary, art, music, media and cultural studies and refers to different processes and emphases of communication and meaning-making. *Rezeption* studies focus on the communicative appropriation of a 'text' (as understood in semiotics, for example, as including visual, audiovisual, musical artefacts etc) by a 'recipient' or a 'reader' (as seen in semiotics, for example, including listening, viewing, reading etc). The concepts *Rezipient* and *Rezeption* provide umbrella terms for different theories (for example, cognitive, semiotic, discourse analytical) within and beyond media and communication studies, which focus on interactive processes of communication (for example, largely within the triad of author-text-reader but including institutional processes).

## Danish (Kirsten Drotner)

Etymologically, Danish is very close to (low) German. As with most other countries, modern media in Denmark such as newspapers, journals and books develop in tandem with urban culture including theatres, salons and reading circles, and in tandem with the struggle for some sort of democratic representation. These developments took form during the eighteenth and nineteenth centuries when Denmark was heavily influenced by German Enlightenment culture. Hence, it is to be expected that there are close similarities between German and Danish conceptualisations of the practices and entities which in English are denoted by the terms 'audience' and 'public' (noun, adjective) as well as between the noun *Öffentlichkeit* (German) and *offentlighed* (Danish).

### *'Audience'*

#### Dictionary translations
*sb* (1) publikum; (theatre etc, also:) tilskuere; tilskuer/skare, -kreds; (at concert, lecture, etc, also:) tilhørere; tilhører/skare, -kreds; (radio, also:) lyttere; lytter/kreds, -skare; (TV, also:) seere; seer/kreds, -skare; (of writer, also:) læsere, læserkreds, -skare; (abt advertising, also:) forum. (2) audiens, foretræde. (3) give hama. ≈ lytte til hvad han har at sige.

## Current established dictionary meaning

In Danish, no word exists for the generic term audience to denote a general positioning of receivers *vis-à- vis* cultural products or processes. The translation offers *publikum* (public) as the generic term, and then specifies the activity in relation to particular media (listener, viewer, etc).

## Typical usage

There are a few words that are related to audience, all derived from latin *audire*, to listen. In *specialist usage*, one finds the noun *audiens* to denote a formal hearing by a king or bishop, who lends ear to petitions. Hence, the activity is on the part of the superior party. A related, and equally specialised term, is the noun *auditør*, who is a public official dealing with e.g. military offences. In specialist, academic usage the noun *reception* is applied as a direct 'loan-word' from Continental literary theory (Jauss 1970/1982) to denote the appropriation of media. Within media studies, its usage has spread with the expansion of audience studies, which in Danish is regularly referred to as *receptionsanalyse* or *receptionteori* (reception analysis, reception theory). The term *recipient* (receiver) as a loan word from Anglo-American audience studies is not as accepted or widely used in academic circles as *reception* and, more importantly, the word carries none of the normative associations of the English term. In *general usage*, the word *reception* means the place where one checks into a hotel. The general meaning of the term *auditorium* is a lecture hall, for example, at a university, and the people gathered here would be termed *publikum* (public). This semantic sliding points to the most important distinction in Danish when attempting to capture the meaning of audience and public, namely that between the nouns *publikum* (public, audience) and *offentlighed* (public or public sphere).

# 'Public'

## Dictionary translations

sb offentlighed; publikum; *adj* offentlig; almen; almen-; samfunds-.

## Current established dictionary meaning

In specialised as well as *general usage*, the noun *publikum* (from lat. *publicus*) covers both the semantic field of public and audience. It derives from the field of drama and has spread to other cultural expressions and settings:

(1) It is a generic term for people in general or for those living in a particular geographical place (a country, a city);

(2) It is a generic term for groups of people who engage in some sort of cultural

activity or are receivers of some form of cultural product, regardless of its performance in the public or the private sphere;

(3) It is a normative term applied to a collective of people who engage in some sort of public event or activity.

## Typical usage and associations

In its generic usage, a group of people appropriating mass media may also be termed *modtagere* (receivers). In reference to specific media *publikum* and *modtagere* may be specified in relation to the medium used, e.g. *tilhører* (listener to (*til*) a public debate) or *tilskuer* (viewers of (*til*) a theatre or cinema performance) when active engagement is stressed; and *lytter* (listener to the radio), *seer* (viewer of a TV programme) or *læser* (reader) when no active engagement is implied. A more normative use may be invoked by adding attributive adjectives such as *dannet* (educated). Historically, the association to something general has carried negative connotations similar to the term mass, and this is particularly evident when used in the plural *publikummer* (archaic). A *publikation* of a book is applied in educated usage where the common term is *udgivelse* (to give out or leave for everybody to use). As a verb, *publicere* (to make public), the term is only applied in relation to print media (as in *publikation*), and, as such, it is closely associated with the public sphere, thanks to the Enlightenment tradition. The adjective, *publik*, is no longer in common use (for the general use of the adjective, see below: *offentlig*). The latin origin only exists in the legal term *notarius publicus*.

## Comment

It is interesting to note that new terms are appropriated to cover the usage of more interactive media such as computers, the Internet and mobile phones. Here, the term *bruger* (user) is the general term that implies a form of active, if not collective, engagement, which the words for radio and television usage do not. A further complication in relation to the term *bruger* is that, in general usage, including journalism, it is used interchangeably with the word *forbruger* (consumer). Hence, attempts to stress more active media engagements may become intimately linked to commercial appropriations. As a positively valued noun, *publikum* is closely bound up with the Enlightenment discourse of an educated and well-informed collective of people actively engaging in the cultural public sphere (theatre, museum, the reading public), while an engagement in the political public sphere will be referred to as *offentlighed*.

Thus, a full definition of the semantic field must encompass the term *offentlighed*. This noun is a direct loan from German *Öffentlichkeit* (from *offen*, open), and it covers three sets of semantic fields: (a) It is a generic term for everybody living in a particular geographical place (a country, a city) and in this definition very similar to *publikum;* (b) It is a generic term denoting what is accessible to and known by everybody, or issues of wide societal significance; (c) It is a legal term pertaining to state matters or to the relations between the state and its citizens. However, in its *specialist usage*, the term *offentlighed* is applied by disciplines such as media studies, political economy and law. In media studies it is mostly used normatively within traditions associated with the Habermasian tradition and second- and third-generations of Critical thought. While *publikum in general usage* is mostly applied in its generic sense, the term *offentlighed* more often carries normative associations, not evident in the dictionary definitions, because of its close association with an Enlightenment discourse, where consensus is perceived to emanate from public debate in the press. In its normative sense, it refers to a collective of people who engage in the political public sphere, and in that part of the cultural public sphere which is traditionally closely associated with the political sphere, namely the press - for example, *i offentlighedens interesse* (in the public interest), *tale på offentlighedens vegne* (speak on behalf of the public).

## Greek (Mirca Madianou)

It is worth noting that two widely used English-Greek dictionaries translate 'audience' and 'public' (*n.*) as '*κοινό*' [pronounced: koino], meaning common/shared (Collins, 1997 and Penguin-Hellenews, 1975). 'Audience' is also translated as '*ακροατήριο*' [akroatirio], which literally means 'audience' (the collective term for 'listeners'), although in Greek this original emphasis on listening still survives. This means that although *ακροατήριο* can be used to describe the audience for radio or for theatre, it does not describe well the television audience; in this case the term *κοινό* is used or, alternatively, the nouns *θεατές* [theates], or *τηλεθεατές* [tiletheates]. *θεατές* means viewers (and in some contexts spectators) and derives from the ancient Greek verb *θέωμαι* [theomai] which means to see (as in 'theatre'). *Τηλεθεατές* means television viewers; the prefix *τηλε-* derives from the ancient Greek word for distance (from which the 'tele' in 'television' derives).

Hence there is no single word for audience, but rather, at least three. On the other hand, the noun 'public' is only translated as *κοινό*. Public as an adjective is translated as *δημόσιο* [dhemosio] from the ancient Greek word *δήμος* [demos] meaning people, public (as in 'democracy').

## 'Audience'

### Dictionary translations

(1) (in theatre etc) *ακροατήριο* [akroatirio]. (2) (radio) *ακροατές* [akroates]. (3) (TV) *τηλεθεατές* [tiletheates]. (4) (public) *κοινό* [koino]. (5) (with queen etc) *ακρόαση* [akroasi]

I group these in the following three:

## Current established dictionary meanings of translated term and its synonyms
(1) *ακροατήριο* [akroatirio, collective], *ακροατές* [akroates, plural] i. collective term for the people attending a concert, a talk, a play; ii. the people attending a trial in court

(2) *θεατές* [theates]. i. people who see/witness something unintentionally. ii. people who watch a spectacle, a show.

(3) *κοινό* [koino] - see also next entry. i. Common: a feature found in more than two people. ii. Collective term for 'citizens', the people in general. iii. Collective term for people who attend an event, the people addressed by this event. iv. Collective term for a group of people who follow/adore an artist (in this context it is a synonym of fan).

## Origin of translated term
(1) *ακροατήριο* [akroatirio] from the ancient Greek verb *ακρόωμαι* [akroomai], to listen. (2) *θεατές* [theates] from the ancient Greek verb *θέωμ 'ι* [theomai], to see. (3) *κοινό* [koino] from the ancient Greek word *κοινός* - similar meaning, see next entry.

## Typical usage
(1) Emphasis on listening. Thus, the term is more appropriately used for theatre and radio, but is increasingly used to describe the television audience (for example in audience research, *έρευνα ακροατηρίου* [ereuvna akroatiriou] and *μέτρηση ακροαματικότητας* [metrisi akroamatikotitas]).

(2) Most commonly used to refer to either the viewers of a performance or a spectacle, or to those who have witnessed an event unintentionally. Often used with an adjective or a prefix to specify the type of performance or spectacle. *Τηλεθεατής* (tiletheatis), television viewer.

(3) Very widely used to both mean audience and public (see following entry).

## Connotations and associations
(1) Relatively neutral. Usually assumed as homogenous.

(2) Strong connotation of passivity as is evident in the phrase, '*θεατής των γεγονότων*' [theatis ton gegonoton] - a spectator of the events.

(3) The term is relatively neutral and quite general, often used to refer to the nation, the society and the people. Homogeneity is assumed which is evident in the lack of plural form (see following entry). Although there is no direct connotation of participation and activity, the term does not connote passivity as in the case of *θεατές* [theates].

## Derivatives

(1) The word itself is a derivative of the ancient Greek word *ακρόωμαι* [akroomai] (to listen). Other derivatives include, *ακρόαση* [akroasi], *ακροαματηκότητα* [akroamatikotita] measurement of listenship, *ακροαματικός* [akroamatikos] the hearing of a trial.

(2) Many: *θέαμα* [theama] (spactacle), *θέατρο* [theatro] (theatre), *αμφιθέατρο* [amphitheatre] *τηλεθεατής* [tiletheatis] (viewer), *φιλοθεάμον κοινό* [filotheamon koino] the spectacle loving public.

(3) Many derivatives, for instance: *κοινότητα* [koinotita] (community), *κοινωνία* [koinonia] (society), *επικοινωνία* [epikoinonia] (communication).

## Relatives:

1, 2, and 3 are relatives, but note the differences in connotations and typical usage (previous sections).

## *'Public'*

### Dictionary translations

*το κοινό* [to koino] Note: 'public' as an adjective is translated as *δημόσιο* [dhemosio].

### Current established dictionary meanings of translated term and its synonyms

(1) Common: a feature found in more than two people; (2) Collective term for the aggregate of citizens, the people; (3) Collective term for people who attend an event, the people addressed by this event. Used with adjectives to specify what type of event/audience, e.g., theatre public; (4) Collective term for a group of people who follow/adore an artist (as in 'fan').

### Origin of translated term

From the ancient Greek word *κοινός*. The ancient and modern words have similar meanings and connotations (see above) with the difference that in ancient Greek the term did not mean audience. The ancient word is the root for the Latin cum- that is the root for common and community [see section on derivatives].

## Typical usage
Very widely used to mean both 'audience' (see previous entry) and 'public'. Interestingly, the plural form, *τα κοινά*, [ta koina] can only be used to mean 'public life' (usually in the context of involvement in public life); it cannot be used to mean multiple publics, audiences or groups of people.

## Connotations and associations
The term is relatively neutral and quite general, often used to refer to the nation, the society and the people. Homogeneity is assumed which is evident in the lack of plural form (see above, 4). Although there is no direct connotation of participation and activity, the term does not connote passivity as in the case of *θεατές* [theates].

## Derivatives
Many derivatives, for instance: *κοινότητα* [koinotita] (community), *κοινωνία* [koinonia] (society), *επικοινωνία* [epikoinonia] (communication).

## Relatives
antonym: *ιδιωτικό* (idiotiko), private.

## Comment
As Sonia Livingstone notes in the English entry, the link to democracy and citizenship made by academics is indirectly present in common/popular use (although in the Greek case there is a strong etymological link). On the other hand, the word *δημόσιο* [dhemosio] which is how pubic as an adjective is translated (hence, *δημόσια γνώμη* [dhemosia gnomi] public opinion, *δημόσιο συμφέρον* [dhemosio simferon] public interest), has a strong (and very obvious etymological) link to democracy and participation. At the same time, the noun *δημόσιο* [dhemosio] has acquired negative connotations in recent years as it has been associated with the government, party politics, patronage relationships and corruption. So, being a 'public servant' *(δημόσιος υπάλληλος* [dhimosios ypallilos]), or to seek for a job in the *δημοσιο*, can have negative connotations of low productivity, vested interests and lack of trust. An example from my own research that is included in my chapter, can highlight this dimension: some of the informants in that study referred to the public service television channels as 'governmental channels' *(κυβερνητικά κανάλια*, [kyvernitika kanalia]).

# Slovenian (Sabina Mihelj)

## 'Audience'

### Dictionary translations
(Grad *et al.* 1971, 1992, 1997)

(1) *občinstvo*. (2) *publika*. (3) *poslualstvo*(n) / *poslušalci* (m)/*poslušalke* (f). (4) *avdienca*.

### Current established dictionary meanings
(Bajec *et al.* 2000)

Noun: (1) *občinstvo*: (1a) people who gather to see a public performance, event; (1b) people who receive or are interested in certain cultural products, regardless of the specific communication channel used. (2) *publika*: synonymous with *občinstvo*.(3) *poslušalstvo*: listeners. (4) *avdienca*: a formal hearing or interview, e.g. with the Pope.

### Origin of term/history
(1) *občinstvo*: derived from the Old Church Slavonic noun *ob_ština* (community), and that from the Ancient Slavonic adjective *obьtь* (common, general). (2) *publika*: appropriated following the examples of German *das Publikum*, English *the public* and Croatian *publika*, originally from the Latin *publicus*. (3) *poslušalstvo*: derived from the Old Church Slavonic noun *sluh* (the sense of hearing) and the verb *slušati* (to listen; to belong; to obey) (Snoj 1997).

### Typical usage
*Občinstvo* and *publika* are used interchangeably to refer to a group of people who are recipients within a communication process, regardless of the channel of communication and regardless of whether they are dispersed or located in the same place.

### Derivatives
While the words *občinstvo* and *publika* are generally used synonymously, their etymologies and derivatives reveal an important semantic difference. The word *občinstvo* is itself a derivative of the adjective *obče* (general, common, public, or basic), and like virtually all other derivatives of this adjective, e.g. *občina* (the basic unit of local government), *občevati* (to engage in a relationship, to communicate, to have sexual intercourse), it is used to refer to something which has to do with a community. By contrast, the derivatives of *publika*, such as *publicirati* (to publish),

*publikacija* (publication), *publicistika* (journalism, especially the activity of writing analytical texts, commentaries), *publicist* (m)/ *publicistka* (f) (journalist, especially if he/she writes analytical texts, commentaries) etc., are all related only to the activity of making something (typically information) available to everyone, without this necessarily leading to the formation of a community.

### Connotations and associations

No specific connotations are directly related to any of the translations given above. However, a slightly negative connotation is related to the hyponym *množica* (crowd), especially in the meaning of lower social strata. Terms for mass media are derived from this noun (*množični mediji, množična občila, sredstva množičnega obveščanja, sredstva množične komunikacije*), as well as the term for mass culture (*množična kultura*). Much more explicitly negative connotations are related to the term *masa*, which means a big quantity of indistinguishable elements. In the adjectival form, this term is sometimes used to refer to mass culture *(masovna kultura)*, mass products *(masovni proizvodi)* mass events *(masovni dogodki)*, and mass media (masovni mediji).

### Relatives

Apart from *poslušalstvo* (listenership of radio), two more nouns are used in Slovenian which differentiate the audience with regard to the channel of communication used: *gledalstvo* (n)/ *gledalci* (m)/ *gledalke* (f) (viewers) and *bralci* (n)/ *bralci* (m)/ *bralke* (f) or *čitateljstvo* (readership). In some contexts, the noun *zbor* is used as a synonym for *publika* or *občinstvo* - yet only in cases where a larger group of people is physically gathered at a specific place. As in other languages examined in the appendix, the Slovenian translations of 'audience', i.e. *občinstvo* and *publika*, would not encompass people involved in computer-mediated communication. In this case, the word *uporabnik* (m)/ uporabnica (f) (user) would most often be used.

In media and communication studies, as well as in literary theory, *občinstvo* and *publika* would often be replaced with the term *prejemniki* (m)/ prejemnice (f) (recipients). In literary theory, this term is strictly used within the analytical and theoretical framework of *recepcijska estetika* (reception aesthetics), borrowed from the (German) Konstanz school of literary theory. By contrast, in the field of media and communication studies, the term *prejemniki* is used within the broader analytical framework of either the French structuralist semiology or the Anglo-American audience studies, and sometimes Lacanian psychoanalysis. Within television theory, the concept of the recipient was further ramified to account for the differences between the addressee and the recipient; in this case, the pair of concepts *potencialni gledalec* (potential viewer) and *virtualni aktualni gledalec* (virtual actual viewer) was introduced.

## 'Public'

### Dictionary translations (Grad *et al.* 1971, 1992, 1997)
Noun: (1) *javnost*. (2) *občinstvo*. (3) *publika*. (4) *občestvo* (appears only in the older English–Slovenian dictionary, i.e. Grad 1971).

Adjective: (1) *javno* (n) *javen* (m) *javna* (f). (2) *ljudsko* (n) *ljudski*, (m)/ *ljudska*(f). (3) *narodno* (n)/ *naroden* (m)/ *narodna*(f).

### Current established dictionary meanings (Bajec *et al.* 2000)
Noun: (1) *javnost*: (1a) members of a socio-political community, especially in relation to an event or a specific issue; (1b) a larger number of people, not just the private sphere, family or individual; (1c) audience; (1d) visitors. (2) and (3) usually used also as translations for the audience, see above. (4) *občestvo*: a community sharing common spiritual values, mentality, traditions.

Adjective: (1) *javno*: (1a) related to a community and not to the individual; (1b) meant to be used by all people, all members of a community; (1c) made in such a way to be accessible to the public; (1d) related to the socio-political activity and/or to the state. (2) *ljudsko*: related to the people. (3) *narodno*: related to the nation.

### Origin of term/history (Snoj 1997)
(1) *javnost, javno*: derived from the from Old Church Slavonic *javiti* (to make known, to make visible). (2) *občestvo*: taken from Russian *obščestvo* (community), derived from the Ancient Slavonic adjective *obьt'ь* (common, general).

### Typical usage
Both *javnost* and especially the adjective *javen* ('public') are used in a wide variety of contexts, usually to refer to something that is linked or accessible to the whole population of a state, but sometimes also extended to include the population of the whole globe. For example, the adjective *javno* (*javen, javna*) is used in phrases such as *javni interesi* (public interests), *javno mnenje* (public opinion), *javni park* (public park), *javna knjižnica* (public library); *javna hiša* (brothel; literally: public house), *javno predvajanje* (public screening), *javni delavec* (state employee) and *javna televizija* (public television). By contrast, the noun *občestvo* is used with reference to a closely bounded community, especially a religious community (*cerkveno občestvo*), but sometimes also with reference to a village (*vaško občestvo*) or national community (*narodno občestvo*).

### Derivatives
The noun *javnost* and the adjective *javen* are themselves derivatives of the verb

*javiti* (to communicate, to give notice, to make known, to announce), which has a number of other derivatives, such as *objaviti* (to make something available to the public, usually by publishing it in the media), *prijaviti* (to denounce, to report a criminal activity; to report, to register something requested officially such as taxes), *brzojavka* (telegram).

### Connotations and associations
The noun *javnost* tends to be charged with positive connotations; it connotes a collective that is to be respected. By contrast, the adjective *javno* may - depending on the exact context - become charged with either positive or negative connotations. For example, within official (state), media and academic discourses on broadcasting, *javna televizija* (public television service) generally has positive connotations, while *zasebna* or *komercialna televizija* (private or commercial television) is associated with negative connotations. By contrast, in the realm of economy, including the official (state) discourses on economy, the connotations of the very same terms often tend to be reversed.

### Relatives
In general usage, both the noun *javnost* as well as the adjective *javno* are often used interchangeably with a number of other terms denoting a specific collective or things linked to that collective. *Javnost* is often conflated with *skupnost* (community), *družba* (society), *narod/ nacija* (nation), *ljudstvo* (people), while *javno* is used interchangeably with *obče* (general, common, public, or basic), *skupno* (common to all), *državno* (belonging to the state), *družbeno* (belonging to the society), *narodno nacionalno* (national) and *ljudsko* (popular, related to the people). It is only within academic discourses, especially within political science, but also within media and communication studies, that attempts have been made to differentiate *javnost* from its relatives.

### Comment
Historically, the Slovenian nation - as many other European nations, particularly in Central and Eastern Europe - has been conceived almost exclusively in terms of ethnicity and/or culture, and was thus not seen as coextensive with the state or the citizenry. Keeping this is mind, the above-mentioned conflation of *javnost* with terms such as *narod* or *nacija* (nation) in general usage obviously runs against the normative sense of *javnost,* stemming from the Enlightenment tradition and closely associated with citizenship. This has been an issue of particular concern within the Slovenian academic sphere, where attempts have been made to link the terms *javnost* as well as *javno* to the state and the community of citizens, and distinguish it from the nation, understood in ethnic/cultural terms. Within the field of media and communication studies, such an understanding of *javnost* is fostered by the academic journal *Javnost* (*Public*), which addresses problems of the public

sphere, public communication, public opinion, public discourse, publicness, publicity, and public life.


## French (Daniel Dayan)

### *'Public' (Adjective)*

#### Current established dictionary meaning
Petit Larousse Dictionary: (1) that which concerns a whole people, e.g. 'public interest'; (2) that which concerns the government of the country: 'public affairs'; (3) that which is manifest, known to everyone: 'public knowledge'; (4) that to which anyone is entitled: 'public meeting'.

Littré Dictionary: (1) that which belongs to, or concerns, a whole people (ex: Public cause; public morals; public interest); (2) that which takes place in presence of everyone (ex. public lecture, public debates).


### *'Public' (Noun)*
Petit Larousse Dictionary: (1) the people in general ('announcement to the public'); (20) a group of gathered individuals that may vary in size (ex. 'the public of a theatre').

Littré dictionary: (1) the public in general; (2) a number of people, of varied size, gathered to attend a spectacle, (3) a ceremony, a meeting (eg. Chamfort "*Combien faut-il de sots pour faire un public?*" How many nitwits does it take to make a public?").


### *'Audience'*

#### Current established dictionary meaning
Littré Dictionary: (1) attention given to a speaker (a King honours you by giving you audience: by hearing your opinion); (2) social occasion devoted to listening to an individual who wishes to be heard by you (the ambassador has requested an audience); (3) social occasion devoted to listening to a group (Kings may grant collective audiences). By extension: all those who attend a given audience (either because the audience is collectively granted, or because their presence is permitted when an individual audience is offered); (4) Spanish colonial courts in Latin America; (5) Session in a French tribunal.


### *'Auditoire' (Noun)*
Littré Dictionary: (1) a space in which assembly gathers to listen to speakers; (2)

in old churches, the part of the church where the congregation gathers; (3) a tribunal; collectively, all those who hear.

### 'Auditeur' (Noun)

Littré Dictionary: (1) a person who listens; (2) an examiner (as in the practice of audit which involves expertise, but no power of decision); (3) an individual allowed to listen to the scriptures, but not to partake in communion, in primitive christianism (a pre-christian); (3) in the judiciary world: (4) an officer present at trials, yet not allowed to partake in deliberations.

### Comment

In the academic lexicon, most French discussions refer to either the notion of 'public' or the notion of 'audience', although some authors have tried to introduce other notions (such as *'Auditoire'*), so far without success.

The notion of 'Audience' is restricted, being mainly used in relation to statistical evaluation. Thus, the philosopher Mikel Duffrenne writes:

> *One is tempted to save the word 'public' just for those groups that exist for a brief duration in a theatre or concert hall. Indeed, it is during such gatherings that a public is most conscious of existing, that sociability is most intense ... Yet, this restriction in the meaning of the word is unwarranted. A museum has a public, albeit dispersed in time. So does a novel. So does cinema, with a public made of solitary spectators ......This is why the scientific study of publics relies on statistical methods and deliberately neglects the phenomena of actual gathering (left to group dynamics).*

> *(Encyclopedia universalis; entry: 'Public and Art').*

Duffrenne points here to publics that are 'scientifically studied' through 'statistical methods'. In such cases publics tend to be called 'audiences'. Yet, even here, Mikel Dufrenne speaks of 'publics', and is in fact entitled to do so, since the French notion of public is ambiguous. On the one hand, it is a generic word, the type of expression that linguists would call 'degree zero', a notion that includes and encompasses that of 'audience'. On the other hand, it is a normative notion, with strong links to the Latin *'res publica'* (both 'republic' and 'common good').

This normative dimension is already present much before the enlightenment. Thus an historian of literature, Hélene Merlin writes :

> *In the beginning of the seventeenth century PUBLIC designates not only Christianity, but the kingdom, the state, taxation, the people, that is: everything that corresponds to the eminently political paradigm of* 'res publica'. *'Public' also designates everything*

*that is* public; *all reality ... considered from the point of view of the common good, and constructed as representation (ceremony, pageantry, etc....).*

*(*Public et litterature en France au XVII° *siécle; Paris Belles Lettres 1994).*

The double status (both generic and normative) of the noun *'public'* has already been noted. Concerning 'audience', an additional semantic feature is manifested indirectly in reference to the uses of the noun *'auditeur'*. As we can see from the Littré entries, most meanings of the notion of *'auditeur'* are characterised by a lack or restriction. *'Auditeur'* therefore carries connotations not of passivity, but of a particular circumscribed activity. *'Auditeur'* suggests attendance minus action: Restriction of exertive power; restriction of participation in deliberations; restriction of access to Christian communion. This restrictive dimension seems at least implicitly present, in the current uses of *'audience'*.

## References

Babinioti, G. (1998) *Αεξικό της Νέας Ελληνικης* [Lexiko tis Neas Ellinikis]. Athens: Centre for Lexicology.

Bajec, Anton *et al. Slovar slovenskega knjnega jezika* [*Dictionary of Slovenian Language*]. Ljubljana: DZS, 2000.

Becker-Christensen, C. (ed.) (2001) *Politikens nudansk ordbog* Copenhagen: Politiken.

Brøndum-Nielsen, J. et al. (eds) (1934) *Ordbog over det danske sprog,* vol. 15 Copenhagen: Gyldendal.

Brøndum-Nielsen, J. et al. (eds) (1937) *Ordbog over det danske sprog* vol. 17 Copenhagen: Gyldendal.

*Collins English Greek Dictionary* (1997) Glasgow: HarperCollins Publishers.

*Collins English/ German* (1994).

*Duden, deutsches Universallexikon* (1996).

*Duden, Deutsches Universalwörterbuch* (1983).

Duffrenne, Mikel (1973). *Public et Art.* Encyclopedia Universalis, vol. 13, .795-8.

Eco, Umberto (2003) *Mouse or Rat. Translation as Negotiation.* London: Weidenfels and Nicholson.

*Encyclopedia Universalis,* France.

Fiske, J. (1992). Audiencing: a cultural studies approach to watching television. *Poetics, 21*, 345-359.

Grad, Anton, and Henry Leeming: *Slovensko-angle_ki slovar* [*Slovenian-English Dictionary*]. Ljubljana: DZS, 1997.

Grad, Anton, Rušena škerlj and Nada Vitorovič: *Veliki angleško-slovenski slovar* [*English-Slovene Dictionary*]. Ljubljana: DZS, 1992.

Grad, Anton: *Angleško-slovenski slovar* [*English-Slovene Dictionary*]. Maribor: Obzorja, 1971, 1 edn 1965.

Jauss, Hans R. (1970/1982). Litteraturgeschichte als Provokation der Litteraturwissenschaft. In his: Litteraturgeschichte als Provokation. Frankfurt/M: Suhrkamp: 144-207. Shortened version tr. as "Literary History as a Challenge to Literary Theory", *New Literary History* 2, 1 (1970): 7-37. Tr. Elizabeth Benzinger. Rpt. in Hans Robert Jauss (1982) *Toward an Aesthetic of Reception*. Minneapolis: University of Minnesota Press. Tr. Timothy Bathi.

Habermas Jürgen (1962) *Strukturwandel der Öffentlichkeit. Berlin: Neuwied.*

Jürgen Habermas (1969/1982) *Structural Transformations of the Public Sphere.*

(1977) *Langenscheidt English/ German.*

*Longman's Dictionary of the English Language.*

Merlin, Hélene (1994). *Public et literature en France au XVII° siécle.* Paris: Les Belles Lettres, 478 (and back cover).

Merriam-Webster online dictionary. See http://www.merriam-webster.com /

Nielsen, B. Kjaerulff (1974) *Engelsk-dansk ordbog* Copenhagen: Gyldendal. Orig. 1964.

*Oxford Duden English/ German* 1997.

Penguin-Hellenews (1975) *Αγγλοελληνικό Λεξικό* [Agglo-Elliniko Lexiko]. Athens: Penguin-Hellenews.

Schanze, H. (2002) *Metzler Lexikon Medientheorie, Medienwissenschaft.* Stuttgart & Weimar: Metzler Verlag.

Snoj, Marko: *Slovenski etimološki slovar* [*Slovenian Etymological Dictionary*] Ljubljana: Mladinska knjiga, 1997.

Stamatakou, I. (1949) *Λεξικό της Αρχαιας Γλώσσης* . [Lexiko Arhaias Ellinikis Glossis]. Athens: Ekdotikos Oikos Dimitrakou.

Tegopoulos-Fytrakis (1989) *Ελληνικο Λεξικό* [Elliniko Lexiko]. Athens: Ekdoseis Armonia.

*The Littré Dictionary of the French Language.*

*The Petit Larousse Dictionary of the French Language.*

Vinterberg, H. & A. C, Bodelsen (1966) *Dansk-engelsk ordbog* Copenhagen: Gyldendal.

Von Wilpert, G. (1969) *Sachwörterbuch der Literatur.* 5. Auflage. Stuttgart: Alfred Kröner Verlag.

Vostanjoglou, T. (1988) *Αντιλεξικό ή Ονομαστικό της Νεοελλήνικής* [Antilexiko I Onomastiko tis Neoellinikis Glossas]. Athens.

# Index

citizenship; multi-culturalist
citizenship

civic culture 31-5, 58, 59, 60, 199-200, 205 *see also* culture

civil society 199-200

collective attention 12, 13 *see also* attention

collective fictions 68 *see also* fiction and reality

commercialisation 174-5

commitment 53

communication
mobile phones 192
online 176

communicative context 15

communities 49-50
imagined 47, 68

connectivity 203

consumer audiences 12, 68, 73, 74 *see also* audiences; cultural consumption

contiguous publics 48 *see also* publics

counter-publics 56 *see also* publics

crowds 48-9, 140

cultural citizenship 14, 143-6 *see also* citizenship; youth culture

cultural consumption 14, 148-9, 150-1, 155-6 *see also* consumer audiences; youth culture

culture
civic 31-5, 58, 59, 60, 199-200, 205
mass 149
youth 167-8, 199

Cyprus 106

**D**

Dama (Zafimahaleo Rasolofondraosolo) 121-2, 123, 126-33

demographers' publics 62 *see also* publics

diffused audiences 26-8 *see also* audiences

diverse audiences 105-6 *see also* audiences

Duran, Lucy 119

**E**

Ebor Gardens 147-8, 157

economy, and personal sphere 172-5

education
and cultural consumption 148-9, 150-1, 155-6
and television 82-3
and theatre attendance 154

ERT 104-5

ethnicity, and news consumption 105-6, 108

Europe, and new media 10, 26, 188-9, 205

exclusion 13, 25, 108-9

experts 90

**F**

feeding 'the soul' 124-5

fiction and reality 87-8 *see also* collective fictions

France
reality television 77-81, 85
world music 118, 120

Freemasons 44

funding/subsidies 142-3, 144, 147

**G**

Germany, radio station 146

governance 177-8

Greek broadcasting 13, 101

**H**

Hall, Sir Peter 139

Harry Potter novels, and A S Byatt 64-5

Hegel, Georg 51

*Hernani* (Victor Hugo) 53

**I**

identity publics 55 *see also* publics

income, and cultural consumption 155-6

individualisation 172-4, 192, 202

individualism 93-5

institutionalising publics 53 *see also* publics

Internet
chat rooms 11, 20, 169
and children 165-6, 168, 173, 176, 178-9
in Greece 101

obvious publics 61, 62-4, 67-8 *see also* publics

online communication 176

op eds 64-5

orphan publics 63 *see also* publics


# P

palaeo-television 82 *see also* television

para-social relationships 141-2

participation 13, 14, 19, 27-8, 177

*Perdu de vue* (Lost from sight) 77, 86-7

performance 13, 52, 65-6, 141, 143 *see also*
        Dama; theatres

performing publics 62-3 *see also* publics

*persona(e) ficta(e)* 43-4, 53-4

personal sphere 172-9 *see also* public/private

Philippines 201

political action 59-60

political publics 44 *see also* publics

political talk 58-9

politics
        and mobile phones 200-1
        and world music 122-3

power
        and audiences 28, 88
        and mobile communication 205-6
        of new media 163-4
        and publics 28

Prague, Velvet Revolution 48

Priestley, J.B., West Yorkshire Playhouse
        production 14, 149-50

privacy 170, 176, 179, 180 *see also*
        public/private

private
        definitions (Williams) 22-3
        dependence of public 28-9
        *see also* public/private

private experiences into the public sphere 83-5
        *see also* public/private

pronounced publics 62, 67-8 *see also* publics

*Psy show* 77

psychology 90, 94-5

publi-graphy 62, 66-7

public debate, and talk shows 20

public discourse, and mobile phones 189-93

public life 100

public service broadcasting 10, 36, 104-5 *see
        also* broadcasting

public sphere 10, 12, 90-3, 170, 175-7 *see also*
        public/private; social spheres

public/audience/nation alignment 10

public/private
        blurring 168-70, 175-6, 180
        and childhood 14, 165-8, 170-1
        distinctions 14, 20, 88-90
        good and bad 140
        interpenetration/intersection 170-1
        and media use 102-3, 108

public/private space 12, 139-40
        blurring 204
        and ideas 92
        and mobile phones 190-1, 193-4, 198
        *see also* space

publics
        advocacy 63
        and audiences 11-12, 17, 21-2, 24-6, 35-
        6, 54-5, 57-8, 126, 205
        as audiences 21-2
        or audiences 19-20
        versus audiences 17-19
        behaviour 52-3
        careers 44
        catalysed 62, 67-8
        conceptualisation 15
        contiguous 48
        counter 48
        definitions 15-16
                Dayan 43-4, 45, 51-2, 54, 233-5
                Drotner 191-2, 201-2, 222-5
                Livingstone 9, 11, 216-19
                Madianou 100, 225-8
                Meinhof 115, 213-16, 219-22
                Mihelj 229-33
                Williams 22-3
        demographers' 62
        dependent on the private 28-9
        discussion 60-1
        and exclusion 13, 25
        identity 55
        and inclusion 25
        institutionalising 53

and social life 86

and theatre audiences 141, 149-50

*see also* reality television; talk shows

*Témoin numéro un* (Witness number one) 77, 86-7

testimony 85, 92

text messaging 188, 198-9, 203-4 *see also* mobile phones

theatres 14

attendance and education 154

audiences 14, 139-40, 141, 149-50, 157-9

dangerous 140

and publics 139-40

and social class 147-8

and television 141, 149-50

ticket prices 135

3G technology 188, 189, 205

time, and mobile communication 194-5

## U

universality 49

unpublics 64 *see also* publics

## V

victim, audience as 30-1

viewers 12, 31-5 *see also* audiences

voter apathy 27-8

## W

West Yorkshire Playhouse 147, 149-59

witnesses 50-2, 83-5, 90

Womad 120

world music

audiences 117-18, 120-1, 122, 125-6, 134-5

content 119-20

definitions 118

and language 119-20, 134

and politics 122-3

*see also* roots music

## Y

young people 11, 176, 177, 179, 180 *see also* children/childhood

youth culture 167-8, 199 *see also* children/childhood; culture